History 3
Student Guide

Part 1

About K12 Inc.

K12 Inc., a technology-based education company, is the nation's leading provider of proprietary curriculum and online education programs to students in grades K–12. K12 provides its curriculum and academic services to online schools, traditional classrooms, blended school programs, and directly to families. K12 Inc. also operates the K12 International Academy, an accredited, diploma-granting online private school serving students worldwide. K12's mission is to provide any child the curriculum and tools to maximize success in life, regardless of geographic, financial, or demographic circumstances. K12 Inc. is accredited by CITA. More information can be found at www.K12.com.

Printed by RR Donnelley/Digital, Kendallville, IN, USA, July 2015

Table of Contents

Unit 4: The Renaissance Elsewhere and the Reformation

Unit 5: Moving From Maps to the World

Unit 6: The Age of Exploration

Unit 7: The World They Found

Student Guide
Lesson 1: Using Maps and Globes

- National Geography Standard 3: How to analyze the spatial organization of people, places, and environments on Earth's surface.
- National Geography Standard 1: How to use maps and other geographic representations, tools, and technologies to acquire, process, and report information.
- National Geography Standard 5: That people create regions to interpret Earth's complexity.

Lesson Objectives

- National Geography Standard 1: How to use maps and other geographic representations, tools, and technologies to acquire, process, and report information.
- National Geography Standard 3: How to analyze the spatial organization of people,places, and environments on Earth's surface.
- National Geography Standard 5: That people create regions to interpret Earth's complexity.
- Explore concepts to be addressed during the year in History 3
- Review the names and locations of the continents and oceans.
- Interpret information on maps by using map keys.
- Describe the purpose of a map key and commonly used symbols.
- Identify differences between globes and maps.

PREPARE

Approximate lesson time is 60 minutes.

Advance Preparation

- It's important that you read the Course Introduction for History 3 before your student begins the course. You can find the course introduction at the beginning of the Using Maps and Globes lesson.

Materials

> For the Student
>
>> History Record Book
>>
>> Understanding Geography: Map Skills and Our World (Level 3)

Keywords and Pronunciation

cardinal directions : The four main directions (north, south, east, and west).

compass rose : A symbol on a map that shows cardinal and intermediate directions.

continent : One of the seven large pieces of land on Earth.

globe : A round model of the Earth.

intermediate directions : The four directions between the cardinal directions: northeast, northwest, southeast, and southwest.

map : A detailed drawing of an area, often showing features such as towns and roads or rivers and mountains.

ocean : A large body of salt water on the Earth's surface.

satellite image : A picture taken from a spacecraft and sent to Earth.

LEARN
Activity 1: Welcome to History 3 (Online)

Activity 2. Optional: Welcome to History (Online)

Activity 3. Optional: Looking Backward (Online)

Activity 4: Using Maps and Globes (Online)

Activity 5: Using Keys to Unlock Maps (Online)

ASSESS
Lesson Assessment: Using Maps and Globes (Offline)

You will complete an online assessment covering the main objectives of this lesson. Your assessment will be scored by the computer.

LEARN
Activity 6. Optional: Using Maps and Globes (Online)

Student Guide
Lesson 2: Directions and Hemispheres

Lesson Objectives
- Name the cardinal and intermediate directions and use them to describe locations.
- Identify and locate the Equator and prime meridian on a map.
- Name and locate the Earth's four hemispheres.
- Locate specified places relative to the Equator, prime meridian, or Earth's hemispheres.
- Recognize the purpose of a compass rose.

PREPARE

Approximate lesson time is 60 minutes.

Materials
> For the Student
> > History Record Book
> > Understanding Geography: Map Skills and Our World (Level 3)

Keywords and Pronunciation
cardinal directions : The four main directions (north, south, east, and west).

compass rose : A symbol on a map that shows cardinal and intermediate directions.

Equator : An imaginary line that goes around the middle of the Earth, dividing it into the Northern and Southern Hemispheres.

hemisphere : One half of the Earth; the Earth can be divided into four hemispheres (Eastern, Western, Northern, and Southern).

intermediate directions : The directions in between the cardinal directions (northwest, northeast, southwest, and southeast).

North Pole : the point on Earth that is as far north as you can go

prime meridian (priym muh-RIH-dee-uhn) : An imaginary line going around the Earth and running through the North and South Poles.

South Pole : The point on Earth that is as far south as you can go.

LEARN
Activity 1: Which Way Is North? *(Online)*

Activity 2: The Four Hemispheres *(Online)*

ASSESS
Lesson Assessment: Directions and Hemispheres (*Online*)

You will complete an online assessment covering the main objectives of this lesson. Your assessment will be scored by the computer.

LEARN
Activity 3. Optional: Directions and Hemispheres *(Online)*

Student Guide
Lesson 3: The Places We Live

Use maps to show where you live and learn to distinguish continents from countries. Use political maps to find countries, states, and capital cities.

Lesson Objectives

- Identify political maps as those showing the borders of countries or states.
- Locate places relative to their borders.
- Locate and name capitals on a political map.
- Identify where one lives from general to specific (for example, continent, country, state, city, neighborhood).
- Distinguish continents from countries.
- Recognize capital cities as places where government officials meet and work.

PREPARE

Approximate lesson time is 60 minutes.

Materials

> For the Student
>> History Record Book
>> Understanding Geography: Map Skills and Our World (Level 3)

Keywords and Pronunciation

border : The dividing line between two places, such as two states or countries, shown as lines on most maps and globes.

capital : The city in a country or state where the government officials meet and work.

community : A group of people who live and work in the same area and who have something in common with each other.

neighborhood : A small area or section of a city or town where people live together.

political map : A map that shows the locations of countries and the borders between them, and often shows the location of states and cities.

LEARN
Activity 1: The Places We Live *(Online)*

Activity 2: Countries, States, and Borders *(Online)*

ASSESS

Lesson Assessment: The Places We Live (*Online*)

You will complete an online assessment covering the main objectives of this lesson. Your assessment will be scored by the computer.

Lesson Assessment: The Places We Live (*Offline*)

You will complete an offline assessment covering the main objectives of this lesson. Your learning coach will score this assessment.

Name _____ Date _____

Lesson Assessment

The Places We Live, Part 2

In order for the student to answer this question, use one or more maps of the world, continent, country, and state in which you live. The student should point to their continent, country, state, and city.

1. Where do you live on the planet, continent, country, state, and city?

Use the world political map on pages 26 of Understanding Geography to answer the following questions.

2. What is the capital of Canada?

3. What is the capital of the Dominican Republic?

Student Guide
Lesson 1: Renaissance Means Rebirth

- Define *Renaissance* as *rebirth,* referring to a rebirth of interest in the classical civilizations of Greece and Rome.
- Characterize the Middle Ages as a dangerous time and an age of faith.
- Identify Christianity as the dominant faith of Europe.
- Describe the late Middle Ages as a time when writers, thinkers, and artists rediscovered classical models.

The Renaissance, approximately 1350-1600, was a period of cultural growth and rebirth. People opened a door to the future by looking back to the past of Greece and Rome.

Lesson Objectives

- Define Renaissance as rebirth, referring to a rebirth of interest in the classical civilizations of Greece and Rome.
- Characterize the Middle Ages as a dangerous time and an age of faith.
- Identify Christianity as the dominant faith of Europe.
- Describe the late Middle Ages as a time when writers, thinkers, and artists rediscovered classical models.
- Explain that *Renaissance* means *rebirth.*
- State that rebirth meant a new interest in the civilizations of ancient Greece and Rome.

PREPARE

Approximate lesson time is 60 minutes.

Materials

For the Student

    History Record Book

    paper, notebook

    pencils, colored 12

    🖳 Ancient Greece to the Renaissance activity sheet

Optional

    Botticelli by Mike Venezia

Keywords and Pronunciation

Persephone (pur-SEH-fuh-nee)

primavera (pree-muh-VAIR-uh)

Renaissance (REH-nuh-sahns) : Literally, rebirth; the time in Europe, beginning in the 1300s, when there was a new interest in the civilizations of ancient Greece and Rome.

zephyr (ZEH-fur)

LEARN

Activity 1: Botticelli and More (Online)

Activity 2: History Record Book (Offline)

Instructions

Choose either A or B.

A. Written Narration

Write two to four sentences explaining what the lesson was about. If necessary, use the Show You Know questions to help get started. Only include the most important parts of the lesson. Write your name, the date, and the lesson title on your written narration, and put it in your History Record Book.

Sample written narration: "The Renaissance came after the Middle Ages. *Renaissance* means *rebirth.* People invented many new things. They thought Greece and Rome were great civilizations."

B. Picture Narration

Draw a picture of the part of the lesson that interested you most. When you have finished drawing, describe the picture. Below your picture, write a description of what you have drawn. Write your name, the date, and the lesson title on your picture narration, and put it in your History Record Book.

Activity 3: From Ancient Greece to the Renaissance (Offline)

Instructions

By the late Middle Ages people were tired of living in dangerous and uncertain times. They were ready for a change. For inspiration, they looked back to the beauty and grandeur of ancient Greece and the glory of ancient Rome. The period immediately after the Middle Ages is called the Renaissance.

The four time periods covered in this activity, in order, are (1) ancient Greece, (2) ancient Rome, (3) the Middle Ages, and (4) the Renaissance.

Follow these directions to make a timeline that goes from ancient Greece to the Renaissance.

1. Add color to the three pictures on the Ancient Greece to the Renaissance activity sheet. Label each picture appropriately.

2. Draw a picture in the fourth rectangle to represent the Renaissance. Think about the painting Primavera. What does Renaissance mean? Rebirth. People in the Renaissance wanted to bring back the art, beauty, architecture, and learning that was part of ancient Greece and Rome. Label this picture.

3. Cut these four pictures out and glue them onto a sheet of construction paper in the correct order, starting with the earliest time period on the left.

10

ASSESS

Lesson Assessment: Renaissance Means Rebirth (*Online*)

You will complete an offline assessment covering the main objectives of this lesson. Your learning coach will score this assessment.

LEARN

Activity 4. Optional: Renaissance Means Rebirth *(Offline)*

Instructions

Learn more about Botticelli, the man who painted *Primavera,* check your library or bookstore for the nicely illustrated book *Botticelli* by Mike Venezia.

As usual, preview the recommended reading material listed here before having the student view it.

Name _____ Date _____

Ancient Greece to the Renaissance

Color and label the pictures. Draw a picture for the Renaissance. Cut the pictures out and glue them, in order, to a sheet of construction paper.

✂ cut

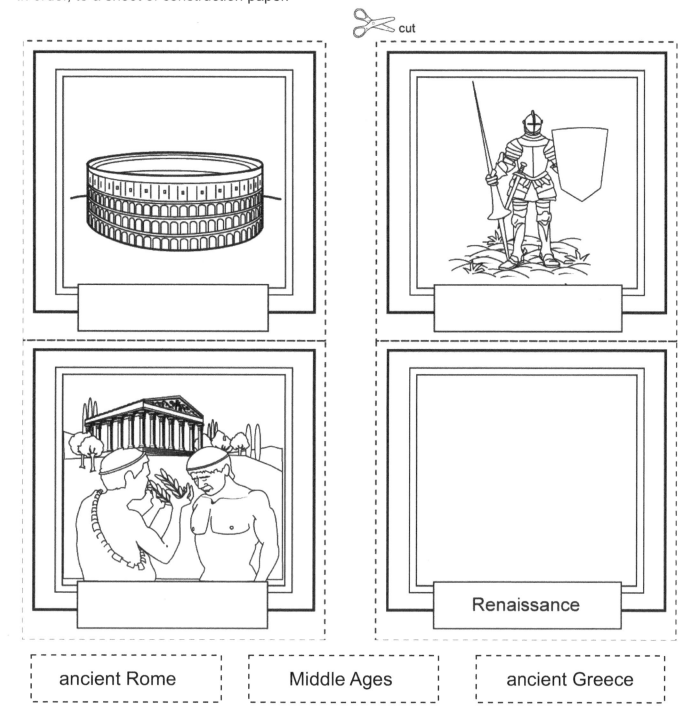

| ancient Rome | Middle Ages | ancient Greece |

Lesson Assessment

Renaissance Means Rebirth

1. What does *Renaissance* mean?_____

2. People in the Renaissance looked back at two ancient civilizations. What were

    they?_____

Student Guide
Lesson 2. Optional: Glories of Greece

Ancient Greece has been called the birthplace of western civilization. The historic home of democracy and a civilization that stressed human potential, Greece left a legacy that is with us still.

Lesson Objectives

- Identify Homer as a Greek poet.
- Identify ancient Greece as the historic home of democracy.
- Recognize Plato and Aristotle as two great Greek thinkers.

PREPARE

Approximate lesson time is 60 minutes.

Materials

For the Student

    🖥 Map of Ancient Greece

    History Record Book

    🖥 Wreath About Greece activity sheet

    glue, children's white

    paper clips

    paper, construction

    pencils, colored 12

    scissors

Optional

    Children of Ancient Athens. AppleSeeds, Cobblestone Publishing, December 1999.

Keywords and Pronunciation

Aristotle (AIR-uh-stah-tl)

democracy : Government by the people.

Iliad (IL-ee-uhd)

Odyssey (AH-duh-see)

Plato (PLAY-toh)

LEARN
Activity 1. Optional: Optional Lesson Instructions *(Online)*

Activity 2. Optional: Let's Go to Ancient Greece *(Online)*

Activity 3. Optional: History Record Book *(Offline)*
Instructions
Choose either A or B.
A. Written Narration
Write two to four sentences explaining what the lesson was about. If necessary, use the Show You Know questions to help get started. Only include the most important parts of the lesson. Write your name, the date, and the lesson title on your written narration, and put it in your History Record Book.
Sample written narration: "The Oak Street Poetry Club went back in time to see ancient Greece. They saw Homer, who was a great Greek poet. They also saw Plato and Aristotle, who were great thinkers."

B. Picture Narration
Draw a picture of the part of the lesson that interested you most. When you have finished drawing, describe the picture. Below your picture, write a description of what you have drawn. Write your name, the date, and the lesson title on your picture narration, and put it in your History Record Book.

Activity 4. Optional: A Wreath About Greece *(Offline)*
Instructions

Review what you know about life in ancient Greece. Think about Homer, the Parthenon, Athena, Plato, Aristotle, and democracy. What were these people, places, and ideas? How did they contribute to Greek life? After discussing these questions, create your own olive branch wreath to show what you have learned.

Measure around your head with a tape measure or piece of string. Then make enough 1½- to 2-inch strips of brown construction paper to fit around your head when stapled or glued together. Once you have made this headband, use the Wreath About Greece activity sheet to trace some olive leaves on green construction paper. Cut them out and glue them to your headband.

Now color and cut out the small pictures that show some of the people, places, and ideas you reviewed about ancient Greece. Glue each picture to one of the leaves.

Then hang each leaf from a paper clip and attach it to your wreath. Put your wreath on your head or show it to someone else while you explain what each of the hanging olive leaves tells us about ancient Greece.

Activity 5. Optional: Glories of Greece *(Offline)*
Instructions

Read all or part of Children of Ancient Athens to learn more about what life was like in ancient Greece. Learn the "Who's Who of Greek Gods." Find out what it's like to "Dress Like an Ancient Athenian," and enjoy "Staying Fit in Ancient Athens."

This magazine is available both in the library and for purchase online at Cobblestone Publishing (http://www.cobblestonepub.com).

As usual, preview the recommended reading material listed here before having your student view it.

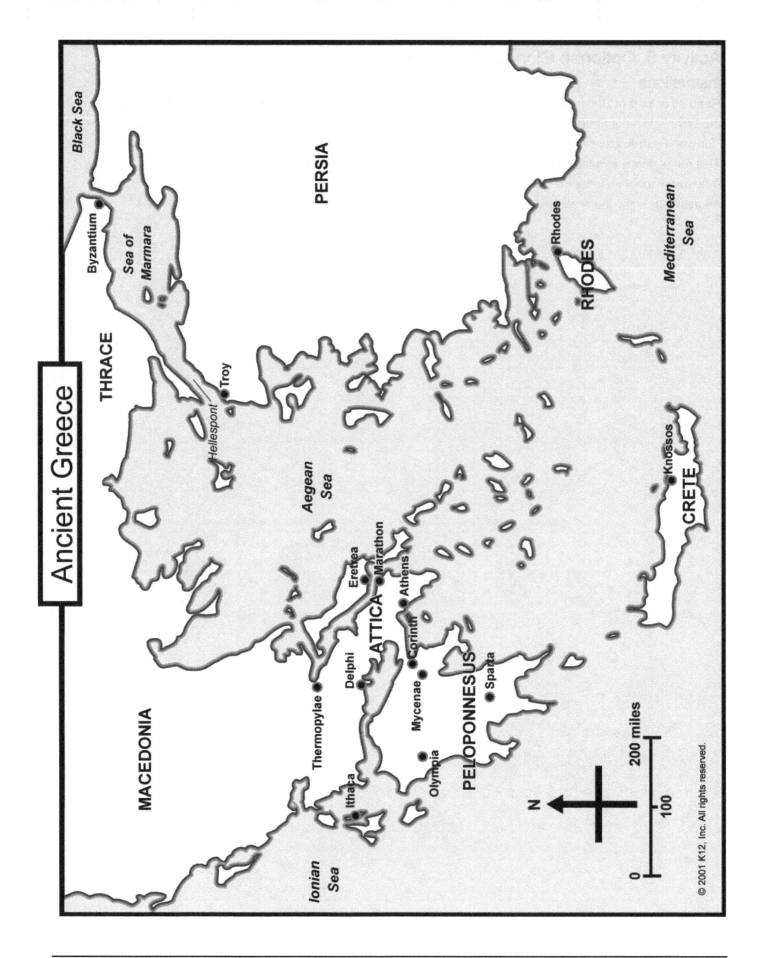

Ancient Greece

Black Sea

THRACE

MACEDONIA

PERSIA

Byzantium

Sea of Marmara

Troy

Hellespont

Aegean Sea

Eretrea

Marathon

Athens

ATTICA

Corinth

Delphi

Thermopylae

Ithaca

Mycenae

Olympia

Sparta

PELOPONNESUS

Ionian Sea

Rhodes

RHODES

Mediterranean Sea

Knossos

CRETE

N

0   100   200 miles

© 2001 K12, Inc. All rights reserved.

Name   Date

Wreath About Greece

Use brown and green construction paper, and the pictures on this page, to create an olive branch wreath about life in ancient Greece. Make a headband from brown construction paper. Use the olive leaf pattern to trace green leaves, and glue them to the headband. Then make six more leaves, color and cut out the pictures at the bottom of the page, and glue one picture to each leaf. Use paper clips to attach these leaves to your headband. Then use your headband to tell someone else about ancient Greek history.

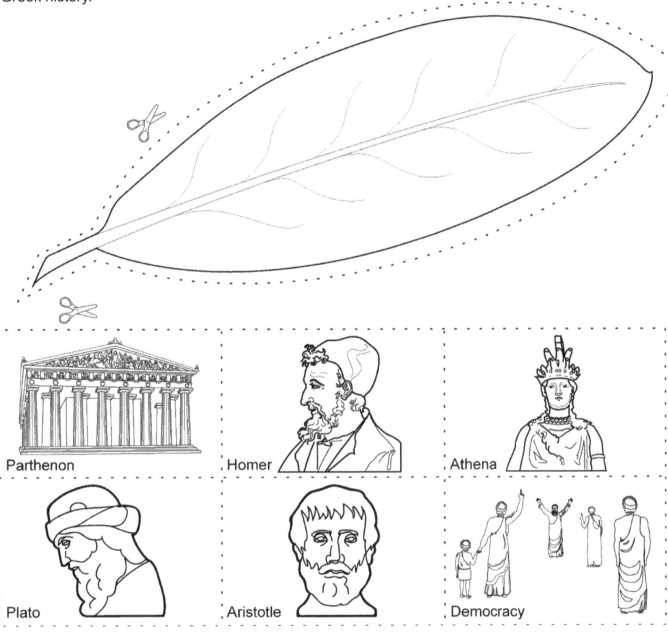

Parthenon   Homer   Athena

Plato   Aristotle   Democracy

Student Guide
Lesson 3. Optional: Remembering Rome

Romans borrowed the gods and ideas of the ancient Greeks, and built a great civilization. Rome gave the world a great literature of its own.

Lesson Objectives

- State that Romans adopted many Greek ideas.
- State that Latin was the language of ancient Rome.
- Identify Cicero and Virgil as great Roman writers.

PREPARE

Approximate lesson time is 60 minutes.

Materials

> For the Student
>> 🖳 Map of Ancient Italy
>>
>> History Record Book
>
> Optional
>> Children of Ancient Rome. AppleSeeds, Cobblestone Publishing, December 2000.

Keywords and Pronunciation

Aeneid (uh-NEE-id)

Athena (uh-THEE-nuh)

Cicero (SIS-uh-roh)

Minerva (muh-NUR-vuh)

Pantheon (PAN-thee-ahn)

republic : A government in which citizens vote for leaders.

Virgil (VUR-juhl)

Zeus (zoos)

LEARN
Activity 1. Optional: Optional Lesson Instructions (Online)

This lesson is OPTIONAL. It is provided for students who seek enrichment or extra practice. You may skip this lesson.

If you choose to skip this lesson, then go to the Plan or Lesson Lists page and mark this lesson "Skipped" in order to proceed to the next lesson in the course.

Activity 2. Optional: Glories of Ancient Rome *(Online)*

Activity 3. Optional: History Record Book *(Online)*
Instructions
Choose either A or B.

A. Written Narration. Write two to four sentences explaining what the lesson was about. If necessary, use the Show You Know questions to help get started. Only include the most important parts of the lesson. Write your name, the date, and the lesson title on your written narration, and put it in your History Record Book.

Sample written narration: "Virgil was a poet in Rome. He went to Rome to see Cicero. Virgil wrote in Latin. The Romans got many great ideas from the Greeks."

B. Picture Narration. Draw a picture of the part of the lesson that interested you most. When you have finished drawing, describe the picture. Below your picture, write a description of what you have drawn. Write your name, the date, and the lesson title on your picture narration, and put it in your History Record Book.

Activity 4. Optional: Virgil, Cicero, and You *(Online)*
Instructions
Virgil noticed many things about Rome as he made way to Cicero's house. Here are some of the things he saw:

- Rome was surrounded by seven hills.
- The city had narrow streets.
- Temples, government buildings, and theaters were everywhere.
- Some buildings were made of white marble and had huge column.

Write a four-line poem about the things Virgil noticed about Rome. If you want, use the following sentence for the first line. You may or may not choose to make your poem rhyme.

"Virgil came to Rome seeking Cicero."

After you finish, try reciting your poem to an audience.

Activity 5. Optional: Remembering Rome *(Online)*
Instructions
The December 2000 issue of AppleSeeds is titled Children of Ancient Rome. This amply illustrated issue has articles about everyday life in Rome, the Colosseum, children's games, and how people got clean.

Perhaps the most interesting article is about what people in ancient Rome ate. You might be surprised!

This issue is available in a library or for purchase online at Cobblestone Publishing (http://www.cobblestonepub.com).

As usual, preview the recommended reading material listed here before having your student view it.

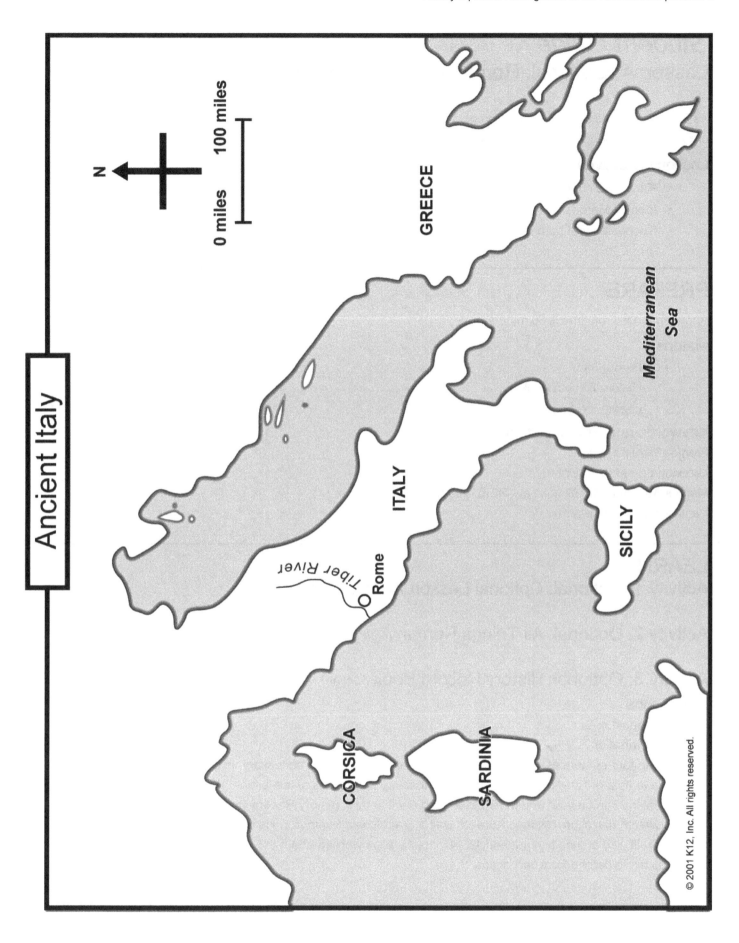

Ancient Italy

N

0 miles

100 miles

GREECE

Mediterranean Sea

ITALY

SICILY

Tiber River

Rome

CORSICA

SARDINIA

Student Guide
Lesson 4. Optional: Roman Greatness, Roman Peril

As Rome grew and became a great empire, the city's art and architecture reflected its wealth. Marcus Aurelius presided over a period of splendor and danger as Rome faced invasions on its east and north.

Lesson Objectives

- Name two characteristics of Roman architecture (such as domes, arches, aqueducts, marble).
- Identify Marcus Aurelius as a great emperor of ancient Rome.
- Recognize that barbarian tribes on Rome's borders threatened Rome.

PREPARE

Approximate lesson time is 60 minutes.

Materials

> For the Student
>> History Record Book
>> paper, notebook

Keywords and Pronunciation

Fronto (FRAHN-toh)

Laocoon (lay-AH-kuh-wahn)

Marcus Aurelius (MAHR-kuhs aw-REEL-yuhs)

Pantheon (PAN-thee-ahn)

LEARN
Activity 1. Optional: Optional Lesson Instructions *(Online)*

Activity 2. Optional: All Things Roman *(Online)*

Activity 3. Optional: History Record Book *(Online)*

Instructions

Choose either A or B.

A. Written Narration

Write two to four sentences explaining what the lesson was about. If necessary, use the Show You Know questions to help get started. Only include the most important parts of the lesson. Write your name, the date, and the lesson title on your written narration, and put it in your History Record Book.

Sample written narration: "Marcus Aurelius was a great Roman emperor. He was very proud of things Romans built, like arches and aqueducts. Marcus Aurelius worried about the Roman Empire. He worried that it was too big to defend from barbarians."

B. Picture Narration

Draw a picture of the part of the lesson that interested you most. When you have finished drawing, describe the picture. Below your picture, write a description of what you have drawn. Write your name, the date, and the lesson title on your picture narration, and put it in your History Record Book.

Activity 4. Optional: Letter from Fronto *(Online)*

Instructions

Marcus Aurelius wrote a letter to Fronto about the glories of Rome and his fears for Rome's future. Have your student imagine that he is Fronto. After Fronto receives the letter from Marcus, he decides that people who come after Rome should know why Rome was great and what its downfall was. He writes an open letter to be put somewhere safe and secure so that future generations will know about Rome.

The letter should include the following key points:

Roman greatness:
- architecture (domes, arches, aqueducts, the forum)
- art (sculptures like the Laocoön)
- government (Rome was a republic)

Roman peril:
- barbarians along the border, hungry for more land
- an empire so large the Roman army couldn't defend it

Activity 5. Optional: Roman Greatness, Roman Peril *(Online)*

Marcus mentioned the Laocoön, a sculpture carved during the height of Roman greatness. Go online and learn more about this work of art.

Student Guide
Lesson 5: A Dangerous Feudal World

When the Roman Empire fell, wars, fighting, and insecurity characterized life in much of Europe. The Middle Ages were a dangerous time, when feudalism offered people some protection, and faith offered most people their only hope for something better.

Lesson Objectives
- Describe the Middle Ages as a dangerous and hard time.
- Define the feudal system as an exchange of protection for service and labor.
- Identify Christianity as the dominant faith of Europe.
- Recognize the functions of castles, cathedrals, and monasteries.

PREPARE

Approximate lesson time is 60 minutes.

Materials
    For the Student
        History Record Book
        🖥 Feudal Mobile activity sheet
        glue, children's white
        paper, construction
        pencils, colored 12
        scissors
    Optional
        The Duke and the Peasant: Life in the Middle Ages by Sister Wendy Beckett

Keywords and Pronunciation
Charlemagne (SHAHR-luh-mayn)
feudalism (FYOO-dl-ih-zuhm) : A political or economic system in which people exchanged land, loyalty, and service in return for protection.

LEARN
Activity 1: Rome Falls and the Middle Ages Begin (Online)

Activity 2: History Record Book (Online)

Instructions
Choose either A or B.

A. Written Narration. Write two to four sentences explaining what the lesson was about. If necessary, use the Show You Know questions to help get started. Only include the most important parts of the lesson. Write your name, the date, and the lesson title on your written narration, and put it in your History Record Book.

Sample written narration: "The Middle Ages were a hard time for people. There was a lot of fighting and disease. People built castles during the Middle Ages. They built big churches called cathedrals, too."

B. Picture Narration. Draw a picture of the part of the lesson that interested you most. When you have finished drawing, describe the picture. Below your picture, write a description of what you have drawn. Write your name, the date, and the lesson title on your picture narration, and put it in your History Record Book.

Activity 3: Feudal Mobile *(Online)*
Instructions

After the fall of the Roman Empire, things fell apart. Cities crumbled, roads practically disappeared, and people forgot how to read and write. Life was hard during the Middle Ages. It was also a dangerous time, with kings and nobles fighting each other for land and power.

Kings like Charlemagne started a system called feudalism to try to stop the fighting. You can think of this system as a triangle, with the king at the top, and nobles below him. Below the nobles were knights, and at the bottom of the triangle were the serfs.

In feudalism, people exchanged land, loyalty, and service for protection. All the people in the feudal system--kings, nobles, knights, and serfs--depended on castles for their safety.

There was something else that helped people get by in these difficult times--the Christian Church. The pope sent priests and bishops across Europe to spread Christianity. Priests built churches and bishops built cathedrals. Monks also traveled across Europe, building monasteries where they lived together and devoted their lives to God. Follow the directions on the Feudal Mobile activity sheet to make a mobile showing the people and buildings of the Middle Ages.

ASSESS
Lesson Assessment: A Dangerous Feudal World (*Online*)

You will complete an offline assessment covering the main objectives of this lesson. Your learning coach will score this assessment.

LEARN
Activity 4. Optional: A Dangerous Feudal World *(Online)*
Instructions

The book *The Duke and the Peasant: Life in the Middle Ages*, by Sister Wendy Beckett and Jean de France, Duc de Berry (New York: Prestel, 1997), gives a detailed account, in text and illustrations, of the lives of nobles and peasants. See how medieval life changed as the seasons changed.

The book is based on the calendar pictures from the *Book of Hours*. This prayer book was owned by the Duc de Berry, a French nobleman from the fourteenth century.

As usual, preview the recommended reading material listed here before having your student view it.

Feudal Mobile

1. Color the pictures of buildings on page 2, cut them out, and glue each one onto a piece of construction paper slightly bigger than the picture itself.
2. Hang the four pictures of buildings from a hanger.
3. Color, cut out, and glue onto pieces of construction paper the pictures of people on page 3.
4. Hang each picture of a person below the building that person is associated with. For the people associated with the castle, hang them below the castle, one below the other, in the order that feudalism placed them.

Example:

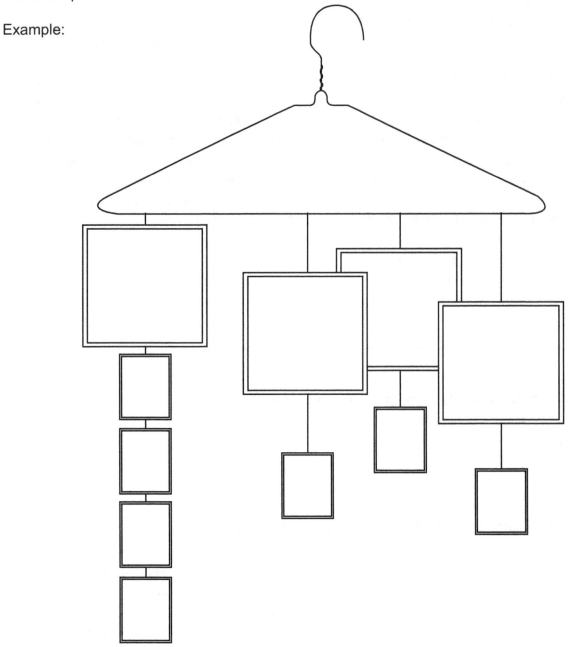

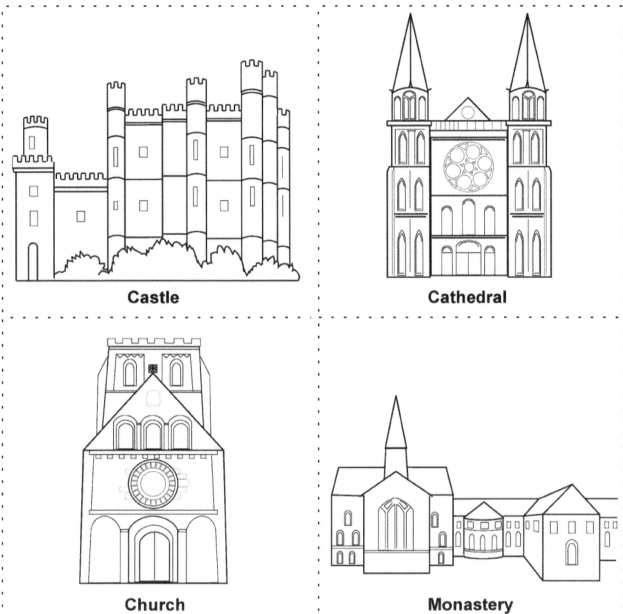

Castle

Cathedral

Church

Monastery

King

Noble

Knight

Serf

Bishop

Priest

Monk

Lesson Assessment

A Dangerous Feudal World

1. Were the Middle Ages a time of peace and plenty, or a dangerous and hard

   time?_____

2. What was the name of the system that traded land or services for protection?_____

3. Why was Europe called Christendom?_____

4. What is another name for fortresses that kings built to protect their lands?_____

5. What do we call the larger churches built by bishops so people could pray for help when life got

   hard during the Middle Ages?_____

6. What was a monastery?_____

Student Guide
Lesson 6: Monks, Islam, and the Light of Classical Learning

Preserved and translated by Muslim scholars, the works of ancient Greek and Roman philosophers survived into the Middle Ages. By the late Middle Ages those works were reaching European monks, who took up their study.

Lesson Objectives

- Explain that in monasteries monks copied books and preserved learning.
- Name Islam as a religion that valued learning and preserved classical works in the Middle Ages.
- Recognize that by the late Middle Ages, European thinkers were rediscovering ancient Greek writers.

PREPARE

Approximate lesson time is 60 minutes.

Materials

For the Student

🖳 Map of Europe and the Middle East

History Record Book

glue, children's white

paper, construction

pencils, colored 12

scissors

Optional

The House of Wisdom by Florence Parry Heide

Keywords and Pronunciation

Baghdad (BAG-dad)

Islam (is-LAHM)

Muhammed (moh-HAM-uhd)

Muslim (MOUZ-luhm)

Thomas Aquinas (uh-KWIY-nuhs)

LEARN
Activity 1: The Light of Classical Learning *(Online)*

Activity 2: History Record Book (Online)

Instructions

Choose either A or B.

A. Written Narration.

Write two to four sentences explaining what the lesson was about. If necessary, use the Show You Know questions to help get started. Only include the most important parts of the lesson. Write your name, the date, and the lesson title on your written narration, and put it in your History Record Book.

Sample written narration: "Thomas Aquinas was a good student, but he was quiet. He lived during the Middle Ages. When he grew up, he liked to read old books by Aristotle. Thomas Aquinas wrote books, too."

B. Picture Narration.

Draw a picture of the part of the lesson that interested you most. When you have finished drawing, describe the picture. Below your picture, write a description of what you have drawn. Write your name, the date, and the lesson title on your picture narration, and put it in your History Record Book.

Activity 3: Learning with Thomas Aquinas and Aristotle (Online)

Instructions

Both St. Thomas Aquinas and Aristotle loved learning. Show that you do, too, by following these directions to create a collage about their ideas and yours.

Copy this saying of St. Thomas Aquinas at the top of a piece of construction paper:

"Wonder...is the cause of delight because it carries the hope of discovery."

Below it, copy this quote from Aristotle:

"Whereas a rattle is a suitable toy for infant children, education serves as a rattle for young people."

Below that, write your own saying about learning.

Now look in magazines for pictures that illustrate all three ideas. Create a collage around the sayings to show what learning means to these famous thinkers and to you.

Extension: Here are two sayings about friendship from these philosophers. Add your own idea and create another collage.

St. Thomas Aquinas: "There is nothing on this Earth more to be prized than true friendship."

Aristotle: "What is a friend? A single soul in two bodies."

ASSESS

Lesson Assessment: Monks, Islam, and the Light of Classical Learning (Online)

You will complete an offline assessment covering the main objectives of this lesson. Your learning coach will score this assessment

LEARN
Activity 4. Optional: Monks, Islam, and the Light of Classical Learning *(Online)*
Instructions

Learn more about the place of learning in Baghdad that housed books but was much more than a library.

Check your library or bookstore for *The House of Wisdom* by Florence Parry Heide and Judith Heide Gilliland, illustrated by Mary Grandpre (New York: Dorling Kindersley Publishing, 1999).

As usual, preview the recommended reading material listed here before having your student view it.

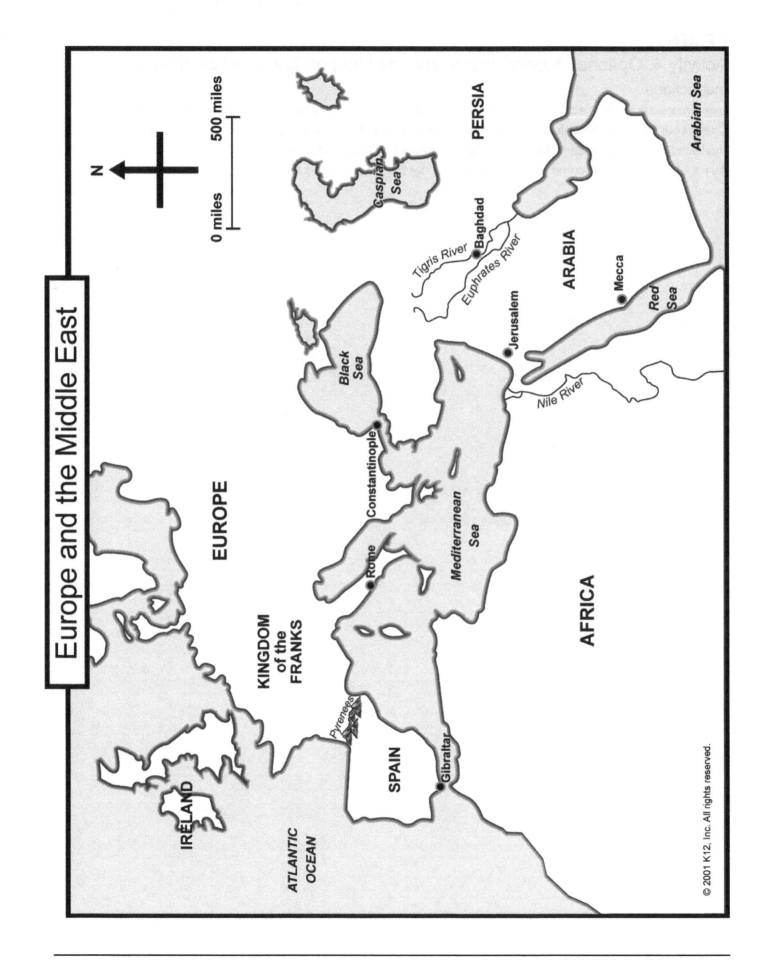

Europe and the Middle East

N

500 miles

0 miles

IRELAND

ATLANTIC OCEAN

EUROPE

KINGDOM of the FRANKS

Pyrenees

SPAIN

Gibraltar

Rome

Constantinople

Black Sea

Mediterranean Sea

Caspian Sea

PERSIA

Tigris River

Baghdad

Euphrates River

Jerusalem

Nile River

AFRICA

ARABIA

Mecca

Red Sea

Arabian Sea

Lesson Assessment

Monks, Islam, and the Light of Classical Learning

1. Who copied old manuscripts and preserved learning in Europe during the Middle Ages?_____

2. What was the religion of the people who translated, copied, and saved the works of the ancient Greeks and Romans in centers of learning on the Arabian peninsula and elsewhere?_____

3. Whose works did Thomas Aquinas use to help him in his thinking?_____

Student Guide
Lesson 7: Dante Writes a Book

Meet Dante Alighieri, a master storyteller and great poet who wrote the most important work of literature of the Middle Ages. In those uncertain times, Dante's imaginative journey through the afterlife to the gates of heaven revealed that faith provided hope.

Lesson Objectives
- Identify Dante as the author of *The Divine Comedy*.
- Describe *The Divine Comedy* as a poem about life after death.
- Explain that the Christian faith provided hope for many Europeans during the Middle Ages.

PREPARE

Approximate lesson time is 60 minutes.

Materials
> For the Student
>> Map of Italy in the Middle Ages
>>
>> History Record Book
>>
>> pencils, colored 12

Keywords and Pronunciation
Dante Alighieri (DAHN-tay ahl-eeg-YEH-ree)
Virgil (VUR-juhl)

LEARN
Activity 1: Dante's Divine Poem *(Online)*

Activity 2: History Record Book *(Online)*
Instructions
Choose either A or B.

A. Written Narration. Write two to four sentences explaining what the lesson was about. If necessary, use the Show You Know questions to help get started. Only include the most important parts of the lesson. Write your name, the date, and the lesson title on your written narration, and put it in your History Record Book.

Sample written narration: "Dante was sad because he had to leave his home. He wrote a poem called *The Divine Comedy*. It was about life after death. In the poem, he meets Beatrice in heaven."

B. Picture Narration. Draw a picture of the part of the lesson that interested you most. When you have finished drawing, describe the picture. Below your picture, write a description of what you have drawn. Write your name, the date, and the lesson title on your picture narration, and put it in your History Record Book.

Activity 3: A *Divine Comedy* Poster *(Online)*
Instructions

Even though *The Divine Comedy* is almost 700 years old, people still read it today. It's one of the greatest poems ever written. But would even more people read this great work if you reminded them about it? Maybe a poster would do the trick.

Your job is to create a poster highlighting Dante's famous work. Begin by reviewing some of the key ideas you learned about this poem.

1. The *Divine Comedy* was a poem about life after death.
2. Beatrice inspired Dante to write it. He thought she looked like an angel.
3. Dante wrote the poem after he had to leave his family and the city of Florence.
4. The poem was called a comedy because it had a happy ending.
5. The poem had a sad beginning.
6. Dante chose his favorite poet, Virgil, to guide him through hell and up to the gates of heaven.
7. Dante wrote The Divine Comedy in Italian, not in Latin.
8. Dante, like other people of his time, looked to Christianity for hope.

Plan your poster on drawing paper before you create it. What do you want people to know about Dante and his poem?

Make a list of the ideas you want to show. Find the right colors and materials for your message. Then create your poster.

Show your poster to someone else and explain what you know about Dante and his famous poem, The Divine Comedy.

ASSESS

Lesson Assessment: Dante Writes a Book (*Online*)

You will complete an offline assessment covering the main objectives of this lesson. Your learning coach will score this assessment.

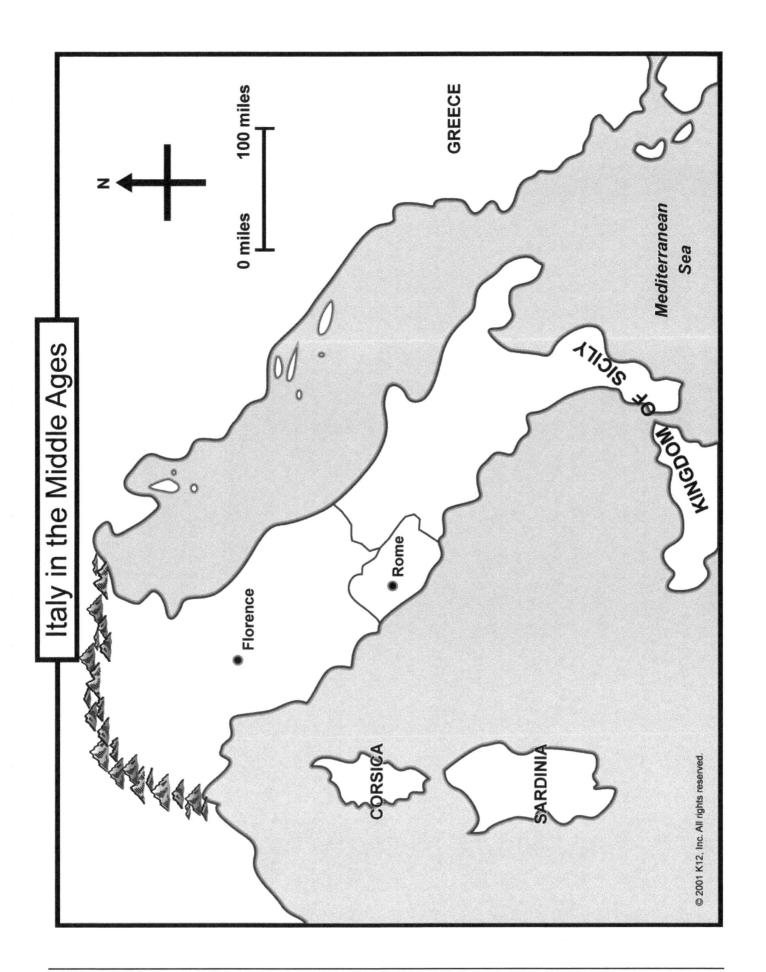

Italy in the Middle Ages

N

100 miles

0 miles

GREECE

Mediterranean Sea

KINGDOM OF SICILY

Florence

Rome

CORSICA

SARDINIA

Lesson Assessment

Dante Writes a Book

1. Who wrote *The Divine Comedy*?_____

2. Was *The Divine Comedy* about life on earth or life after death?_____

3. During the hard and dangerous Middle Ages in Europe, what gave people

   hope?_____

Student Guide
Lesson 8: Giotto Breaks with the Past

In the late Middle Ages, while monks pursued learning and scholarship, town life began to flourish once more. The church commissioned more art for churches, convents, monasteries, and palaces. From the Italian hillsides came a shepherd boy named Giotto, who awed his patrons with his lifelike art.

Lesson Objectives
- Name Giotto as a great artist of the late Middle Ages.
- State that Giotto painted realistic figures and showed emotions.
- Contrast Giotto's style with that of medieval art.

PREPARE

Approximate lesson time is 60 minutes.

Materials
For the Student
- Map of Italy in the Middle Ages
- History Record Book

Keywords and Pronunciation
Giotto di Bondone (JAWT-toh dee bohn-DOH-nay)

LEARN
Activity 1: Giotto: The Artist *(Online)*

Activity 2: History Record Book *(Online)*
Instructions
Choose either A or B.

A. Written Narration
Write two to four sentences explaining what the lesson was about. If necessary, use the Show You Know questions to help get started. Only include the most important parts of the lesson. Write your name, the date, and the lesson title on your written narration, and put it in your History Record Book.

Sample written narration: "Giotto was a shepherd. He liked to paint pictures of animals like sheep. He went to Florence and Rome and painted in new ways. His paintings looked more real than the ones people painted before."

B. Picture Narration
Draw a picture of the part of the lesson that interested you most. When you have finished drawing, describe the picture. Below your picture, write a description of what you have drawn. Write your name, the date, and the lesson title on your picture narration, and put it in your History Record Book.

Activity 3: A Painting Inspired by Giotto *(Online)*

Try your hand at painting like Giotto.

ASSESS

Lesson Assessment: Giotto Breaks with the Past *(Online)*

You will complete an offline assessment covering the main objectives of this lesson. Your learning coach will score this assessment.

LEARN

Activity 4. Optional: Giotto Breaks with the Past *(Online)*

Here's your chance to choose a favorite work by Giotto.

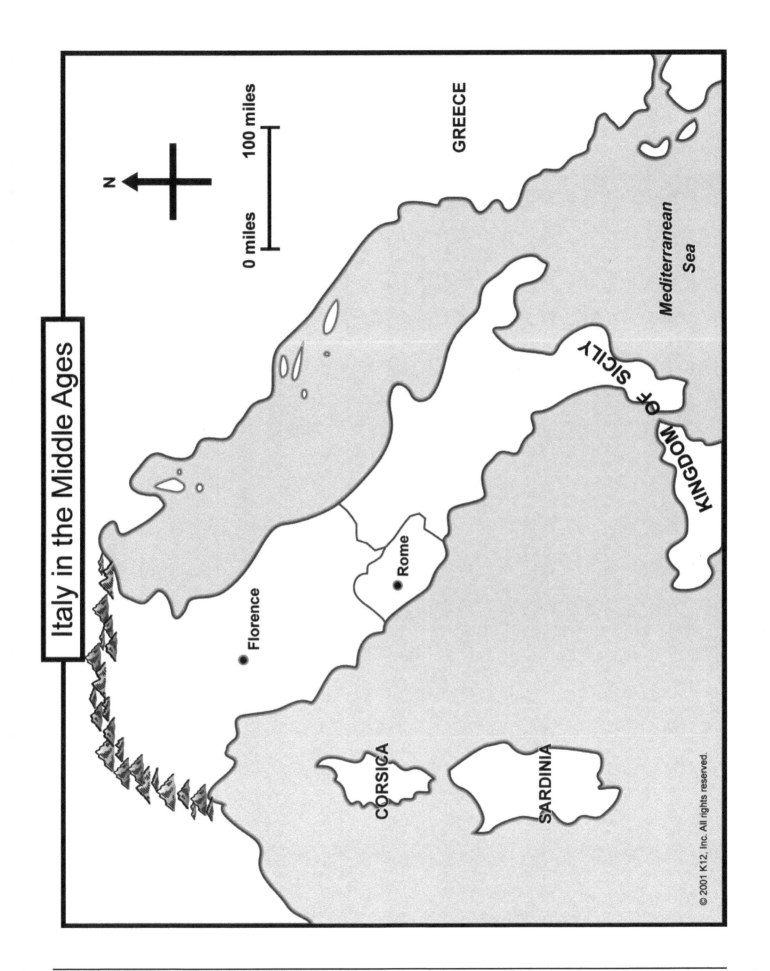

Italy in the Middle Ages

N

100 miles

0 miles

GREECE

Mediterranean Sea

KINGDOM OF SICILY

Florence

Rome

CORSICA

SARDINIA

Lesson Assessment

Giotto Breaks with the Past

1. What is the name of the great artist of the late Middle Ages who broke with the old ways of painting? _____

2. How do you describe Giotto's style? _____

3. What are some of the differences between Giotto's paintings and those of medieval artists? _____

Student Guide
Lesson 9: Petrarch: The Treasure Hunter

Meet Petrarch, a scholar and poet who paved the way for the Renaissance. He described the time he lived in as a "dark age," and urged a rediscovery of the humanistic works of ancient Greece and Rome.

Lesson Objectives
- Identify Petrarch as a writer and poet inspired by classical writers.
- Identify humanism as the idea that humans are good and capable of great things.
- Name Petrarch as the first humanist.

PREPARE

Approximate lesson time is 60 minutes.

Materials
> For the Student
>> History Record Book
>>
>> paper, notebook

Keywords and Pronunciation
humanism (HYOO-muh-nih-zuhm) : The idea that humans are good and capable of great things.
Petrarch (PEH-trahrk)

LEARN
Activity 1: Meet Petrarch *(Online)*

Activity 2: History Record Book *(Online)*
Instructions
Choose either A or B.
A. Written Narration
Write two to four sentences explaining what the lesson was about. If necessary, use the Show You Know questions to help get started. Only include the most important parts of the lesson. Write your name, the date, and the lesson title on your written narration, and put it in your History Record Book.
Sample written narration: "Petrarch liked to write letters. He wrote poems, too. He liked the Greeks and Romans. He believed that people were good and could do great things."

B. Picture Narration
Draw a picture of the part of the lesson that interested you most. When you have finished drawing, describe the picture. Below your picture, write a description of what you have drawn. Write your name, the date, and the lesson title on your picture narration, and put it in your History Record Book.

Activity 3: A Letter to Petrarch (Online)
Instructions

In the story "A Letter from Petrarch," you learned a lot about this famous writer and poet. Petrarch explained that he liked writing letters and poetry. He described his love of learning, reading, and travel. He mentioned his interest in the works of classical Greek and Roman writers, especially Cicero and Virgil.

Petrarch believed that human beings are good and capable of doing great things. His writing described his great faith in humanity. People have called Petrarch the first humanist.

Now it's your turn. Think about what you enjoy and how you like to learn. Then write a letter to Petrarch about your ideas. Explain what you marvel at and what you think people can do and be.

ASSESS
Lesson Assessment: Petrarch: The Treasure Hunter (Online)

You will complete an offline assessment covering the main objectives of this lesson. Your learning coach will score this assessment.

LEARN
Activity 4. Optional: Petrarch: The Treasure Hunter (Online)
Instructions

Petrarch believed that human beings are capable of great things. He believed that people can express themselves in beautiful ways--through painting, sculpting, building, and writing wonderful poems.

People remember Petrarch for both his letters and his poetry. Here is the first verse of one of his poems. The first line is written both in Italian and in English, so that you can see Petrarch's language. You might want to try reading both the English and the Italian versions aloud together.

Vago augelletto che cantando vai,
Little wandering bird that goes singing,

Then read the whole verse aloud in English and think about what it says. Do you think this poem is about a small bird that is missing summer and is sad about winter coming?

Little wandering bird that goes singing,
Your time gone by, with weeping notes,
Seeing the night and the winter near,
And the day and all the joyful months behind....

Now it's your turn to write some poetry. Decide what should come next in this poem. Then write one or two more verses of four lines each. What will happen to the little bird in your poem? After you finish, read your poem aloud to a friend and explain that you have been writing poetry with Petrarch, the first humanist.

Lesson Assessment

Petrarch: The Treasure Hunter

1. What was Petrarch known for?_____

2. What other writers inspired Petrarch?_____

3. What do we call the idea that humans are good and capable of great things?_____

4. Who was the first humanist?_____

Student Guide
Lesson 10: Unit Review and Assessment

You've completed this unit, and now it's time to review what you've learned and take the unit assessment.

Lesson Objectives

- Demonstrate mastery of important knowledge and skills in this unit.
- Explain that *Renaissance* means *rebirth*.
- State that rebirth meant a new interest in the civilizations of ancient Greece and Rome.
- Describe the Middle Ages as a dangerous and hard time.
- Define the feudal system as an exchange of protection for service and labor.
- Explain that in monasteries monks copied books and preserved learning.
- Name Islam as a religion that valued learning and preserved classical works in the Middle Ages.
- Recognize that by the late Middle Ages, European thinkers were rediscovering ancient Greek writers.
- Identify Dante as the author of *The Divine Comedy*.
- State that Giotto painted realistic figures and showed emotions.
- Identify humanism as the idea that humans are good and capable of great things.
- Identify Christianity as the dominant faith of Europe.

PREPARE

Approximate lesson time is 60 minutes.

Materials

> For the Student
>> History Record Book

Keywords and Pronunciation

aqueducts (AK-wuh-dukts)

Aquinas (uh-KWIY-nuhs)

Aristotle (AIR-uh-stah-tl)

Athena (uh-THEE-nuh)

Cicero (SIS-uh-roh)

Dante Alighieri (DAHN-tay ahl-eeg-YEH-ree)

Giotto di Bondone (JAWT-toh dee bohn-DOH-nay)

Petrarch (PEH-trahrk)

Renaissance (REH-nuh-sahns) : Literally, rebirth; the time in Europe, beginning in the 1300s, when there was a new interest in the civilizations of ancient Greece and Rome.

Virgil (VUR-juhl)

LEARN
Activity 1: A Look Back (Online)
Instructions

We've said that history is like a good book. It's a grand connected story. To understand one chapter, like the Renaissance, you need to know the chapter that's gone before. In these last nine lessons we've been taking a quick look back as we get ready to move forward and study the Renaissance.

Do you remember what *Renaissance* means? If you said "rebirth," you've been paying attention. But what was reborn and what was left behind? Let's review.

In the first lesson you created a time line of history. We could put more civilizations and other periods on that time line, but we've been looking at the stretch from ancient Greece to the Middle Ages. We've almost reached the Renaissance.

What do you remember about ancient Greece? Do you remember the poet Homer with his tales of adventure? Do you think about the noisy Greek democracy? Or Athena in the white marble Parthenon? Maybe you remember those great thinkers, Plato and Aristotle. Ancient Greece came first on our time line.

Next came the mighty civilization of ancient Rome. The Romans borrowed a lot from the Greeks: gods and goddesses, and ideas about what human beings could do. What do you remember about Rome? Its domed Pantheon filled with statues of gods and goddesses? Its arches and aqueducts? Do you remember Rome's republic or its great Latin writers such as Virgil and Cicero?

The ancient civilizations of Greece and Rome are often called "classical" civilizations. These two great civilizations shared many things in common. They shared a belief that human beings were capable of thinking great thoughts and doing great things. They found ways for men to govern themselves and not be ruled by kings. They wrote wonderful poems and dramas. They built amazing buildings, and the Romans built a whole empire.

But then what happened? The Roman Empire collapsed. Barbarian tribes swept out of the north, and in A.D. 476 the last Roman emperor was overthrown. That's what we call the "fall of Rome." What period came next? If you said "the Middle Ages," you're right.

"The Middle Ages" is a funny name. What were they in the middle of? The Middle Ages stand like a long bridge between ancient and modern times. Some people who lived at the end of the Middle Ages, like Aquinas and Dante, might say it was a long, bright bridge. Others like Petrarch and Giotto, who longed for something different, might say it was a long, dark bridge. But here's what we know about the Middle Ages. People lived very hard lives. They didn't wake up knowing they were safe and going to have a good day. From the moment those barbarian tribes swept down the Italian peninsula and toppled the Roman Empire, life got harder. It was a time of fighting, danger, and plague. Kings and nobles built castles for protection. Bishops and priests built cathedrals and churches to pray for safety. The Christian faith grew. Dante's poem shows us how Christianity gave people hope of a better life after death. They needed that hope.

But by 1350 something new was in the air. Books were being written. Towns were being built. Think back to the painting we studied at the beginning of these lessons. Do you remember that picture of spring? It was bright and graceful. It was full of trees, flowers, gentle breezes, and handsome gods and goddesses. The painting itself is a story of rebirth. *Renaissance* means "rebirth."

So what was reborn? Interest in ancient Greece and Rome. Thinkers like Thomas Aquinas had studied Aristotle. Writers like Dante had admired Virgil. Now artists like Giotto said we could learn something from Roman painting. Poets like Petrarch said it was time to reread Cicero and Virgil. Those ancient writers could teach us about humanism, the idea that humans are good and capable of great things.

You might think, "Well, what difference could it make if a lot of people sat around reading old Greek and Roman books? So what if they looked at old Greek and Roman art?" In the next unit you'll discover that it made a big difference. Europe was about to be reborn.

Activity 2: History Record Book Review *(Online)*

Instructions

Use the contents of your History Record Book to review the unit on Background to the Renaissance. Take some time to revisit the narrations, activity sheets, writing activities, and pictures in the History Record Book. Read the narrations aloud. Don't hurry this part of the review; it will refresh your memory and give you a sense of just how much you've already learned.

Activity 3: Online Interactive Review *(Online)*

ASSESS

Unit Assessment: Unit Review and Assessment (*Offline*)

Complete an offline Unit Assessment. Your learning coach will score this part of the Assessment.

Name _____   Date _____

Background to the Renaissance

Read each question and its answer choices. Fill in the bubble in front of the word or words that best answer the question.

1. What does the word *Renaissance* mean?
   ⓐ reread
   ⓑ rebirth
   ⓒ study
   ⓓ write

2. During the Renaissance there was a renewed interest in which two ancient civilizations?
   ⓐ Mesopotamia and Egypt
   ⓑ Greece and Rome
   ⓒ Japan and China
   ⓓ India and Arabia

3. Complete this sentence: The Middle Ages could best be described as a time of _____.
   ⓐ peace and plenty
   ⓑ danger and hardship
   ⓒ law and order
   ⓓ inventions and progress

4. What did some European thinkers, like Thomas Aquinas, rediscover during the late Middle Ages?
   ⓐ ancient Greek writers
   ⓑ ancient Egyptian treasures
   ⓒ ancient African kingdoms
   ⓓ ancient Chinese tombs

5. Who was an artist of the late Middle Ages who painted in a realistic style?
    ⓐ Thomas Aquinas
    ⓑ Dante Aligihieri
    ⓒ Giotto di Bondone
    ⓓ Francesco Petrarch

6. This religion valued learning and spread through Arabia,
   Mesopotamia, and North Africa during the Middle Ages.
    ⓐ Judaism
    ⓑ Christianity
    ⓒ Islam
    ⓓ Buddhism

7. Humanists believe that _____.
    ⓐ animals should be more like humans.
    ⓑ humans can do great things.
    ⓒ the human body should be studied.
    ⓓ plants can be made to look like humans.

8. During the Middle Ages, which people copied books and helped keep
   learning alive?
    ⓐ bishops
    ⓑ knights
    ⓒ monks
    ⓓ serfs

9. What do we call the period in history between 476 and about 1350?
    ⓐ the Age of Darkness
    ⓑ the Middle Years
    ⓒ the Time of Danger
    ⓓ the Middle Ages

10. John lived on Lord William's land and worked in the fields outside the castle. In exchange for John's work, Lord William protected John and his family. This is an example of a system that was popular during the Middle Ages. What system was it?

ⓐ republicanism

ⓑ humanism

ⓒ democracy

ⓓ feudalism

11. Who was the great medieval poet who wrote *The Divine Comedy* in Italian?

ⓐ Thomas Aquinas

ⓑ Dante Aligihieri

ⓒ Giotto di Bondone

ⓓ Francesco Petrarch

12. What was the faith of most people in Europe during the Middle Ages?

ⓐ Judaism

ⓑ Islam

ⓒ Christianity

ⓓ Buddhism

Student Guide
Lesson 1: Italy: The Hub of the Renaissance

- Identify Italy, with its numerous competing city-states, as the place where the Renaissance began.
- Identify Florence, Venice, and Rome as centers of Renaissance learning.
- Recognize that artists and scholars were inspired by ancient Greece and Rome.
- Describe the Renaissance ideal of a well-rounded individual (the "Renaissance man").
- Identify key figures, characteristics, and accomplishments of the Italian Renaissance.

Italy, with its central location and competing city-states, gave birth to the Renaissance and became its dynamic center.

Lesson Objectives

- Identify Italy, with its numerous competing city-states, as the place where the Renaissance began.
- Identify Florence, Venice, and Rome as centers of Renaissance learning.
- Recognize that artists and scholars were inspired by ancient Greece and Rome.
- Describe the Renaissance ideal of a well-rounded individual (the "Renaissance man").
- Identify key figures, characteristics, and accomplishments of the Italian Renaissance.
- Locate the Italian peninsula on a map.
- Identify city-states as main political units of Renaissance Italy.
- Identify trade as key to the growth of the Italian city-states.
- Name one major Italian city-state.

PREPARE

Approximate lesson time is 60 minutes.

Materials

For the Student

    📖 Map of Renaissance Italy, A.D. 1450

    History Record Book

    📖 City-States of Renaissance Italy activity sheet

    cardboard

    glue, children's white

    scissors

Keywords and Pronunciation

Alberti (ahl-BAIR-tee)

Cicero (SIS-uh-roh)

city-state : A state consisting of an independent city and its surrounding territory.

Colosseum (kah-luh-SEE-uhm)

Cosimo (KAW-zee-moh)

Pietro (PYEH-troh)

LEARN
Activity 1: Italy's Many States *(Online)*

Activity 2: History Record Book *(Online)*
Instructions
Choose either A or B.

A. Written Narration
Write two to four sentences explaining what the lesson was about. If necessary, use the Show You Know questions to help get started. Only include the most important parts of the lesson. Write your name, the date, and the lesson title on your written narration, and put it in your History Record Book.

Sample written narration: "There were many city-states in Italy. They liked to fight and argue. People came to the city-states to trade. Florence and Venice were important city-states."

B. Picture Narration
Draw a picture of the part of the lesson that interested you most. When you have finished drawing, describe the picture. Below your picture, write a description of what you have drawn. Write your name, the date, and the lesson title on your picture narration, and put it in your History Record Book.

Activity 3: Italy Jigsaw Puzzle *(Online)*
Instructions

At the beginning of this lesson, you were asked to imagine a jigsaw puzzle of the Italian city-states. Now you will have a chance to make one.

Use The City-States of Renaissance Italy activity sheet to say the names and point to the locations of the Italian city-states. The full names of some were longer, such as the Republic of Florence or Kingdom of Naples, but only the last parts of their names--the parts that are also the city names-- are on this map.

Color each city-state a different color, and fill in the map key or legend to show your choices. Look carefully at all the names of the city-states. Some of them are in more than one place, so be sure to make your colors match.

Glue the activity sheet to a piece of lightweight cardboard. Cut it into pieces along any lines you wish. Now reassemble your puzzle and note how the city-states fit together to make up Renaissance Italy around 1450.

ASSESS
Lesson Assessment: The Hub of the Renaissance (*Online*)
You will complete an offline assessment covering the main objectives of this lesson. Your learning coach will score this assessment.

LEARN
Activity 4. Optional: Italy: The Hub of the Renaissance *(Online)*

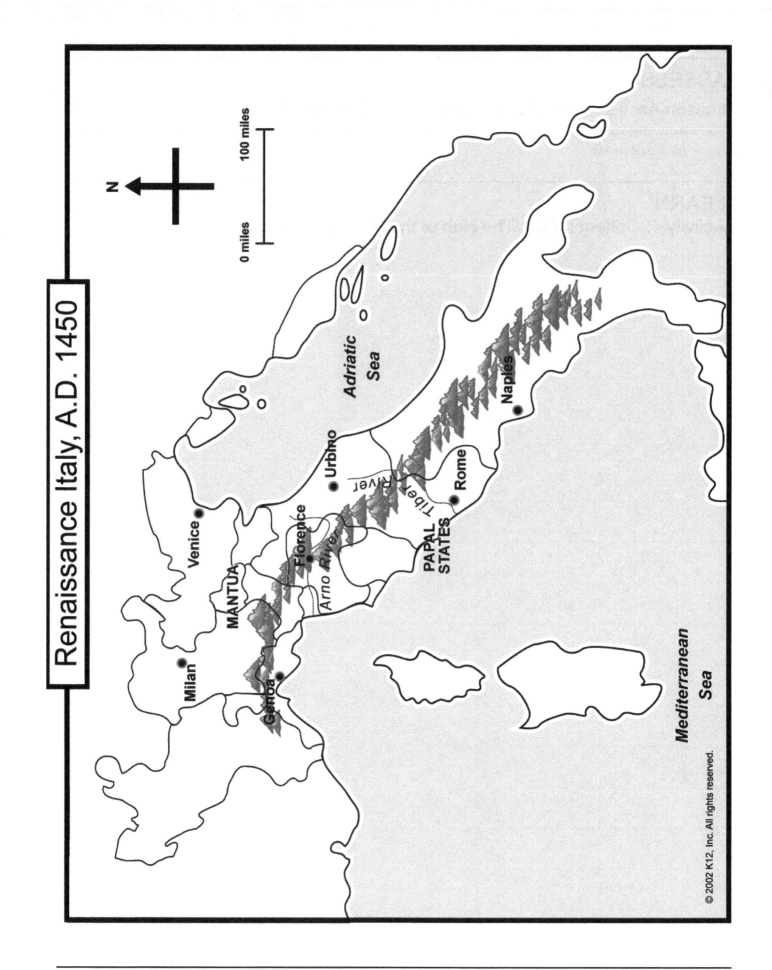

Renaissance Italy, A.D. 1450

N

100 miles

0 miles

Adriatic Sea

Milan

Venice

MANTUA

Genoa

Florence

Arno River

Urbino

Tiber River

PAPAL STATES

Rome

Naples

Mediterranean Sea

The City-States of Renaissance Italy

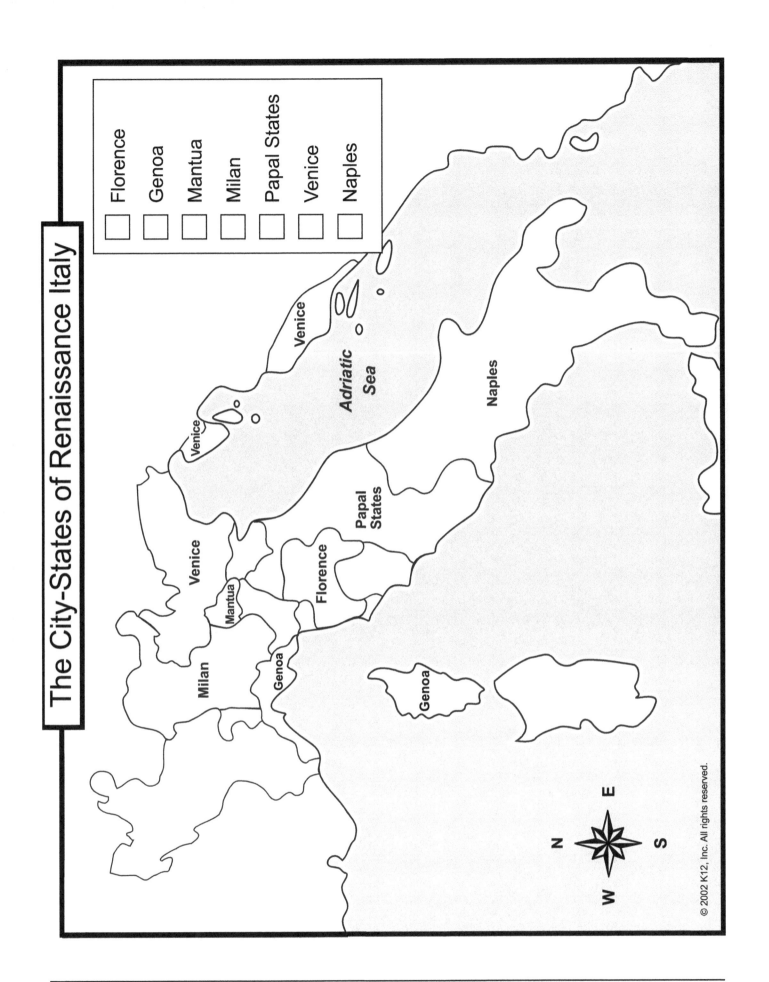

Florence ☐
Genoa ☐
Mantua ☐
Milan ☐
Papal States ☐
Venice ☐
Naples ☐

Lesson Assessment

The Hub of the Renaissance

1. **In order to answer this question you will need to use the map of Renaissance Italy.**
   Where is the Italian peninsula located?

2. Renaissance Italy was divided into many different parts. What were they called?_____

3. Why did Italian city-states grow and become wealthy at the beginning of the

   Renaissance?_____

4. Name one of the important city-states in Italy._____

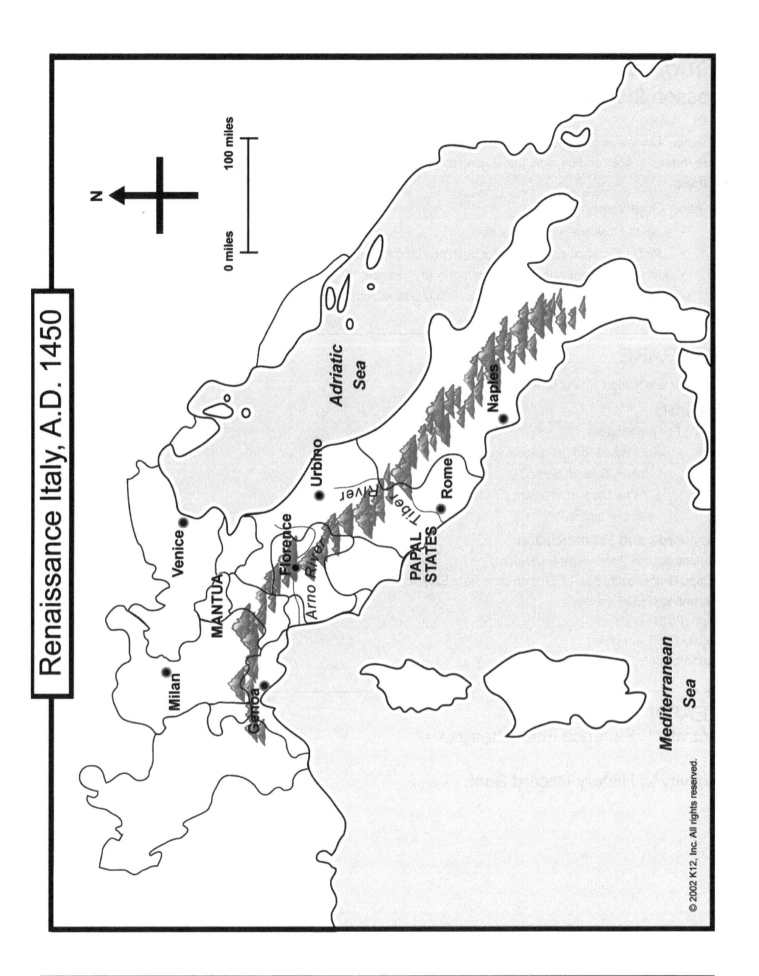

Renaissance Italy, A.D. 1450

N

100 miles

0 miles

Adriatic Sea

Mediterranean Sea

Venice

Milan

MANTUA

Florence

Arno River

Genoa

Urbino

Tiber River

PAPAL STATES

Rome

Naples

Student Guide
Lesson 2: Florence and the Medici

Florence, birthplace of the Renaissance, was a center of cloth-making and banking. The Medici family made their fortune in both and became the leading family of Florence. They patronized the arts and classical learning.

Lesson Objectives

- Locate Florence on a map of Italy.
- Identify Florence as a center for cloth production and banking.
- Identify the Medici as the leading family of Florence.
- Give an example of how the Medici family patronized learning and art.

PREPARE

Approximate lesson time is 60 minutes.

Materials

For the Student

  🖥 Map of Renaissance Italy, A.D. 1450

  History Record Book

  🖥 The Medici of Florence activity sheet

  pencils, colored 12

Keywords and Pronunciation

Constantinople (kahn-stant-n-OH-puhl)

Filippo Brunelleschi (fee-LEEP-poh broo-nehl-ES-kee)

Florentine (FLOR-en-teen)

florin (FLOR-uhn)

Medici (MED-uh-chee)

platonic (pluh-TAH-nik)

LEARN
Activity 1: Florence Flourishes *(Online)*

Activity 2: History Record Book *(Online)*

Instructions

Choose either A or B.

A. Written Narration

Write two to four sentences explaining what the lesson was about. If necessary, use the Show You Know questions to help get started. Only include the most important parts of the lesson. Write your name, the date, and the lesson title on your written narration, and put it in your History Record Book.

Sample written narration: "Florence was a great city in Italy. A family called the Medici lived there. They were rich and powerful. They made money from wool and helped lots of artists."

B. Picture Narration

Draw a picture of the part of the lesson that interested you most. When you have finished drawing, describe the picture. Below your picture, write a description of what you have drawn. Write your name, the date, and the lesson title on your picture narration, and put it in your History Record Book.

Activity 3: Medici - Art and Money *(Online)*
Instructions

The florin, a gold coin, is a reminder that the Medici family enriched life in Florence. Review *Cosimo's Secrets* to discuss some of the ways the Medici earned florins and some of the ways the Medici spent florins.

Then use the Medici of Florence activity sheet to illustrate what you learned about how the Medici earned and spent their money.

ASSESS
Lesson Assessment: Florence and the Medici (*Online*)

You will complete an offline assessment covering the main objectives of this lesson. Your learning coach will score this assessment.

LEARN
Activity 4: Florence and the Medici *(Online)*

Visit the Medici Villas in Florence to learn more about their history and how they look today.

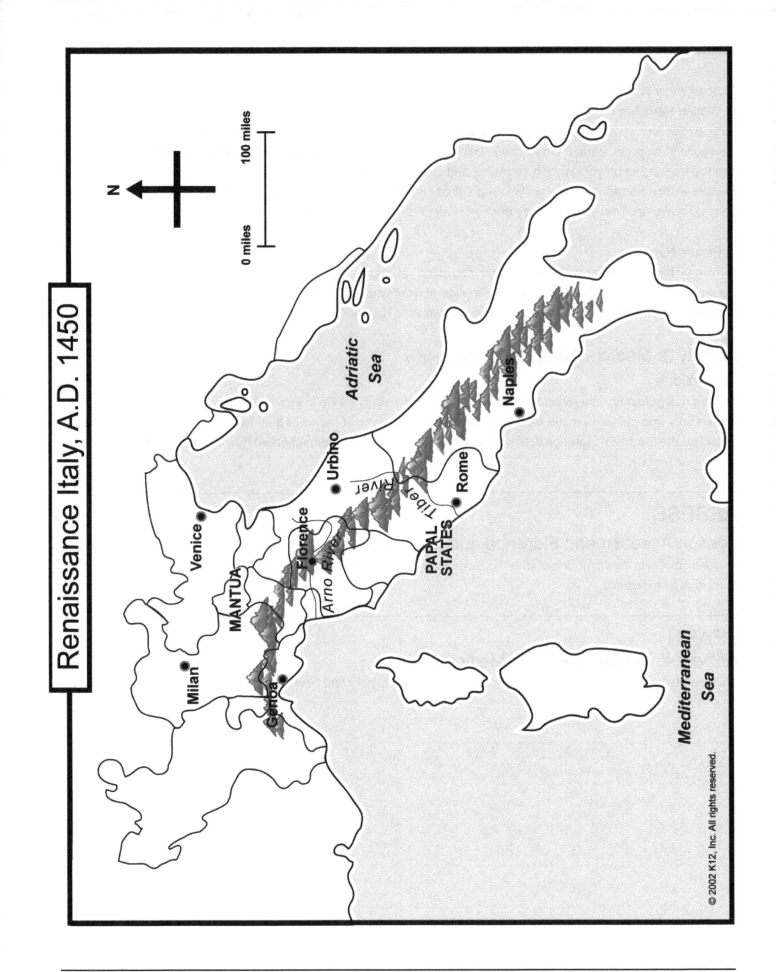

Renaissance Italy, A.D. 1450

N

100 miles

0 miles

Milan

Venice

MANTUA

Genoa

Florence

Arno River

Urbino

Tiber River

Adriatic Sea

PAPAL STATES

Rome

Naples

Mediterranean Sea

Name _____   Date _____

The Medici of Florence

How the Medici Made Money

How the Medici Spent Money

Lesson Assessment

Florence and the Medici

1. **In order to answer this question you will need to use the map of Renaissance Italy.**
   Where is Florence located?

2. Name the leading family that made the decisions in Florence._____

3. Because of the Medici, Florence became the center for two things. What were

   they?_____

4. What is one thing that the Medici family did for Florence to help make it a center of art and

   learning?_____

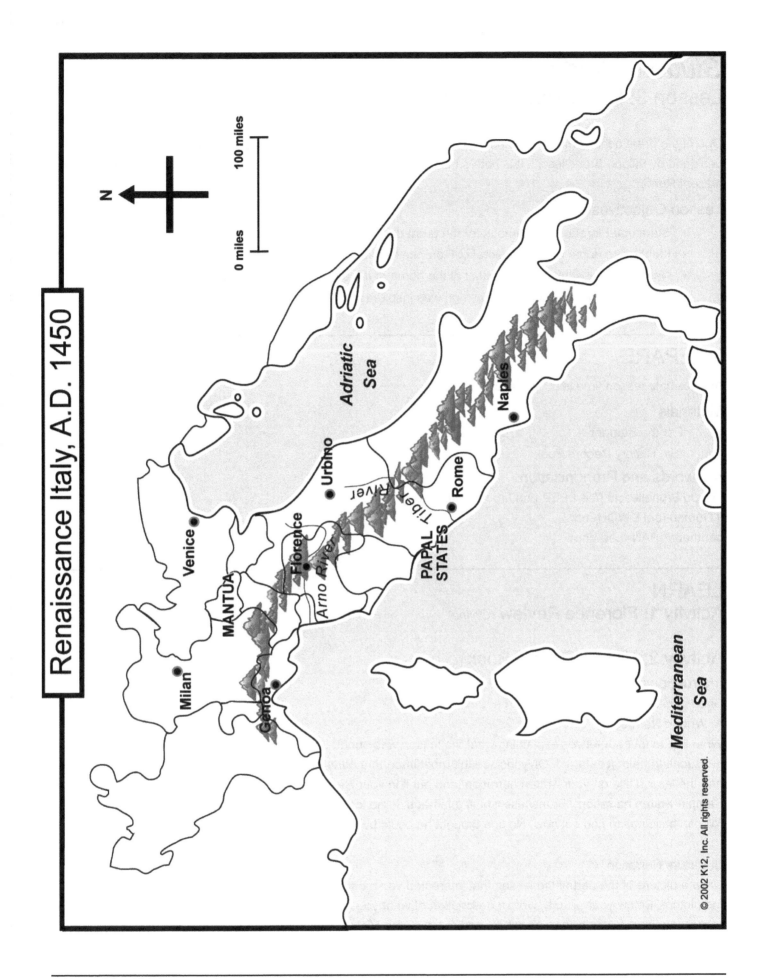

Renaissance Italy, A.D. 1450

N

100 miles

0 miles

Milan

Venice

MANTUA

Genoa

Florence

Arno River

Urbino

Adriatic Sea

Tiber River

PAPAL STATES

Rome

Naples

Mediterranean Sea

Student Guide
Lesson 3: Brunelleschi's Dome

One of the great achievements of Renaissance architecture was the dome of the Cathedral of Florence, designed by Filippo Brunelleschi. It is both a triumph of original thought and a tribute the architectural glory of ancient Rome.

Lesson Objectives

- State that Florence was famous for the great dome on its cathedral.
- Identify the dome of the cathedral of Florence from pictures.
- Name Brunelleschi as the architect of the dome of the cathedral of Florence.
- Explain that Brunelleschi's new design was inspired by the buildings of ancient Rome.

PREPARE

Approximate lesson time is 60 minutes.

Materials
> For the Student
>> History Record Book

Keywords and Pronunciation

Filippo Brunelleschi (fee-LEEP-poh broo-nehl-ES-kee)

Il Duomo (eel DWOH-moh)

pantheon (PAN-thee-ahn)

LEARN
Activity 1: Florence Review *(Online)*

Activity 2: History Record Book *(Online)*
Instructions
Choose either A or B.

A. Written Narration
Write two to four sentences explaining what the lesson was about. If necessary, use the Show You Know questions to help get started. Only include the most important parts of the lesson. Write your name, the date, and the lesson title on your written narration, and put it in your History Record Book.

Sample written narration: "Brunelleschi built a famous dome for the cathedral in Florence. He studied old Roman buildings to find out how. No one thought he could build his dome, but he did."

B. Picture Narration
Draw a picture of the part of the lesson that interested you most. When you have finished drawing, describe the picture. Below your picture, write a description of what you have drawn. Write your name, the date, and the lesson title on your picture narration, and put it in your History Record Book.

Activity 3: Dome Sweet Dome *(Online)*

ASSESS
Lesson Assessment: Brunelleschi's Dome (*Online*)

You will complete an offline assessment covering the main objectives of this lesson. Your learning coach will score this assessment.

LEARN
Activity 4. Optional: Brunelleschi's Dome *(Online)*

Name _____   Date _____

Lesson Assessment

Brunelleschi's Dome

1. What made the cathedral in Florence so wonderful and unique? _____

2. Which ancient civilization did Brunelleschi study to find the inspiration for his new

   design?_____

3. What is shown in this picture?_____

4. Who was the architect of the dome of the cathedral of Florence?_____

Student Guide
Lesson 4: Lorenzo the Magnificent

A leader of Renaissance Florence, Lorenzo de Medici was also known as Lorenzo the Magnificent. He was a statesman who prized classical learning, wrote poetry, patronized the arts, and led Florence at a time of cultural flourishing.

Lesson Objectives

- Identify Lorenzo de Medici as an energetic, skillful leader of Renaissance Florence.
- Identify Lorenzo as an international banker and a patron of the arts and learning.
- Give an example of Lorenzo de Medici's love for the classics and poetry.

PREPARE

Approximate lesson time is 60 minutes.

Materials

For the Student

History Record Book

🖳 Lorenzo Was Magnificent! activity sheet

glue, children's white

scissors

Keywords and Pronunciation

Lorenzo (loh-RENT-soh)

Michelangeo Buonarroti (miy-kuh-LAN-jeh-loh bwaw-nahr-RAW-tee)

Renaissance man : Someone who does many things well.

LEARN
Activity 1: Meet Lorenzo the Magnificent *(Online)*

Activity 2: History Record Book *(Online)*
Instructions
Choose either A or B.
A. Written Narration
Write two to four sentences explaining what the lesson was about. If necessary, use the Show You Know questions to help get started. Only include the most important parts of the lesson. Write your name, the date, and the lesson title on your written narration, and put it in your History Record Book.

Sample written narration: "Lorenzo de Medici liked to sing and write songs and plays. He lived in Florence. He liked to help artists. People called him Lorenzo the Magnificent."

B. Picture Narration

Draw a picture of the part of the lesson that interested you most. When you have finished drawing, describe the picture. Below your picture, write a description of what you have drawn. Write your name, the date, and the lesson title on your picture narration, and put it in your History Record Book.

Activity 3: Lorenzo Was Magnificent! *(Online)*

Instructions

Lorenzo was called "the Magnificent" because he did so many wonderful things. Your challenge is to show his magnificence by creating a collage highlighting as many of his talents and interests as possible.

Surround the drawing of Lorenzo on the activity sheet with items and pictures that illustrate Lorenzo's many talents. Collect, arrange, draw, and glue the things you select. Then color his image to make him look even more magnificent.

ASSESS

Lesson Assessment: Lorenzo the Magnificent (*Online*)

You will complete an offline assessment covering the main objectives of this lesson. Your learning coach will score this assessment.

Lorenzo Was Magnificent!

Draw or glue objects and pictures around Lorenzo to show why he was called magnificent. Review the story for ideas.

Lesson Assessment

Lorenzo the Magnificent

1. What city did Lorenzo the Magnificent lead skillfully and energetically?_____

2. What business did Lorenzo help run throughout Europe just as his father and grandfather had

   before him?_____

3. Why did Lorenzo have scribes make copies of ancient manuscripts?_____

4. How do you know Lorenzo loved the classics and poetry?_____

Student Guide
Lesson 5: Venice: Queen of the Adriatic

Venice, a city of canals, was another center of Renaissance cultural life. At the crossroads between the east and west, this city-state, led by the doge, grew into an empire with lands stretching along the Adriatic coast.

Lesson Objectives

- Locate Venice and the Adriatic Sea.
- Describe Venice as a city of canals.
- Identify Venice as a trading republic and empire led by the doge.

PREPARE

Approximate lesson time is 60 minutes.

Materials

> For the Student
>> 🖳 Map of the Venetian Empire, A.D. 1450
>>
>> pencils, colored 12
>>
>> History Record Book
>>
>> 🖳 Venice: City of Canals activity sheet
>>
>> crayons 8

Keywords and Pronunciation

Adriatic (ay-dree-A-tik)

doge (dohj) : The leader of Venice.

gondola (GAHN-duh-luh)

gondolier (gahn-duh-LIR)

Rialto (ree-AL-toh)

LEARN
Activity 1: Queen of the Adriatic *(Online)*

Activity 2: History Record Book *(Online)*
Instructions
Choose either A or B

A. Written Narration

Write two to four sentences explaining what the lesson was about. If necessary, use the Show You Know questions to help get started. Only include the most important parts of the lesson. Write your name, the date, and the lesson title on your written narration, and put it in your History Record Book.

Sample written narration: "Venice was a great center of trade. It was a beautiful city built on the water. People rode on the canals in boats called gondolas."

B. Picture Narration

Draw a picture of the part of the lesson that interested you most. When you have finished drawing, describe the picture. Below your picture, write a description of what you have drawn. Write your name, the date, and the lesson title on your picture narration, and put it in your History Record Book.

Activity 3: Venice, City of Canals *(Online)*
Instructions

Because of its location on the Adriatic Sea, the city of Venice was both beautiful and rich. Review your trip along the Grand Canal to discuss some of the most interesting features of this city.

Then complete the Venice: City of Canals activity sheet and add another paragraph to Carlo's story on the back.

ASSESS

Lesson Assessment: Venice: Queen of the Adriatic (*Online*)

You will complete an offline assessment covering the main objectives of this lesson. Your learning coach will score this assessment.

LEARN

Activity 4. Optional: Venice: Queen of the Adriatic *(Online)*

Take a virtual tour of Venice.

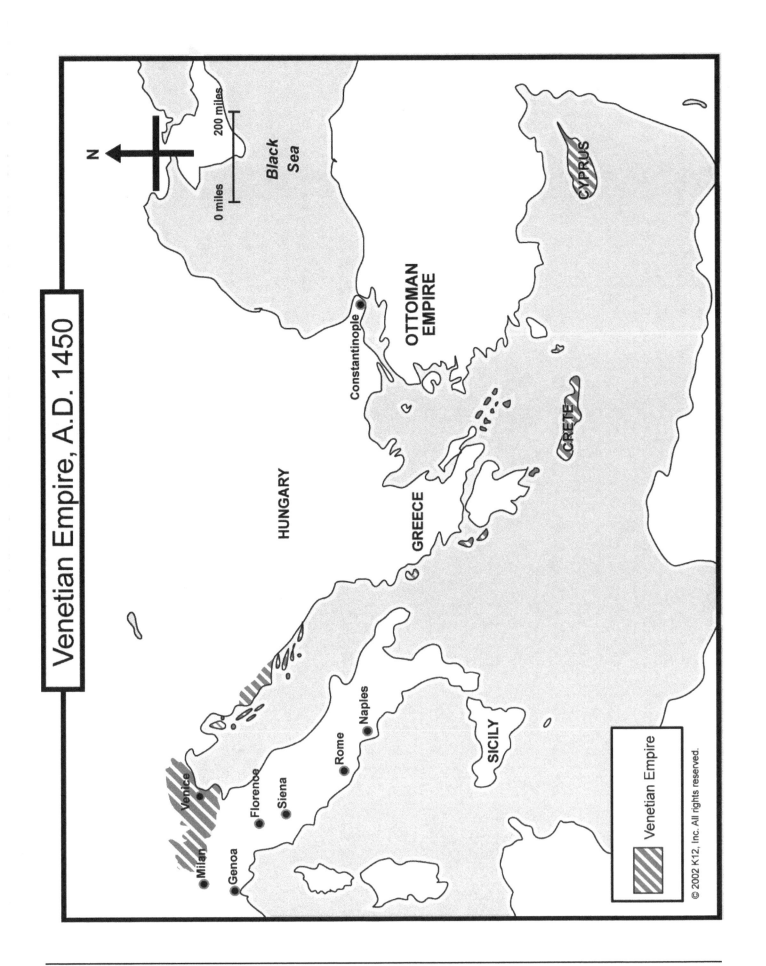

Venetian Empire, A.D. 1450

N

200 miles

0 miles

Black Sea

CYPRUS

OTTOMAN EMPIRE

Constantinople

HUNGARY

GREECE

CRETE

Venice

Milan

Genoa

Florence

Siena

Rome

Naples

SICILY

Venetian Empire

© 2002 K12, Inc. All rights reserved.

Name _____   Date _____

Venice: City of Canals

Add color to bring this picture of Venice to life. Make it as beautiful as possible. Then add another paragraph to Carlo's story on the back.

Lesson Assessment

Venice: Queen of the Adriatic

1. **To answer this question, please use your map of Venetian Empire, A.D. 1450.**
   Where is Venice located?

2. **To answer this question, please use your map of Venetian Empire, A.D. 1450.**
   Where is the Adriatic Sea located?

3. What was special about the way the people of Venice traveled around the

   city?_____

4. Venice was a republic. What was the ruler of Venice called?_____

5. Why did the doge build lots of ships?_____

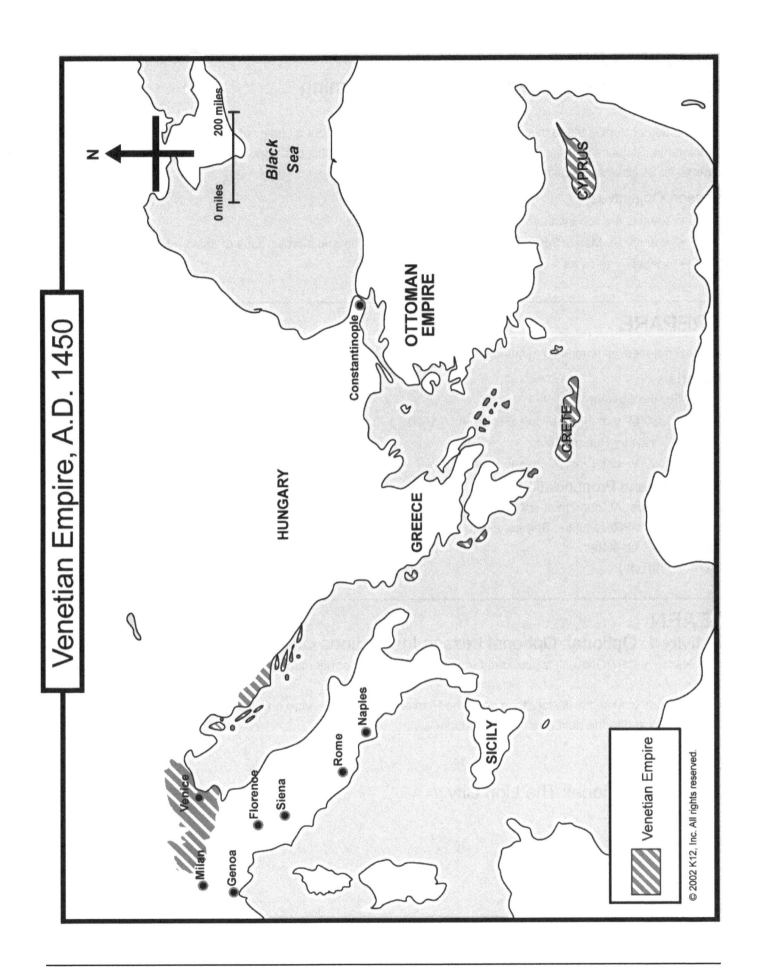

Venetian Empire, A.D. 1450

Student Guide
Lesson 6. Optional: Venice: Lion of Learning

The location of Venice made this city-state not only a hub of trade, but a center of learning and scholarship. Scholars and printers from east and west gathered in this cosmopolitan city, which claimed the evangelist St. Mark as its patron.

Lesson Objectives
- Identify the lion symbol with St. Mark and with Venice.
- Identify St. Mark's Square as the center of Venetian life and a crossroads of east and west.
- Identify Venice as a center of scholarship and books.

PREPARE

Approximate lesson time is 60 minutes.

Materials
For the Student
- Map of the Venetian Empire, A.D. 1450
- History Record Book
- Piero's Diary, Continued activity sheet

Keywords and Pronunciation
Aldus Manutius (AL-duhs muh-NYOO-shee-uhs)
apprentice (uh-PREN-tuhs) : Someone who is learning a trade or art.
Aristotle (AIR-uh-stah-tl)
Piero (PYAIR-oh)

LEARN
Activity 1. Optional: Optional Lesson Instructions *(Online)*
This lesson is OPTIONAL. It is provided for students who seek enrichment or extra practice. You may skip this lesson.

If you choose to skip this lesson, then go to the Plan or Lesson Lists page and mark this lesson "Skipped" in order to proceed to the next lesson in the course.

Activity 2. Optional: The Lion City *(Online)*

Activity 3. Optional: History Record Book *(Online)*

Instructions

Choose either A or B

A. Written Narration

Write two to four sentences explaining what the lesson was about. If necessary, use the Show You Know questions to help get started. Only include the most important parts of the lesson. Write your name, the date, and the lesson title on your written narration, and put it in your History Record Book

Sample written narration: "Piero was a boy who lived in Venice. He took some pages to his friend Hektor near St. Mark's Square. The people of Venice liked books and learning. Venice was the Lion City."

B. Picture Narration

Draw a picture of the part of the lesson that interested you most. When you have finished drawing, describe the picture. Below your picture, write a description of what you have drawn. Write your name, the date, and the lesson title on your picture narration, and put it in your History Record Book.

Activity 4. Optional: Piero's Diary, Continued *(Online)*

Activity 5. Optional: Venice: Lion of Learning *(Online)*

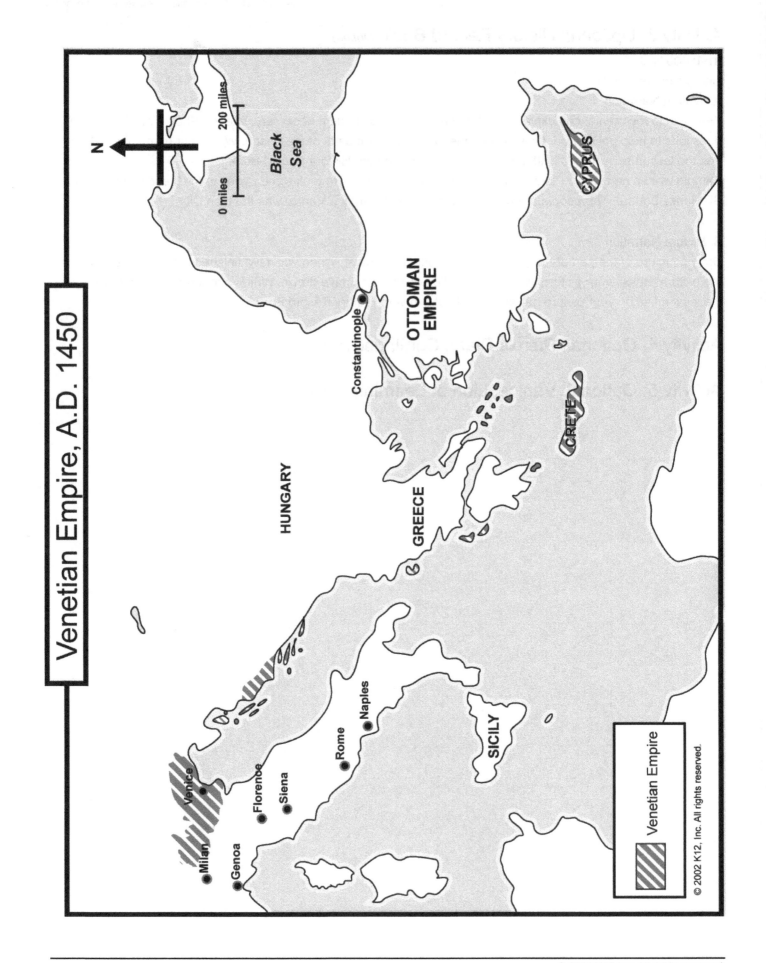

Venetian Empire, A.D. 1450

Black Sea

CYPRUS

OTTOMAN EMPIRE

Constantinople

HUNGARY

GREECE

CRETE

Naples

SICILY

Rome

Siena

Florence

Venice

Milan

Genoa

200 miles

0 miles

N

Venetian Empire

Piero's Diary, Continued

Think about Piero's life in the Lion City. What else could he write in his diary about Venice? Add this information to his diary and color the lions.

Student Guide
Lesson 7: Rome Revived

By the end of the Middle Ages, Rome--the heart of a great classical civilization and historic home of the popes--had fallen into disrepair. Renaissance popes returned to Rome and revived the city, making it one of the most important centers of the Italian Renaissance.

Lesson Objectives

- Identify Rome as the historic center of a great civilization.
- Identify Rome as the historic home of the popes.
- Describe the revival of Rome as a time when the popes returned and the city again became an artistic and cultural center.

PREPARE

Approximate lesson time is 60 minutes.

Materials

For the Student

    📖 Map of Renaissance Italy, A.D. 1450

    History Record Book

    📖 The Popes Revive Rome activity sheet

    pencils, colored 12

Keywords and Pronunciation

Alberti (ahl-BAIR-tee)

Pietro (PYEH-troh)

Sistine Chapel (SIS-teen CHA-puhl)

LEARN
Activity 1: Rome Is Revived *(Online)*

Activity 2: History Record Book *(Online)*
Instructions
Choose either A or B

A. Written Narration

Write two to four sentences explaining what the lesson was about. If necessary, use the Show You Know questions to help get started. Only include the most important parts of the lesson. Write your name, the date, and the lesson title on your written narration, and put it in your History Record Book

Sample written narration: "The popes came back to Rome. They tried to make it a beautiful city again. They bought books and built libraries. They built many new buildings and fixed the city."

B. Picture Narration

Draw a picture of the part of the lesson that interested you most. When you have finished drawing, describe the picture. Below your picture, write a description of what you have drawn. Write your name, the date, and the lesson title on your picture narration, and put it in your History Record Book.

Activity 3: The Popes Revive Rome (Online)

The revival of Rome began with books. But what happened next?

Review the lesson to recall what several Renaissance popes did to help bring the city back to life.

Then write or draw your ideas on The Popes Revive Rome activity sheet.

Extension: Research the achievements of another Renaissance pope. Add these to the back of your activity sheet.

ASSESS

Lesson Assessment: Rome Revived (*Online*)

You will complete an offline assessment covering the main objectives of this lesson. Your learning coach will score this assessment.

LEARN

Activity 4. Optional: Rome Revived (Online)

Visit a website to learn more about the Vatican Library and the revival of Rome.

Name _____   **Date** _____

The Popes Revive Rome

Review the lesson to remember what the Renaissance popes did to bring Rome back to life. Write or draw your ideas in each box below.

Pope Nicholas

Pope Sixtus

Lorenzo de Medici's son - Pope Leo X

Other Popes

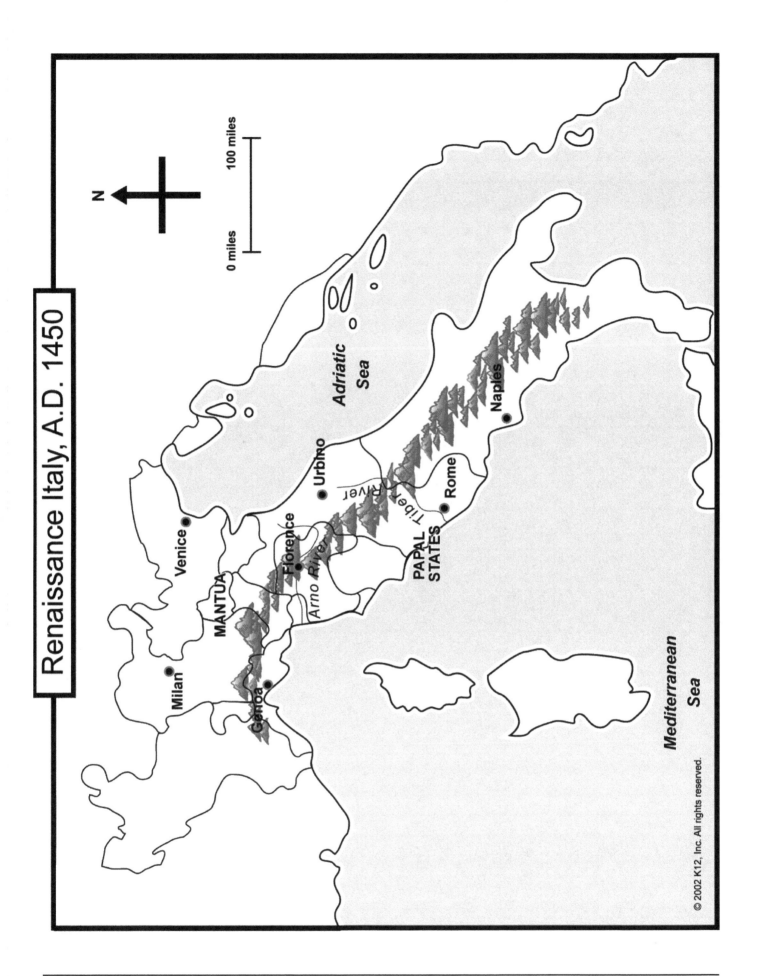

Renaissance Italy, A.D. 1450

N

100 miles

0 miles

Adriatic Sea

Mediterranean Sea

Milan

Venice

MANTUA

Genoa

Florence

Arno River

Urbino

Tiber River

PAPAL STATES

Rome

Naples

Lesson Assessment

Rome Revived

1. What did looking at ruins remind people about Rome? _____

2. Why had Rome been important during the Middle Ages? _____

3. What happened to help bring Rome back to life? _____

4. When the popes returned to Rome, what did they do? _____

Student Guide
Lesson 8: Da Vinci: The Renaissance Man

The greatest genius of the Renaissance, Leonardo da Vinci was a pathbreaking artist, inventor, and engineer. His numerous interests and inventions made him the quintessential "Renaissance man."

Lesson Objectives

- Identify Leonardo da Vinci as a great artist and inventor.
- Define the phrase *Renaissance man* as one who does many things well.
- Name one famous painting by Leonardo da Vinci (*The Mona Lisa* or *The Last Supper*).

PREPARE

Approximate lesson time is 60 minutes.

Materials

For the Student

    🖳 Map of Renaissance Italy, A.D. 1450

    History Record Book

    pencils, colored 12

    ruler

Optional

    Da Vinci by Mike Venezia

    Leonardo da Vinci by Diane Stanley

Keywords and Pronunciation

Leonardo da Vinci (lay-uh-NAHR-doh duh VIN-chee)

Michelangelo Buonarroti (miy-kuh-LAN-jeh-loh bwaw-nahr-RAW-tee)

Milan (muh-LAHN)

Renaissance man : Someone who does many things well.

LEARN
Activity 1: Da Vinci, Renaissance Man (Online)

Activity 2: History Record Book (Online)

It's time to add another chapter to the story of our past. Create a new entry in your History Record Book by completing a written or picture narration.

Activity 3: Da Vinci's Notebook and Yours *(Online)*

Examine some of Leonardo da Vinci's notebook drawings. Then make some of your own.

ASSESS

Lesson Assessment: Da Vinci: The Renaissance Man (*Online*)

You will complete an offline assessment covering the main objectives of this lesson. Your learning coach will score this assessment.

LEARN

Activity 4. Optional: Da Vinci: The Renaissance Man *(Online)*

Read books and visit a website to learn more about Leonardo da Vinci, the ultimate Renaissance man.

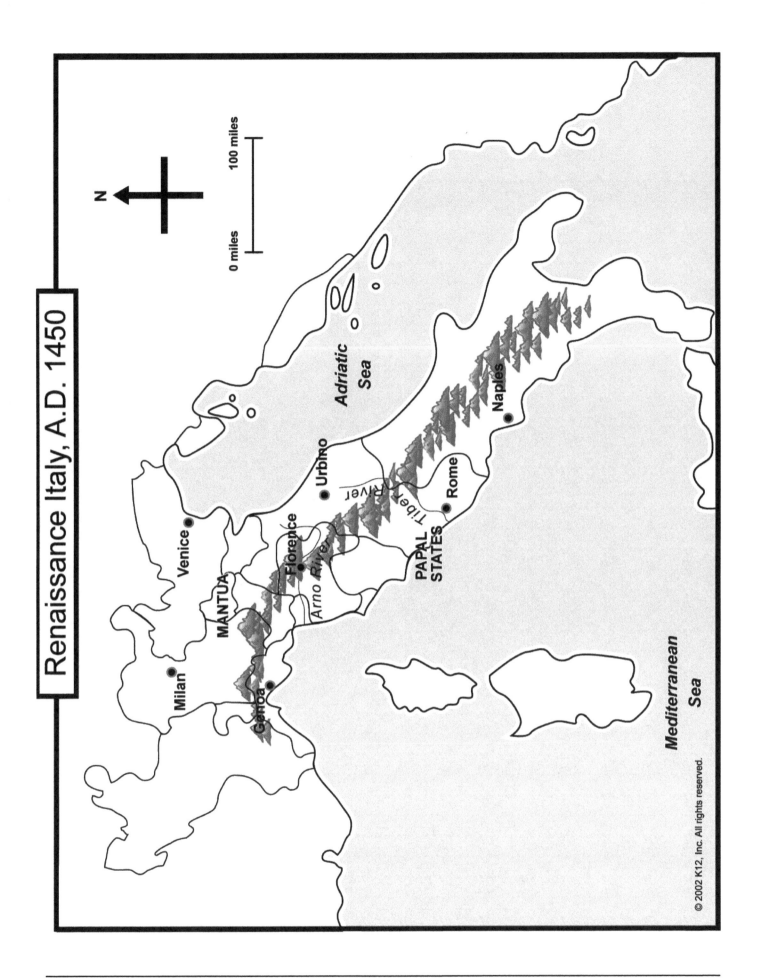

Renaissance Italy, A.D. 1450

N

100 miles

0 miles

Milan
Venice
MANTUA
Genoa
Florence
Arno River
Urbino
Adriatic Sea
Tiber River
PAPAL STATES
Rome
Naples
Mediterranean Sea

Lesson Assessment

Da Vinci: The Renaissance Man

1. Da Vinci could be described as being great at what two things?_____

2. What is a Renaissance man?_____

3. Name one famous painting by da Vinci._____

Student Guide
Lesson 9: Meet Michelangelo

The only Renaissance artist to rival Leonardo da Vinci, fellow Florentine Michelangelo left an unsurpassed legacy of sculpture and painting.

Lesson Objectives

- Identify Michelangelo as a great sculptor and painter from Florence.
- Describe Michelangelo's style as lifelike.
- Recognize the Pietà and the David as two of Michelangelo's greatest works.

PREPARE

Approximate lesson time is 60 minutes.

Materials

For the Student

 📖 Michelangelo Discussion Questions

 Michelangelo by Mike Venezia

 History Record Book

 paper, 8 1/2" x 11"

 pencils, colored 12

Optional

 Michelangelo by Diane Stanley

Keywords and Pronunciation

fresco : a painting made on wet plaster with water-based paint

Leonardo da Vinci (lay-uh-NAHR-doh duh VIN-chee)

Michelangelo Buonarroti (miy-kuh-LAN-jeh-loh bwaw-nahr-RAW-tee)

Pietà (pee-ay-TAH)

sculptor : Someone who carves a work of art.

LEARN
Activity 1: Michelangelo (Online)

Instructions

Get Ready

What does the expression "Renaissance man" mean? [1]

Which great artist and inventor from Florence do we often refer to as a Renaissance man? [2]

What was the name of the great Florentine family who patronized the arts? [3]

Which Medici ran a school for young artists? [4]

Today we're going to learn about another great artist who was also a Renaissance man. He wrote poetry, sculpted, and painted. His name was Michelangelo Buonarroti (miy-kuh-LAN-jeh-loh bwaw-nahr-RAW-tee).

One year, when Leonardo da Vinci (lay-uh-NAHR-doh duh-VIN-chee) was in the great city of Rome, he saw a statue in Saint Peter's church that took his breath away. The statue was by a gifted young sculptor named Michelangelo Buonarroti.

From one block of stone, Michelangelo had carved a story about Jesus. In the story, Mary, the mother of Jesus, holds her son after he has been crucified. The sculpture is called the *Pietà* (pee-ay-TAH).

This was not the first time someone had carved the *Pietà*. Artists from the north had long been telling the same story in wood. But when Michelangelo carved it from marble, it seemed to come alive.

The body of Jesus shows muscles, veins, and bones. The face of Mary shows deep love for her son and sorrow over his death. The *Pietà* looks more real than real life.

How could someone so young carve something so beautiful? Let's read the book *Michelangelo* and find out about an artist often called the greatest of all time.

Read and discuss *Michelangelo* by Mike Venezia.

Teacher tips

Pietà means "pity" in Italian. The sculpture is called the *Pietà* because it depicts Mary mourning over the body of Christ.

Show You Know

After you've read and discussed *Michelangelo* by Mike Venezia, answer the following questions.

What city was Michelangelo from? [5]

How would you describe Michelangelo? [6]

How would you describe Michelangelo's works? [7]

Which statue made by Michelangelo shows Mary, the mother of Jesus, holding her son after he has been crucified? [8]

What famous statue did Michelangelo carve for the people of Florence? [9]

What works of Michelangelo did you like? [10]

Activity 2: History Record Book (Online)

Instructions

Choose either A or B.

A. Written Narration

Write two to four sentences explaining what the lesson was about. If necessary, use the Show You Know questions to help get started. Only include the most important parts of the lesson. Write your name, the date, and the lesson title on your written narration, and put it in your History Record Book.

Sample written narration: Acceptable written narrations could include: "Michangelo was a great artist. He made a sculpture of Jesus and Mary called the Pietà. He made a big statue of David, too."

B. Picture Narration

Draw a picture of the part of the lesson that interested you most. When you have finished drawing, describe the picture. Below your picture, write a description of what you have drawn. Write your name, the date, and the lesson title on your picture narration, and put it in your History Record Book.

Activity 3: Copy Michelangelo *(Online)*
Instructions
Look at the illustrations in Michelangelo again. Choose one and try making your own copy of it.

If you choose a painting, use either colored pencils or watercolors on drawing paper.

Use clay to make a sculpture, or create a shaded pencil drawing of it on white paper.

ASSESS
Lesson Assessment: Meet Michelangelo (*Online*)
You will complete an offline assessment covering the main objectives of this lesson. Your learning coach will score this assessment.

LEARN
Activity 4. Optional: Meet Michelangelo *(Online)*
To learn more about the life of this famous artist, read *Michelangelo* by Diane Stanley (New York: HarperCollins, 2000).

Name _____   Date _____

Michelangelo Discussion Questions:

1. After reading page 6: Look closely at the eyes of the statue. What do you notice about them?

2. After reading page 7: How do the chisel marks near this statue's left eye help it seem alive?

After reading pages 12 and 13: Look at each piece of art closely. Point to Giotto's fresco. Then point to the works of Masaccio, Donatello, and Ghiberti.

3. *Optional:* Now mention one thing Michelangelo might have liked about each of these artworks.

4. After reading page 16: Look closely at the sculpture of the Madonna of the Stairs. What is something that Lorenzo dé Medici might have seen in it to make him keep thinking that Michelangelo's talent was special?

5. After reading page 18: What are some of the things you see that make the statue of the *Pietà* so amazing?

6. After reading page 21: Why did the people of Florence like the *David*?

7. *Optional:* What are some things you see in the statue of David that have helped it become Michelangelo's most famous sculpture?

8. After reading page 23: Why didn't Michelangelo want to paint the ceiling of the Sistine Chapel?

9. After reading page 27: Look at the pictures on pages 24 through 27. What do you see that makes you think Pope Julius made the right decision in asking Michelangelo to paint the ceiling?

10. After reading page 29: What do you see in the sculpture that makes Moses seem to have "special energy and strength"?

11. After reading page 31: Point to and describe something in the painting of the Last Judgment that makes it seem lifelike.

Lesson Assessment

Meet Michelangelo

1. What city was Michelangelo from?_____

2. How would you describe Michelangelo?_____

3. How would you describe Michelangelo's works?_____

4. Which statue made by Michelangelo shows Mary, the mother of Jesus, holding her son after he has

   been crucified?_____

5. What famous statue did Michelangelo carve for the people of Florence?_____

Student Guide
Lesson 10: Julius II, Michelangelo, and the Sistine Chapel

One of the most important works of the Renaissance, the ceiling of the Sistine Chapel is the product of a great artist and a very determined but frugal pope!

Lesson Objectives

- Name Julius II as an important Renaissance pope who hired Michelangelo to paint the Sistine Chapel ceiling.
- Summarize the conflict between Julius and Michelangelo on painting the ceiling.
- State that the Sistine Chapel ceiling is a fresco.
- Recognize the Creation of Adam from a photograph.

PREPARE

Approximate lesson time is 60 minutes.

Materials

For the Student

History Record Book

Keywords and Pronunciation

fresco : a painting made on wet plaster with water-based paint

Sistine Chapel (SIS-teen CHA-puhl)

LEARN
Activity 1: The Artist and the Pope *(Online)*

Activity 2: History Record Book *(Online)*
Instructions
Choose either A or B.
A. Written Narration
Write two to four sentences explaining what the lesson was about. If necessary, use the Show You Know questions to help get started. Only include the most important parts of the lesson. Write your name, the date, and the lesson title on your written narration, and put it in your History Record Book.

Sample written narration: "Pope Julius told Michelangelo to paint the ceiling of the Sistine Chapel. They argued a lot. The pope thought Michelangelo was slow. Michelangelo painted some beautiful stories from the Bible on the ceiling.

B. Picture Narration
Draw a picture of the part of the lesson that interested you most. When you have finished drawing, describe the picture. Below your picture, write a description of what you have drawn. Write your name, the date, and the lesson title on your picture narration, and put it in your History Record Book.

Activity 3: Letter from the Sistine Chapel *(Online)*
Instructions

Imagine you're visiting Rome in 1512. You've been going to the Sistine Chapel to watch Michelangelo finish his masterpiece. Write a letter to a friend encouraging him or her to come to Rome and see what Michelangelo has created.

Include some or all of the following points in your letter:

- Pope Julius II hired Michelangelo to paint the ceiling.
- The ceiling of the Sistine Chapel is a fresco.
- One of the scenes on the ceiling, the Creation of Adam, shows God bringing Adam to life by touching his finger.

You may want to read through the lesson again before writing your letter.

ASSESS

Lesson Assessment: Julius II, Michelangelo, and the Sistine Chapel (*Online*)

You will complete an offline assessment covering the main objectives of this lesson. Your learning coach will score this assessment.

LEARN

Activity 4. Optional: Julius II, Michelangelo, and the Sistine Chapel *(Online)*

See what Michelangelo really painted by viewing photographs of the Sistine Chapel frescoes after they were restored.

Lesson Assessment

Julius II, Michelangelo, and the Sistine Chapel

1. Which pope hired Michelangelo to paint the Sistine Chapel ceiling?_____

2. Why was Michelangelo frustrated with the pope?_____

3. Why was the pope frustrated with Michelangelo?_____

4. What is the name for the kind of painting on the Sistine Chapel ceiling?_____

5. This photograph shows a scene from the Sistine Chapel ceiling. What is this scene

    called?_____

Student Guide
Lesson 11: Isabella d'Este: Renaissance Woman

Known for her intelligence, mastery of the classics, and political skill, Isabella d'Este ruled Mantua during her husband's captivity, and captivated almost everyone who met her.

Lesson Objectives

- Name Isabella d'Este as one of the most important women of the Renaissance.
- Describe Isabella d'Este as a leader of Mantua.
- Explain how Isabella d'Este made the court of Mantua a center of art and learning.

PREPARE

Approximate lesson time is 60 minutes.

Materials

    For the Student

        🖳 Map of Renaissance Italy, A.D. 1450

        History Record Book

        pencils, colored 12

    Optional

        Outrageous Women of the Renaissance by Vicki Leon

Keywords and Pronunciation

Cicero (SIS-uh-roh)

Francesco (frahn-CHAY-skoh)

Isabella d´Este (ee-zah-BEL-lah DES-tay)

Mantua (MAHN-too-ah)

LEARN
Activity 1: Isabella Takes Charge *(Online)*

Activity 2: History Record Book *(Online)*

Instructions

Choose either A or B.

A. Written Narration

Write two to four sentences explaining what the lesson was about. If necessary, use the Show You Know questions to help get started. Only include the most important parts of the lesson. Write your name, the date, and the lesson title on your written narration, and put it in your History Record Book.

Sample written narration: "Isabella d'Este was a Renaissance woman. She ruled Mantua while her husband was prisoner. She brought books and artists to the palace. She started a school for women."

B. Picture Narration

Draw a picture of the part of the lesson that interested you most. When you have finished drawing, describe the picture. Below your picture, write a description of what you have drawn. Write your name, the date, and the lesson title on your picture narration, and put it in your History Record Book.

Activity 3: Isabella's School *(Online)*

Isabella d'Este was one of the most important women of the Renaissance. She led the small city-state of Mantua after her husband, Francesco, was captured by the Venetians. Later, under her direction, the court of Mantua became a center of art and learning. Isabella also started a school for young women. Until this time, only boys were allowed to go to higher schools and learn subjects like Latin and mathematics. Now girls could go to Isabella's school and study those same subjects.

Design and make a pamphlet that advertises and provides information about Isabella's school for young women. The purpose of the pamphlet is to provide the reader with facts about Isabella and her school and to persuade the reader to send his or her daughter to this school.

Add color and some simple drawings and/or illustrations to the pamphlet to convey facts and information and to make it visually appealing.

ASSESS

Lesson Assessment: Isabella d'Este: Renaissance Woman *(Online)*

You will complete an offline assessment covering the main objectives of this lesson. Your learning coach will score this assessment.

LEARN

Activity 4. Optional: Isabella d'Este: Renaissance Woman *(Online)*

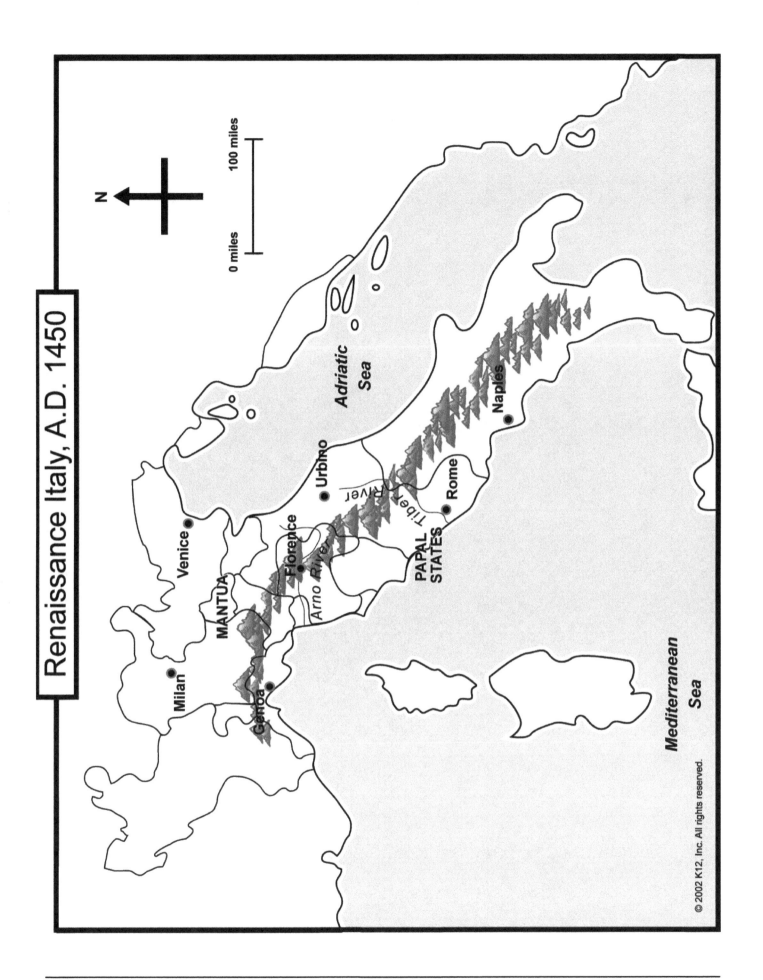

Renaissance Italy, A.D. 1450

N

100 miles

0 miles

Milan

Venice

MANTUA

Genoa

Florence

Arno River

Urbino

Tiber River

PAPAL
STATES

Rome

Naples

Adriatic
Sea

Mediterranean
Sea

Lesson Assessment

Isabella d'Este: Renaissance Woman

1. Who was one of the most important women of the Renaissance?_____

2. Which city-state did Isabella help rule?_____

3. Give an example of something Isabella did to make Mantua a center for art and

   learning._____

Student Guide
Lesson 12. Optional: Castiglione and The Book of the Courtier

All ages have ideals. While the code of chivalry provided ideals for medieval knights, Baldassare Castiglione's *The Book of the Courtier* helped define the ideal Renaissance man and woman.

Lesson Objectives

- Define *courtier* as one who serves a prince.
- Explain that *The Book of the Courtier* defined Renaissance ideals, especially for courtiers.
- Name Castiglione as the author of *The Book of the Courtier*.
- Name three Renaissance ideals, such as good character; grace; classical education; and ability to play an instrument, draw, or paint.

PREPARE

Approximate lesson time is 60 minutes.

Advance Preparation

- If you decide to do the Revisiting the Duchess activity in this lesson, you'll need to gather costumes and props. Read through "At Court With the Duchess" to get an idea of what you'll need.

Materials

    For the Student

        History Record Book

Keywords and Pronunciation

Barnardo (bahr-NAHR-doh)

Castiglione (kahs-teel-YOH-nay)

courtier (KOHR-tee-ur) : One who serves a prince or some other ruler.

Gasparo (GAHS-pahr-oh)

Giuliano (jool-YAHN-oh)

Lodovico (loh-doh-VEE-koh)

LEARN
Activity 1. Optional: Optional Lesson Instructions *(Online)*

This lesson is OPTIONAL. It is provided for students who seek enrichment or extra practice. You may skip this lesson.

If you choose to skip this lesson, then go to the Plan or Lesson Lists page and mark this lesson "Skipped" in order to proceed to the next lesson in the course.

Activity 2. Optional: At Court with the Duchess *(Online)*

Activity 3. Optional: History Record Book *(Online)*
Instructions
Choose either A or B.
A. Written Narration
Write two to four sentences explaining what the lesson was about. If necessary, use the Show You Know questions to help get started. Only include the most important parts of the lesson. Write your name, the date, and the lesson title on your written narration, and put it in your History Record Book.

Sample written narration: "People who served a prince were called courtiers. They liked to visit court and have arguments about how to act. A good courtier was good with weapons and could read Greek and Latin. A courtier was polite."

B. Picture Narration
Draw a picture of the part of the lesson that interested you most. When you have finished drawing, describe the picture. Below your picture, write a description of what you have drawn. Write your name, the date, and the lesson title on your picture narration, and put it in your History Record Book.

Activity 4. Optional: Revisiting the Duchess *(Online)*

Student Guide
Lesson 13: Rebuilding St. Peter's

The largest Christian church in the world, St. Peter's basilica was first commissioned by Julius II and is one of the great architectural achievements of the Renaissance. Michelangelo designed its famous dome, and popes spent lavishly on it.

Lesson Objectives

- Identify St. Peter's Basilica as the largest Christian church in the world.
- Name Julius II as the pope who ordered the rebuilding of St. Peter's Basilica.
- Name Michelangelo as the architect of St. Peter's dome.
- Describe the construction of St. Peter's as being very expensive.

PREPARE

Approximate lesson time is 60 minutes.

Materials

> For the Student
>
> > History Record Book
> >
> > 💻 Hello from St. Peter's activity sheet
> >
> > pencils, colored 12

Keywords and Pronunciation

basilica (buh-SIH-lih-kuh)
Vincenzo (veen-CHENT-soh)

LEARN
Activity 1: A New Church for Rome *(Online)*

Activity 2: History Record Book *(Online)*

Instructions

Choose either A or B.

A. Written Narration

Write two to four sentences explaining what the lesson was about. If necessary, use the Show You Know questions to help get started. Only include the most important parts of the lesson. Write your name, the date, and the lesson title on your written narration, and put it in your History Record Book.

Sample written narration: "Pope Julius decided to build a new Saint Peter's church. It took a lot of gold and marble. Michelangelo planned the dome. Saint Peter's is the biggest Christian church in the world."

B. Picture Narration

Draw a picture of the part of the lesson that interested you most. When you have finished drawing, describe the picture. Below your picture, write a description of what you have drawn. Write your name, the date, and the lesson title on your picture narration, and put it in your History Record Book.

Activity 3: Hello from St. Peter's Basilica *(Online)*

Instructions

St. Peter's Basilica is the largest Christian church in the world. Michelangelo, the great Renaissance sculptor and painter, designed the dome for the church. Each year, thousands of people visit St. Peter's and marvel at the beauty of this famous church.

Complete the Hello from St. Peter's activity sheet:

- Think about the lesson and what you learned about St. Peter's.
- At the bottom of the back of the postcard, write a couple of short sentences describing St. Peter's. If possible, look at some postcards to see how facts and information about a place are presented on the back of a postcard.
- Imagine you visited St. Peter's and want to send this postcard to a friend back home. Write your friend a short note about your visit to St. Peter's.

ASSESS

Lesson Assessment: Rebuilding St. Peter's *(Online)*

You will complete an offline assessment covering the main objectives of this lesson. Your learning coach will score this assessment.

LEARN

Activity 4. Optional: Rebuilding St. Peter's *(Online)*

Explore St. Peter's online. Two websites provide interesting facts and beautiful photographs.

To:

St. Peter's Basilica:

Lesson Assessment

Rebuilding St. Peter's

1. What is the biggest Christian church in the world?_____

2. Who ordered the rebuilding of St. Peter's Basilica?_____

3. Who designed the dome for St. Peter's? _____

4. Was the construction of St. Peter's very expensive?_____

Student Guide
Lesson 14: Unit Review and Assessment

You've completed this unit, and now it's time to review what you've learned and take the unit assessment.

Lesson Objectives

- Demonstrate mastery of important knowledge and skills in this unit.
- Demonstrate mastery of important knowledge and skills taught in previous lessons.
- Explain that *Renaissance* means *rebirth.*
- Locate the Italian peninsula on a map.
- Identify Florence as a center for cloth production and banking.
- Identify the Medici as the leading family of Florence.
- Identify the dome of the cathedral of Florence from pictures.
- Name Brunelleschi as the architect of the dome of the cathedral of Florence.
- Identify Lorenzo as an international banker and a patron of the arts and learning.
- Describe Venice as a city of canals.
- Identify Venice as a trading republic and empire led by the doge.
- Define the phrase *Renaissance man* as one who does many things well.
- Name one famous painting by Leonardo da Vinci (*The Mona Lisa* or *The Last Supper*).
- Identify Michelangelo as a great sculptor and painter from Florence.
- Describe Michelangelo's style as lifelike.
- Recognize the Pietà and the David as two of Michelangelo's greatest works.
- Name Julius II as an important Renaissance pope who hired Michelangelo to paint the Sistine Chapel ceiling.
- Recognize the Creation of Adam from a photograph.
- Describe Isabella d'Este as a leader of Mantua.
- Identify St. Peter's Basilica as the largest Christian church in the world.

PREPARE

Approximate lesson time is 60 minutes.

Materials

> For the Student
> > History Record Book

Keywords and Pronunciation

Castiglione (kahs-teel-YOH-nay)

Filippo Brunelleschi (fee-LEEP-poh broo-nehl-ES-kee)

gondolas (GAHN-duh-luhs)

Isabella d´Este (ee-zah-BEL-lah DES-tay)

Laocoon (lay-AH-kuh-wahn)

Leonardo da Vinci (lay-uh-NAHR-doh duh VIN-chee)

Medici (MED-uh-chee)

Michelangeo Buonarroti (miy-kuh-LAN-jeh-loh bwaw-nahr-RAW-tee)

Petrarch (PEH-trahrk)

Pietà (pee-ay-TAH)

LEARN
Activity 1: A Look Back (Online)

Italy, the boot-shaped peninsula sticking into the Mediterranean Sea, has seen a lot of history. Long ago it was home to the mighty Roman Empire. A thousand years later it gave birth to a new period called the Renaissance. We've learned that *Renaissance* means "rebirth." Let's think about what was reborn during the Renaissance.

First came towns. At the end of the Middle Ages, towns were springing up all over Europe, and merchants were returning to sell their wares. Italy led the way. Italy was not one large country during the Renaissance. It was made up of towns or cities that often ruled themselves. Do you remember what we call these cities that ruled themselves and the areas around them? [1]

Renaissance Italy was made up of hundreds of city-states, big and little, powerful and weak. What are some city-states we've studied? [2]

Which city-state was home to those bankers and patrons of the arts, the Medici family? [3]

Which city-state had canals and gondolas and was led by the doge? [4]

Where did the pope live, and from which city did he rule the Papal States? [5]

Towns and cities were reborn in the Renaissance, and learning was reborn, too. A new kind of learning took place. Which civilizations did people start to study? [6]

The Medicis, Filippo Brunelleschi, Isabella d'Este, Venetian scholars, and many others studied the classical writers. They collected ancient books and art. Renaissance people got excited by the ideas of Greece and Rome.

What did they like about these classical writers? Petrarch could have told you: their fascination with human beings. During the dangerous Middle Ages, people thought a lot about God, about how weak humans were, and about life after death. During the Renaissance, that changed. People still thought a lot about God, but they thought that if God created them, maybe God created something good. The writers of ancient Greece and Rome reminded them of that.

Renaissance means "rebirth," but the Renaissance wasn't about people looking back to the past and longing for the old days. It was about learning from the past and using knowledge in new ways. The Renaissance was a time of incredible *ingenuity.* Do you know that word? It means people using knowledge and imagination to make new things.

Let's think about the people of Florence wanting a dome for their cathedral. Why did they want a dome? [7]

Had the Romans ever built a dome like that? No. The Romans built the amazingly large dome of the Pantheon, but the Florentines had a problem that had never been solved before. They wanted an enormous, tall dome. Who solved that problem? [8]

Brunelleschi looked to Rome for inspiration. He studied Roman ruins. He visited the Pantheon. He thought hard, used all the mathematics he knew, and figured out how to build that amazing dome. He did something brand-new.

You could say the same thing about Leonardo da Vinci or Michelangelo. These great artists created paintings and sculptures inspired by the past. Nobody was more excited than Michelangelo when Pope Julius's men dug up the statue called the *Laocoön*. But Leonardo and Michelangelo created works that were unique, never created before, and some would say never since equaled.

Think about Leonardo's *Mona Lisa.* Think about Michelangelo's *David* or his *Pieta.* Think about the ceiling of the Sistine Chapel or the dome on St. Peter's. Those works told the human and Christian stories in a new way. Their beauty was unique and new.

Why was there so much ingenuity during the Renaissance? Why was this period full of great artists, writers, and thinkers? Nobody knows, but part of the answer has to do with Renaissance ideals. When Castiglione wrote *The Book of the Courtier,* he explained those ideals. He said the ideal person had studied classical writers, knew Latin and Greek, and could play an instrument, write poetry, draw or paint, speak with grace, remain calm in an argument, and offer his opinions humbly. As you can imagine, not everyone in the Renaissance could do all these things. But many people tried.

We think about Michelangelo as a great sculptor and painter. But in his free time, he wrote poetry. He was a Renaissance man. What does that expression, "Renaissance man," mean? [9]

It's not surprising that the Italian Renaissance was full of Renaissance men and women. Their ideas would soon spread to the rest of Europe.

Activity 2: History Record Book Review *(Online)*

Activity 3: Online Interactive Review *(Online)*

ASSESS

Unit Assessment: Unit Review and Assessment *(Offline)*

Complete an offline Unit Assessment. Your learning coach will score this part of the Assessment.

Name _____   Date _____

The Italian Renaissance

Read each question and its answer choices. Fill in the bubble in front of the word or words that best answer the question.

1. Where did the Renaissance begin?
   - ⓐ England
   - ⓑ Italy
   - ⓒ Egypt
   - ⓓ France

2. What does the word *Renaissance* mean?
   - ⓐ rename
   - ⓑ rebirth
   - ⓒ revisit
   - ⓓ review

3. Michelangelo designed the dome of this church. It is the largest Christian church in the world.
   - ⓐ the cathedral in Florence
   - ⓑ St. Mark's Square
   - ⓒ the Parthenon
   - ⓓ St. Peter's Basilica

4. What was the name of the powerful banking family in Florence that supported the arts and learning?
   - ⓐ Medici
   - ⓑ Brunelleschi
   - ⓒ Castiglione
   - ⓓ Julius

5. Who was the architect of the famous dome on the cathedral in Florence?
   ⓐ da Vinci
   ⓑ Giotto
   ⓒ Castiglione
   ⓓ Brunelleschi

6. Which of the following was an Italian city-state known for its canals and led by a doge?
   ⓐ Rome
   ⓑ Venice
   ⓒ London
   ⓓ Florence

7. What is Lorenzo de' Medici famous for?
   ⓐ He created lifelike sculptures.
   ⓑ He wrote a book about Renaissance ideals.
   ⓒ He was a patron of the arts in Florence.
   ⓓ He ordered the rebuilding of St. Peter's.

8. Which painting by Michelangelo shows God's finger reaching toward a man, bringing him to life?
   ⓐ *Mona Lisa*
   ⓑ *The Creation of Adam*
   ⓒ *The Last Supper*
   ⓓ *David*

9. How would you describe the people in Michelangelo's paintings?
   ⓐ flat
   ⓑ lifelike
   ⓒ tiny
   ⓓ imaginary

10. Which of the following is a painting by Leonardo da Vinci?
  - ⓐ *The Creation of Adam*
  - ⓑ the *Pietà*
  - ⓒ *The Last Supper*
  - ⓓ *The Courtier*

11. What does the phrase "Renaissance man" mean?
  - ⓐ a person who was born during the Renaissance
  - ⓑ a person who does many things well
  - ⓒ a person who studies ancient Rome and Greece
  - ⓓ a person who designs domes

12. Who was the greatest sculptor of the Renaissance?
  - ⓐ Julius II
  - ⓑ Leonardo da Vinci
  - ⓒ Isabella d'Este
  - ⓓ Michelangelo

13. Who hired Michelangelo to paint the Sistine Chapel ceiling?
  - ⓐ Pope Julius II
  - ⓑ Leonardo da Vinci
  - ⓒ Isabella d'Este
  - ⓓ Lorenzo de' Medici

14. Who was Isabella d'Este?
  - ⓐ an artist who illustrated books for the popes
  - ⓑ a queen from Venice
  - ⓒ a painter and sculptor who moved to Florence
  - ⓓ an important leader of Mantua who made it a center of art and learning

15. Which of the following are two of Michelangelo's greatest works?
  ⓐ the *Mona Lisa* and the *Primavera*
  ⓑ the *David* and the *Pietà*
  ⓒ *The Last Supper* and the *David*
  ⓓ *The Creation of Adam* and *The Last Supper*

16. What ancient civilizations inspired Renaissance artists and scholars?
  ⓐ Egypt and Mesopotamia
  ⓑ Arabia and India
  ⓒ Greece and Rome
  ⓓ Japan and China

17. Which of the following were Renaissance ideals?
  ⓐ fluency in Italian, ability to sing loudly, pride
  ⓑ study of classical writers, ability to paint and draw, humility
  ⓒ ability to swim and sail, knowledge of how to use a compass
  ⓓ ability to juggle, kindness to animals, compassion

18. During the Renaissance, Florence was known as a center of what?
  ⓐ cloth and banking
  ⓑ shipbuilding and theater
  ⓒ porcelain and silk
  ⓓ sports and art

19. Draw a circle around the Italian peninsula on this map.

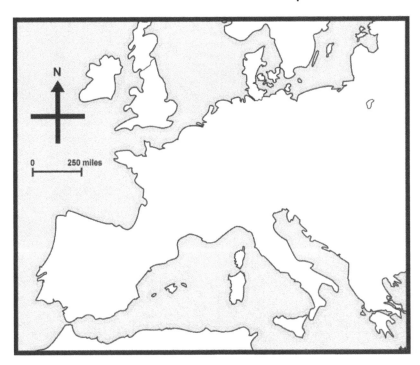

20. What dome is shown in this picture?
  ⓐ the cathedral in Florence
  ⓑ the Pantheon
  ⓒ the Parthenon
  ⓓ the capital of Venice

Student Guide
Lesson 1: Gutenberg Breaks into Print

- Identify Martin Luther as a German monk who led the Reformation.
- State that the Reformation created political and religious splits in Europe.
- Identify the development of the printing press as key to the spread of Renaissance ideas and ideals.
- Recognize the role of Italy in the spread of Renaissance ideas to northern Europe.
- State that strong monarchs emerged in England, France, and Spain.
- Identify key artistic and scientific advances in northern Europe.
- Define the Reformation as a split within Christianity.

German goldsmith Johannes Gutenberg invented a system of movable type in the 1450s that made mass printing possible. Within a decade of his invention, printing presses could be found all over Europe, facilitating the mass production of books and the rapid exchange of ideas.

Lesson Objectives

- Identify the development of the printing press as key to the spread of Renaissance ideas and ideals.
- Recognize the role of Italy in the spread of Renaisssance ideas to northern Europe.
- State that strong monarchs emerged in England, France, and Spain.
- Identify key artistic and scientific advances in northern Europe.
- Define the Reformation as a split within Christianity.
- Identify Martin Luther as a German monk who led the Reformation.
- State that the Reformation created political and religious splits in Europe.
- Name Johannes Gutenberg as the inventor of the printing press.
- Name the Bible as the first important book Gutenberg printed.
- Explain that printing large numbers of books was one of the most important results of Gutenberg's invention.

PREPARE

Approximate lesson time is 60 minutes.

Materials

For the Student

　📖 Map of Europe, A.D. 1450

　History Record Book

　paper, 8 1/2" x 11"

　pencils, colored 12

　📖 Renaissance Printing activity sheet

Keywords and Pronunciation

Johannes Gensfleisch (yoh-HAHN-uhs GENZ-fliysh)
Johannes Gutenberg (yoh-HAHN-uhs GOOT-n-burg)
Mainz (miynts)

LEARN
Activity 1: Johannes Gutenberg *(Online)*

Activity 2: History Record Book *(Online)*
Instructions
Choose either A or B.
A. Written Narration
Write two to four sentences explaining what the lesson was about. If necessary, use the Show You Know questions to help get started. Only include the most important parts of the lesson. Write your name, the date, and the lesson title on your written narration, and put it in your History Record Book.
Sample written narration: "Johannes Gutenberg invented the printing press. The Bible was his first book. The printing press could make lots of books."

B. Picture Narration
Draw a picture of the part of the lesson that interested you most. When you have finished drawing, describe the picture. Below your picture, write a description of what you have drawn. Write your name, the date, and the lesson title on your picture narration, and put it in your History Record Book.

Activity 3: Renaissance Printing *(Online)*
Instructions
If you had a great idea, how would you let other people know about your idea? Write a letter? Send email? Call people on the phone? Write a book? One way to spread your idea would be to write a book. People all over the world could buy your book, read it, and learn about your idea. Your idea would spread quickly to people all over.
This was the result of Gutenberg's invention of the printing press. Books could be printed in large numbers and sent to people in other kingdoms and empires. The ideas in those books would spread as well.
But just how was a book printed? Look at the Renaissance Printing activity sheet to see the steps involved in printing a book during the Renaissance. Then create a mural showing these steps. Display your finished mural on a wall.

ASSESS

Lesson Assessment: Gutenberg Breaks into Print (*Online*)
You will complete an offline assessment covering the main objectives of this lesson. Your learning coach will score this assessment.

LEARN
Activity 4. Optional: Gutenberg Breaks into Print *(Online)*
Instructions

Gutenberg's printing press used small squares of lead on which the letters of the alphabet were formed. Before Gutenberg, the Chinese were carving Chinese characters on wood blocks. In fact, there are a lot of things you can use to print--including potatoes!

Here's how you do it:

- Use a plastic knife to carefully cut a large raw potato in half.
- Use something with a point (such as a pencil) to draw a design, letter, or word on the exposed end of one of the potato halves.
- Have an adult carve away the part of the potato that is not part of the design, letter, or word that you have drawn.
- Spread a thin layer of ink or paint on a paper plate.
- Press the potato into the ink or paint, being careful to keep it flat.
- Stamp a sheet of paper with the potato. Your design, letter, or word will be printed on the paper!

Name _____ **Date** _____

Renaissance Printing

1. Letter blocks are assembled to form words to print.

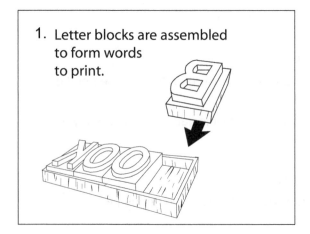

2. The blocks are inked.

ink

3.

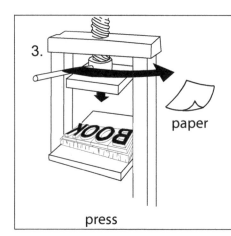

press

4. The page is set aside for the ink to dry.

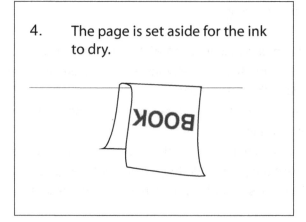

5. Once the ink is dry, the finished page can be bound with other pages into a book.

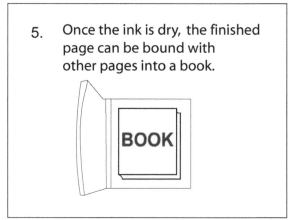

Once the letters have been inked, they are placed on the press table, and beneath a sheet of paper.

The lever is turned to clamp down on the blocks with great pressure to transfer the ink to the paper.

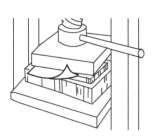

paper

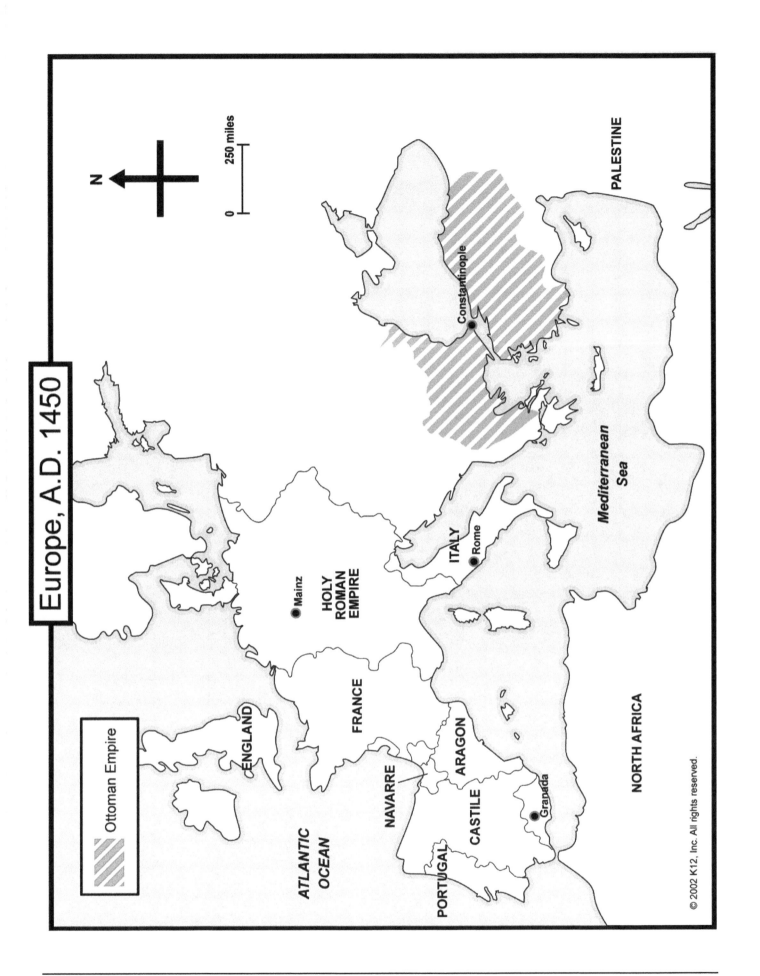

Europe, A.D. 1450

N

250 miles

0

Ottoman Empire

PALESTINE

Constantinople

Mediterranean Sea

Mainz

HOLY ROMAN EMPIRE

ITALY
Rome

ENGLAND

FRANCE

NAVARRE

ARAGON

CASTILE

Granada

PORTUGAL

ATLANTIC OCEAN

NORTH AFRICA

© 2002 K12, Inc. All rights reserved.

Lesson Assessment

Gutenberg Breaks into Print

1. Who invented the printing press?_____

2. What was the first important book Gutenberg printed?_____

3. What was one of the most important results of Gutenberg's

    invention?_____

Student Guide
Lesson 2: Crescent Versus Cross

The confrontation between Christianity and Islam begun in the eighth century lasted well into the Renaissance. European powers contended against Muslim empires with mixed results: Ottoman Turks were triumphant in the east, while Christian monarchs prevailed in Spain.

Lesson Objectives

- State that wars between Christians and Muslims lasted into the Renaissance.
- Identify the Ottoman Turks as the victors in the battle for Constantinople.
- Name Ferdinand and Isabella as the king and queen who ousted the Moors from Spain.
- Locate Christian and Muslim domains on a map.

PREPARE

Approximate lesson time is 60 minutes.

Materials

For the Student

    🖳 Map of Europe, A.D. 1450

    crayons 8 - red

    History Record Book

    🖳 Hagia Sophia as a Mosque activity sheet

    pencils, colored 12

Optional

    Isabel, Jewel of Castilla, Spain, 1466 by Carolyn Meyer

Keywords and Pronunciation

Aragon (AIR-uh-gahn)

Castile (ka-STEEL)

Granada (grah-NAH-dah)

Navarra (nah-VAH-rah)

Ottoman (AH-tuh-muhn)

LEARN
Activity 1: Muslim Constantinople and Christian Spain *(Online)*

Activity 2: History Record Book (Online)

Instructions

Choose either A or B.

A. Written Narration

Write two to four sentences explaining what the lesson was about. If necessary, use the Show You Know questions to help get started. Only include the most important parts of the lesson. Write your name, the date, and the lesson title on your written narration, and put it in your History Record Book.

Sample written narration: "The Muslims and the Christians fought during the Renaissance. The Ottoman Turks used big cannons to capture Constantinople. Ferdinand and Isabella beat the Muslims in Spain."

B. Picture Narration

Draw a picture of the part of the lesson that interested you most. When you have finished drawing, describe the picture. Below your picture, write a description of what you have drawn. Write your name, the date, and the lesson title on your picture narration, and put it in your History Record Book.

Activity 3: Hagia Sophia Changes Hands (Online)

When the Ottoman Turks, who were Muslim, captured Constantinople, they made the Hagia Sophia a mosque. By this time, most mosques had minarets. So what did the new rulers of the city do? They built minarets!

Complete the Hagia Sophia as a Mosque activity sheet.

ASSESS

Lesson Assessment: Crescent Versus Cross (Online)

You will complete an offline assessment covering the main objectives of this lesson. Your learning coach will score this assessment.

LEARN

Activity 4. Optional: Crescent Versus Cross (Online)

You might know Isabella as the queen who sponsored Christopher Columbus's voyage in search of a shorter route to the West Indies. The events in this fictionalized diary take place before 1492, and provide an interesting look into the life of this future queen of Spain.

As usual, preview the recommended reading material listed here before having your student view it.

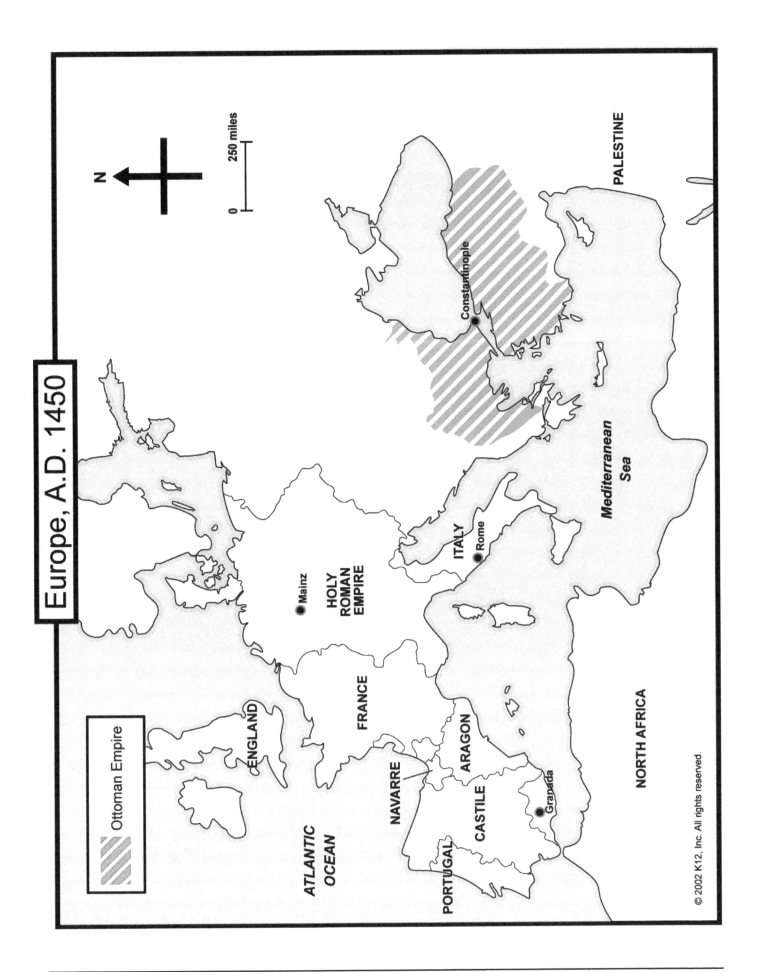

Europe, A.D. 1450

N

250 miles

0

Ottoman Empire

PALESTINE

Constantinople

Mediterranean Sea

ITALY

Rome

Mainz

HOLY ROMAN EMPIRE

FRANCE

ENGLAND

ATLANTIC OCEAN

NAVARRE

PORTUGAL

CASTILE

ARAGON

Granada

NORTH AFRICA

© 2002 K12, Inc. All rights reserved.

Name _____   Date _____

Hagia Sophia as a Mosque

What happened when Constantinople fell to the Ottoman Turks? Among other things, Hagia Sophia was turned into a mosque. Add minarets to this illustration of Hagia Sophia and draw a crescent at the top of the dome, then color it. Complete the sentences below.

1. Wars between _____ and _____ lasted into the Renaissance.

2. The Ottoman Turks conquered _____.

3. _____ and _____ drove the Moors out of Spain.

Name _____ Date _____

Lesson Assessment

Crescent Versus Cross

1. Did wars between Christians and Muslims end with the Crusades, or did they last into the
   Renaissance?_____

2. What group of people captured Constantinople for Islam?_____

3. What were the names of the king and queen of Spain who drove the Moors from
   Spain?_____

4. **To answer this question, please use your map of Europe, 1450 A.D.**

   What area belonged to the Christians, and what area belonged to the

   Muslims?_____

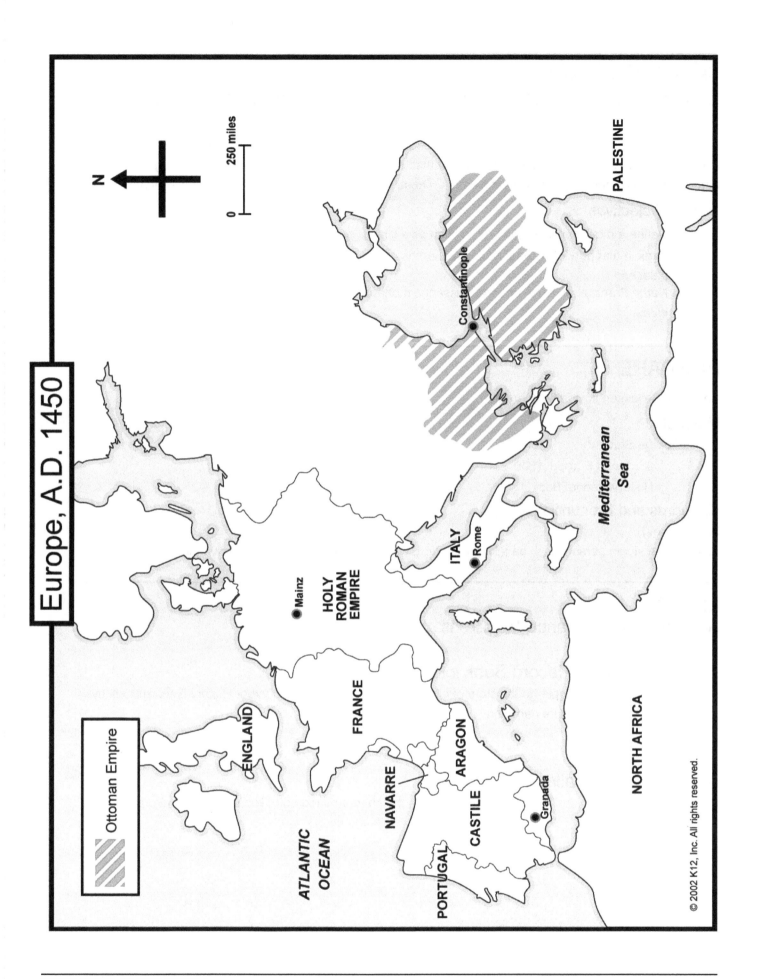

Europe, A.D. 1450

N

250 miles

0

Ottoman Empire

ENGLAND

ATLANTIC
OCEAN

HOLY
ROMAN
EMPIRE

Mainz

FRANCE

NAVARRE

PORTUGAL

ARAGON

CASTILE

Granada

ITALY

Rome

Mediterranean
Sea

NORTH AFRICA

Constantinople

PALESTINE

© 2002 K12, Inc. All rights reserved.

Student Guide
Lesson 3: Renaissance Monarchs and the Changing Face of Europe

While competing city-states in Italy spurred the Renaissance, strong monarchies emerged in England, France, and Spain. Attempting to inspire awe and assert their might, these "new monarchs" enlisted large armies, fought frequently, and built magnificent palaces. These monarchies formed the basis of some modern nations.

Lesson Objectives

- Define a monarch as a single ruler, such as a king or queen.
- Explain that powerful Renaissance monarchs established large armies and built magnificent palaces.
- Name Francis I as a powerful Renaissance monarch of France who imported Italian artists and ideas.

PREPARE

Approximate lesson time is 60 minutes.

Materials

For the Student

💻 Map of Europe, 1500

History Record Book

Keywords and Pronunciation

Louvre (loov)

monarch : A single person, such as a king or queen, who rules over a kingdom or an empire.

LEARN
Activity 1: Renaissance Monarchs *(Online)*

Activity 2: History Record Book *(Online)*

It's time to add another chapter to the story of our past. Create a new entry in your History Record Book by completing a written or picture narration.

Activity 3: Loire Valley Tour *(Online)*

No time to hop on the plane to France for a trip down the chateau-lined Loire River. Instead, take a virtual tour!

ASSESS

Lesson Assessment: Renaissance Monarchs and the Changing Face of Europe (*Online*)

You will complete an offline assessment covering the main objectives of this lesson. Your learning coach will score this assessment.

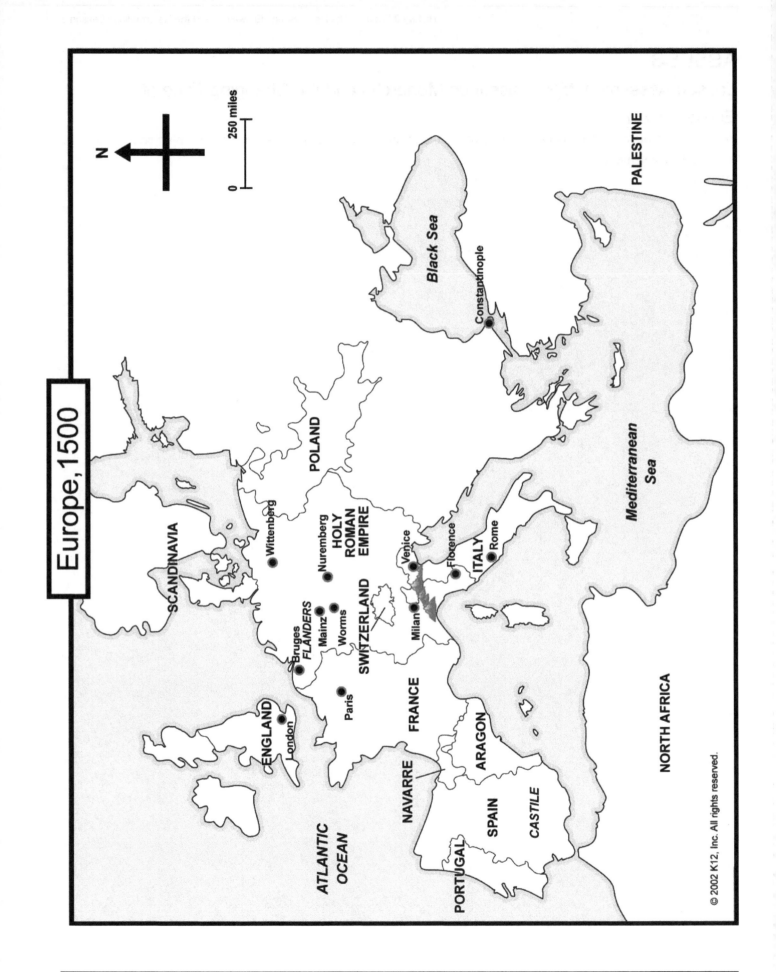

Europe, 1500

250 miles

N

SCANDINAVIA

POLAND

Wittenberg

Nuremberg

HOLY
ROMAN
EMPIRE

Black Sea

Constantinople

PALESTINE

Mediterranean
Sea

Bruges
FLANDERS

Mainz

Worms

SWITZERLAND

Venice

Milan

Florence

Rome

ITALY

London

ENGLAND

Paris

FRANCE

NAVARRE

ARAGON

SPAIN

CASTILE

PORTUGAL

ATLANTIC
OCEAN

NORTH AFRICA

Lesson Assessment

Renaissance Monarchs and the Changing Face of Europe

1. What is a monarch?_____

2. How did powerful Renaissance monarchs show they were

   powerful?_____

3. Name the powerful Renaissance king of France who invaded Italy and brought back Italian artists

   and ideas._____

Student Guide
Lesson 4. Optional: Making Music in the Renaissance

Grand courts and wealthy merchants demanded grand music. For the first time, composers began to write music that was not just church music, but could be sung at court and treated everyday concerns such as love and money.

Lesson Objectives

- Describe the Renaissance as a period when people sang new kinds of songs and played new kinds of musical instruments.
- Describe madrigals as Renaissance songs for four or five voices.

PREPARE

Approximate lesson time is 60 minutes.

Materials

For the Student

⊞ Map of Europe, 1500

History Record Book

paper, 8 1/2" x 11"

pencils, colored 12

⊞ Greensleeves lyric sheet

⊞ Renaissance Instruments activity sheet

Keywords and Pronunciation

madrigal (MA-drih-guhl) : A Renaissance song for four or five voices.

LEARN
Activity 1. Optional: Optional Lesson Instructions *(Online)*

This lesson is OPTIONAL. It is provided for students who seek enrichment or extra practice. You may skip this lesson.

If you choose to skip this lesson, then go to the Plan or Lesson Lists page and mark this lesson "Skipped" in order to proceed to the next lesson in the course.

Activity 2. Optional: Renaissance Music *(Online)*

Activity 3. Optional: History Record Book (Online)

It's time to add another chapter to the story of our past. Create a new entry in your History Record Book by completing a written or picture narration.

Activity 4. Optional: Listening to Renaissance Music (Online)

Don't worry if you don't have the *Greatest Hits of the Renaissance* CD at home. Go online to hear some of the music that was popular at the court of Charles V.

Activity 5. Optional: Making Music in the Renaissance (Online)

Instructions

Two popular instruments in the Renaissance were the lute and the flute. Do a little research to learn more about these two instruments. Check the public library for books on Renaissance music and the history of musical instruments. You can also search the Internet for information on Renaissance instruments. You could start with the site, A Guide to Medieval and Renaissance Instruments.

On the Renaissance instruments activity sheet, write three to five sentences about each instrument. Now do some more research to find another Renaissance musical instrument. Draw a picture of this instrument in the bottom row, and write three to five sentences about it.

Greensleeves

Alas, my love, you do me wrong
To cast me off discourteously;
And I have loved you so long,
Delighting in your company.

Chorus:

Greensleeves was all my joy,
Greensleeves was my delight,
Greensleeves was my heart of gold,
And who but my Lady Greensleeves.

I have been ready at your hand
To grant whatever you would crave;
I have both wagered life and land
Your love and good will for to have.

Chorus

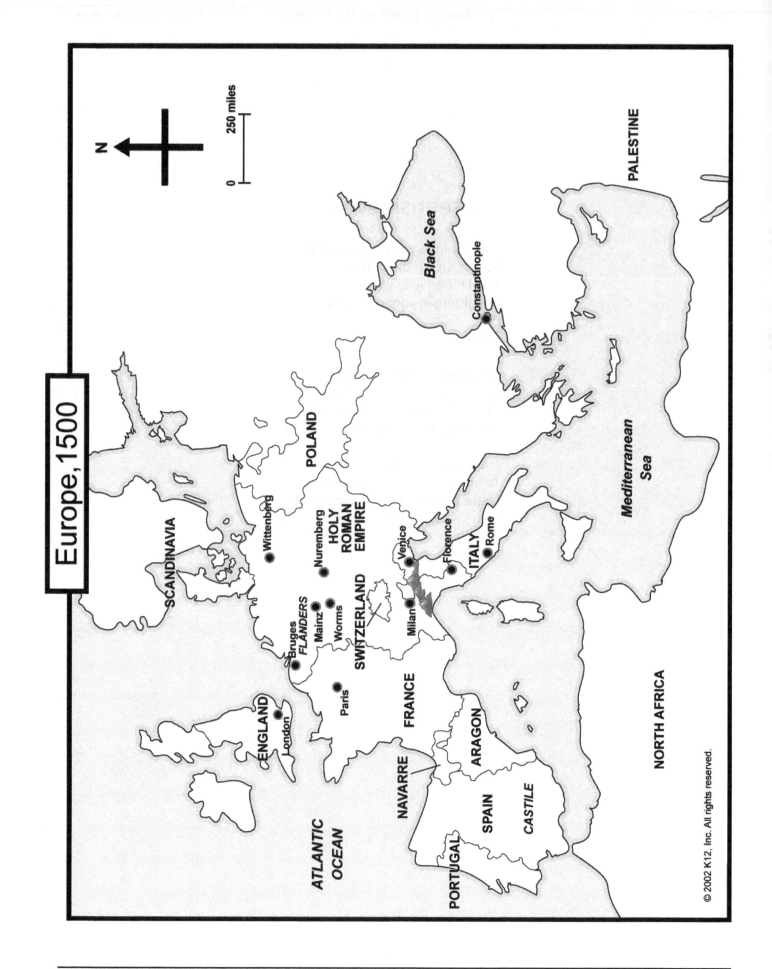

Europe, 1500

N

250 miles

0

PALESTINE

Black Sea

Constantinople

Mediterranean
Sea

SCANDINAVIA

POLAND

Wittenberg

Nuremberg

HOLY
ROMAN
EMPIRE

Venice

Florence

Rome

ITALY

Mainz

Worms

SWITZERLAND

Milan

Bruges

FLANDERS

Paris

ENGLAND

London

FRANCE

NAVARRE

ARAGON

SPAIN

CASTILE

PORTUGAL

ATLANTIC
OCEAN

NORTH AFRICA

Name _____   Date _____

Renaissance Instruments

Follow the directions in the activity instructions to complete this activity sheet.

lute	
flute	

Student Guide
Lesson 5: An Eye for Detail: Van Eyck and Dürer

As trade revived in northern Europe during the 1400s, the arts flourished. Painters like Jan van Eyck and Albrecht Dürer rendered detailed portraits of the life around them and gave the Renaissance in northern Europe a new twist.

Lesson Objectives

- Explain that the printing press made it possible for ideas and prints of Italian art to spread to northern Europe.
- Name van Eyck and Dürer as major Renaissance artists from northern Europe.
- Describe Northern European Renaissance painting as very detailed and realistic.

PREPARE

Approximate lesson time is 60 minutes.

Materials

For the Student

    🖳 Map of Europe, 1500

    History Record Book

    🖳 Durer's Hare activity sheet

Keywords and Pronunciation

Albrecht Dürer (AHL-brekt DYOUR-ur)

Bruges (brouzh)

engraving : Making designs by cutting metal, wood, or another hard surface, and then printing the design.

Giovanni Arnolfini (jee-oh-VAH-nee ahr-nohl-FEE-nee)

Jan van Eyck (yahn van IYK)

LEARN
Activity 1: The Artists van Eyck and Dürer *(Online)*

Activity 2: History Record Book *(Online)*

It's time to add another chapter to the story of our past. Create a new entry in your History Record Book by completing a written or picture narration.

Activity 3: Dürer's Hare *(Online)*

ASSESS

Lesson Assessment: An Eye for Detail: Van Eyck and Dürer *(Online)*

You will complete an offline assessment covering the main objectives of this lesson. Your learning coach will score this assessment.

LEARN

Activity 4. Optional: An Eye for Detail: Van Eyck and Dürer *(Online)*

Take a look at another Northern European Renaissance artist, Pieter Brueghel (PEE-tuhr BROY-guhl). His *Peasant Wedding* is a great example of a very detailed and realistic painting.

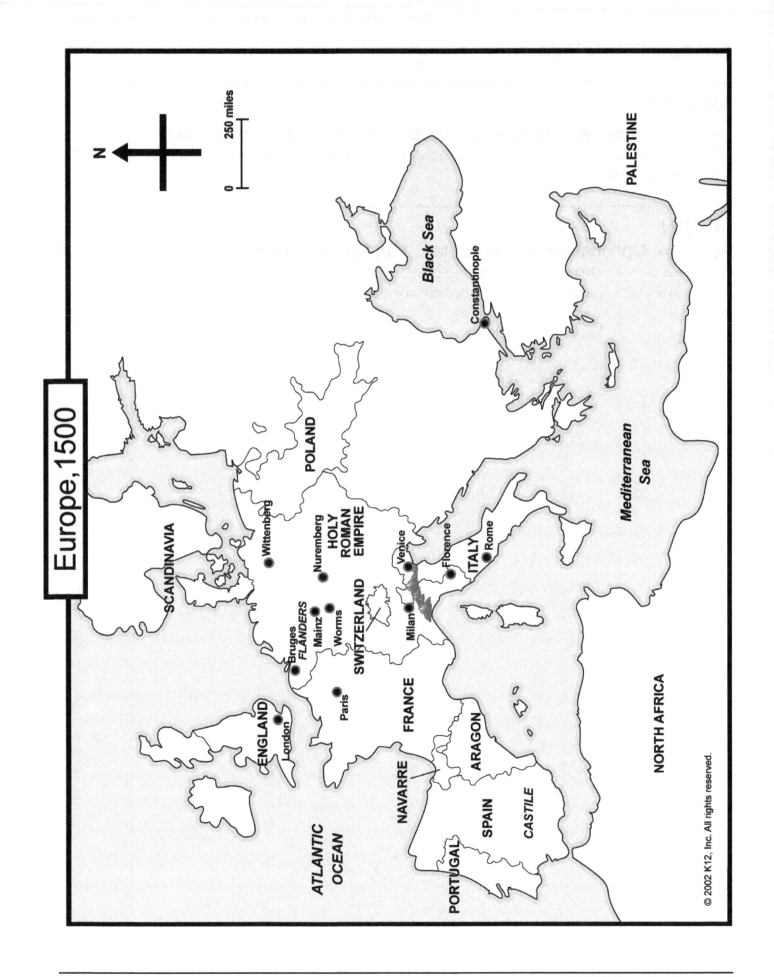

Europe, 1500

250 miles

N

PALESTINE

Black Sea

Constantinople

Mediterranean Sea

POLAND

SCANDINAVIA

Wittenberg

HOLY ROMAN EMPIRE

Nuremberg

Venice

Florence

Rome

ITALY

Bruges
FLANDERS
Mainz
Worms

SWITZERLAND

Milan

Paris

FRANCE

ENGLAND
London

NAVARRE

ARAGON

SPAIN

CASTILE

PORTUGAL

ATLANTIC OCEAN

NORTH AFRICA

© 2002 K12, Inc. All rights reserved.

Name _____   Date _____

Dürer's Hare

Study the image of *A Young Hare*. Look at all of the detail Dürer included in his painting. Now add details to the outline of the hare below to complete the drawing.

Lesson Assessment

An Eye for Detail: Van Eyck and Dürer

1. How did those living north of the Alps learn about Renaissance ideas and Italian

    art?_____

2. What are the names of the two great artists from northern Europe we just learned

    about?_____

3. How would you describe Northern European Renaissance painting?_____

Student Guide
Lesson 6: Copernicus Moves the Earth

Polish astronomer Nicolaus Copernicus is known as the founder of modern astronomy. Breaking with conventional wisdom, he used mathematics and observation to show that the sun, not the Earth, was the center of our solar system, and that the Earth was a planet that moved around the sun.

Lesson Objectives

- Describe the Renaissance as an age of learning and invention in science and math.
- Tell that in the Middle Ages, most people believed that the sun moved around the Earth.
- Tell that Copernicus believed the Earth moved around the sun.

PREPARE

Approximate lesson time is 60 minutes.

Materials

For the Student

    🖳 Map of Europe, 1500

    History Record Book

    🖳 Two Views of the Heavens activity sheet

    crayons 8

Optional

    Copernicus: Founder of Modern Astronomy by Catherine M. Andronik

Keywords and Pronunciation

astronomy : The study of the planets and stars.

Nicolaus Copernicus (NIK-uh-luhs kuh-PUR-nih-kuhs)

LEARN
Activity 1: The Man Who Stopped the Sun and Moved the Earth *(Online)*

Activity 2: History Record Book *(Online)*

Instructions

Choose either A or B.

A. Written Narration

Write two to four sentences explaining what the lesson was about. If necessary, use the Show You Know questions to help get started. Only include the most important parts of the lesson. Write your name, the date, and the lesson title on your written narration, and put it in your History Record Book.

Sample written narration: "Before Copernicus, most people believed that the sun went around the Earth. But Copernicus believed that the Earth went around the sun. He showed it with mathematics. He wrote it all in a book."

B. Picture Narration

Draw a picture of the part of the lesson that interested you most. When you have finished drawing, describe the picture. Below your picture, write a description of what you have drawn. Write your name, the date, and the lesson title on your picture narration, and then put it in your History Record Book.

Activity 3: Two Views of the Heavens *(Online)*

ASSESS

Lesson Assessment: Copernicus Moves the Earth (*Online*)

You will complete an offline assessment covering the main objectives of this lesson. Your learning coach will score this assessment.

LEARN
Activity 4. Optional: Copernicus Moves the Earth *(Online)*

Learn more about Copernicus and the role he played in laying the groundwork for modern astronomy. Read all or part of *Copernicus: Founder of Modern Astronomy* (Great Minds of Science Series) by Catherine M. Andronik (Berkeley Heights, NJ: Enslow Publishers, Inc., 2002).

Name _____   Date _____

Two Views of the Heavens

Circle the Earth in the same color on each model of the heavens. Choose another color to draw a circle around the sun on each model. On the back, write one to three sentences describing how Copernicus's model and the popular one of his time were different.

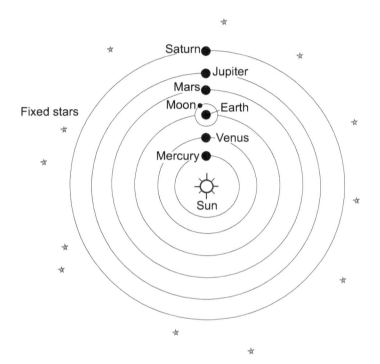

Copernican view of the heavens

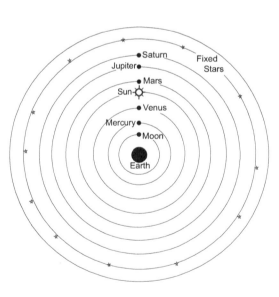

View of the universe
before Copernicus

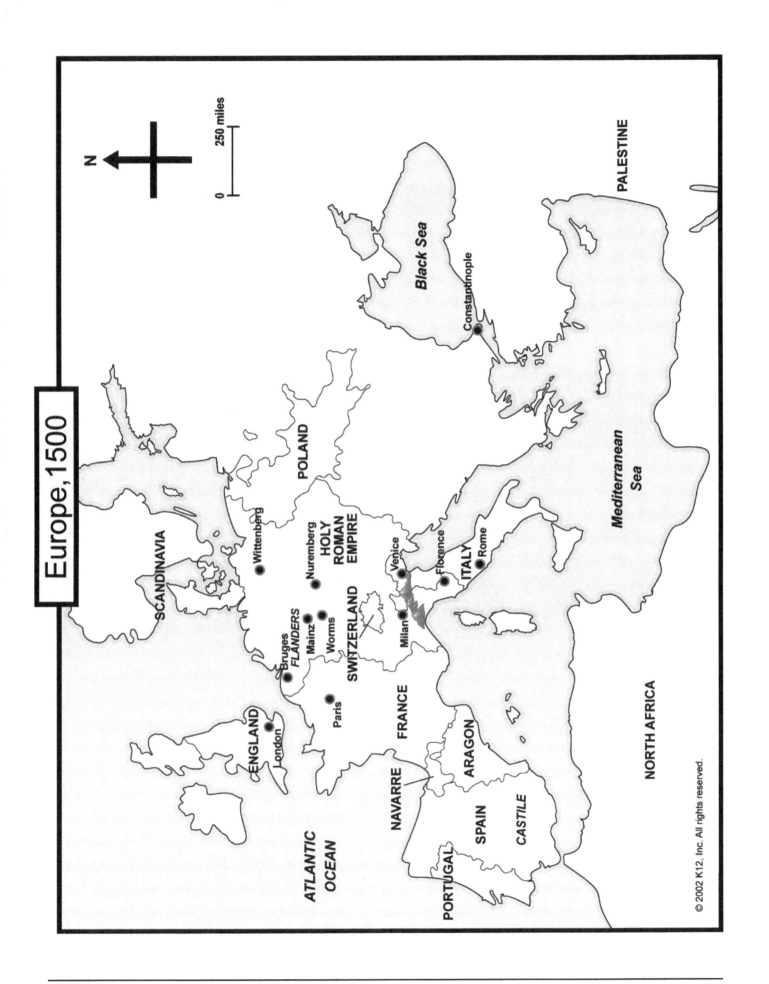

Europe, 1500

N

250 miles

0

SCANDINAVIA

POLAND

Wittenberg

Nuremberg

HOLY ROMAN EMPIRE

Bruges
FLANDERS

Mainz
Worms

SWITZERLAND

Black Sea

Constantinople

Venice

Milan

Florence

ITALY

Rome

Mediterranean Sea

PALESTINE

London

ENGLAND

Paris

FRANCE

NAVARRE

ATLANTIC OCEAN

ARAGON

SPAIN

CASTILE

PORTUGAL

NORTH AFRICA

Lesson Assessment

Copernicus Moves the Earth

1. During the Middle Ages, before the time of Copernicus, did most people believe that the sun moved around the Earth, or that the Earth moved around the sun?_____

2. What did Copernicus believe about the Earth and the sun?_____

3. During the Renaissance, were mathematicians and scientists like Copernicus content to believe what people had always believed?_____

Student Guide
Lesson 7: Martin Luther and the 95 Theses

German monk Martin Luther sought to reform the worldly church. When he posted his 95 Theses criticizing church practices, he set off one of the major changes in world history.

Lesson Objectives

- Name Martin Luther as a monk who wished to reform the Christian Church.
- Identify the 95 Theses as a document that criticized church practices.
- Explain that the printing press helped spread Martin Luther's ideas.

PREPARE

Approximate lesson time is 60 minutes.

Materials

    For the Student

        History Record Book

        💻 Martin Luther Crossword Puzzle

Keywords and Pronunciation

indulgences : Pardons which promised people they would not be punished for their sins after death.

Johann Tetzel (yoh-HAHN TET-suhl)

purgatory (PUR-guh-tohr-ee)

theses (THEE-seez) : Points made in a discussion or argument.

Wittenberg (VIT-n-burg)

LEARN
Activity 1: Luther Picks Up a Hammer and Starts a Fire *(Online)*

Activity 2: History Record Book *(Online)*
Instructions

Choose either A or B.

A. Written Narration

Write two to four sentences explaining what the lesson was about. If necessary, use the Show You Know questions to help get started. Only include the most important parts of the lesson. Write your name, the date, and the lesson title on your written narration, and put it in your History Record Book.

Sample written narration: "Martin Luther thought the church needed to be reformed. He nailed a paper to a church door. He had 95 reasons to fix the church. The printing press helped people read the 95 Theses."

B. Picture Narration

Draw a picture of the part of the lesson that interested you most. When you have finished drawing, describe the picture. Below your picture, write a description of what you have drawn. Write your name, the date, and the lesson title on your picture narration, and then put it in your History Record Book.

Activity 3: Martin Luther Crossword Puzzle *(Online)*

Print and solve the Martin Luther Crossword Puzzle. Place the completed work in your History Record Book.

ASSESS

Lesson Assessment: Martin Luther and the 95 Theses *(Online)*

You will complete an offline assessment covering the main objectives of this lesson. Your learning coach will score this assessment.

Name _____   Date _____

Martin Luther Crossword Puzzle

Solve this crossword puzzle to help you remember the meanings of some of the words from this lesson.

Across

3. pardons issued by the church

5. a monk who sold indulgences

6. ideas that someone makes known and stands by

7. Martin Luther was a _____.

Down

1. where Martin Luther lived

2. an attempt to reform the church

4. The printing _____ helped spread Martin Luther's ideas.

Across 3. indulgences, 5. Tetzel, 6. theses, 7. professor **Down** 1. Wittenberg, 2. Reformation, 4. press

Lesson Assessment

Martin Luther and the 95 Theses

1. Who wanted to reform, or change, the Christian Church?_____

2. What were the 95 Theses?_____

3. What helped spread Martin Luther's ideas so that many people found out about his 95

   Theses?_____

Student Guide
Lesson 8: A Diet of Worms? The Reformation Splits Christianity

What began as a movement for church reform led within four years to a major religious and political split in Europe. "Lutheranism" became its own religion, and the Christian Church split into Catholic and Protestant divisions.

Lesson Objectives

- Define the Reformation as a religious movement that divided the Christian Church into Catholic and Protestant branches.
- Explain the origin of the word *Protestant.*
- State that Luther's protests caused a break with the established church and that he gained support among German princes.

PREPARE

Approximate lesson time is 60 minutes.

Materials

For the Student

 📕 Map of Europe, 1500

 History Record Book

 📕 Martin Luther's Protests activity sheet

 📕 Steps in Martin Luther's Protests activity sheet

 glue, children's white

 paper, construction

 pencils, colored 12

 scissors

LEARN
Activity 1: Martin Luther at the Diet of Worms *(Online)*

Activity 2: History Record Book *(Online)*
Instructions
Choose either A or B.
A. Written Narration
Write two to four sentences explaining what the lesson was about. If necessary, use the Show You Know questions to help get started. Only include the most important parts of the lesson. Write your name, the date, and the lesson title on your written narration, and put it in your History Record Book.

Sample written narration: "Martin Luther went to the Diet of Worms. He would not take back what he said. The emperor made him an outlaw. Then the Christian Church split into Protestant and Catholic parts."

B. Picture Narration

Draw a picture of the part of the lesson that interested you most. When you have finished drawing, describe the picture. Below your picture, write a description of what you have drawn. Write your name, the date, and the lesson title on your picture narration, and then put it in your History Record Book.

Activity 3: Martin Luther Protests (Online)

Instructions

The story of Martin Luther is very important but very complicated. Here is one way of telling it.

Martin Luther thought a lot about what he saw happening in the Catholic Church. Then he wrote down his ideas about changing the church. Because Luther had so many ideas, they became known as the 95 Theses. Martin Luther's ideas made the pope, who was the leader of the church, very angry. So he threw Martin Luther out of the church.

Emperor Charles V was also angry about what Martin Luther did. He made Luther come to a meeting in a city named Worms. Charles wanted Martin Luther to take back what he said, but Luther wouldn't. He ran away to a castle instead.

Martin Luther kept protesting about the Catholic Church. The protestors who agreed with him became known as Protestants. They separated from the Catholic Church.

Martin Luther had tried to reform the Catholic Church. But Martin Luther's Reformation divided the Catholic Church into two parts instead.

Another way of telling Martin Luther's story is in pictures with captions. Do this by printing the activity sheets and following the directions on them.

If you want to extend this activity, think of another way to tell Martin Luther's story. You might even want to write a play or poem about it.

ASSESS

Lesson Assessment: A Diet of Worms? The Reformation Splits Christianity

(Online)

You will complete an offline assessment covering the main objectives of this lesson. Your learning coach will score this assessment.

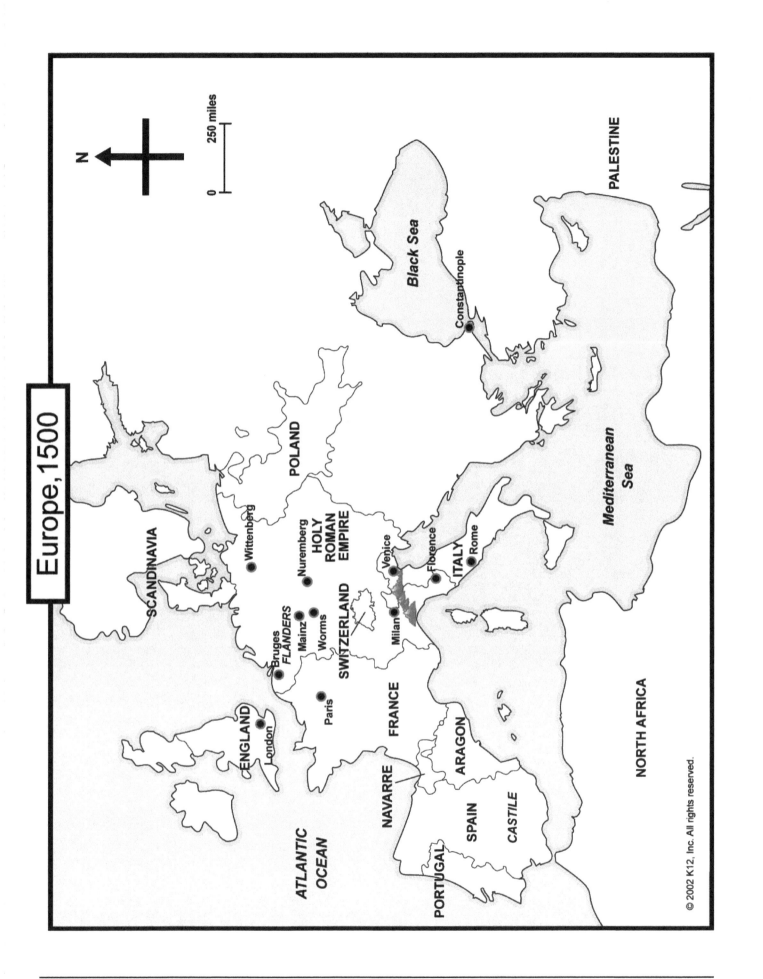

Europe, 1500

250 miles

N

PALESTINE

Black Sea

Constantinople

Mediterranean Sea

POLAND

SCANDINAVIA

Wittenberg

Nuremberg

HOLY ROMAN EMPIRE

Venice

Florence

Mainz

Worms

Milan

Rome

ITALY

Bruges

FLANDERS

SWITZERLAND

Paris

FRANCE

ENGLAND

London

ATLANTIC OCEAN

NAVARRE

ARAGON

SPAIN

CASTILE

PORTUGAL

NORTH AFRICA

Name _____   Date _____

Illustrating Martin Luther's Protests

Cut out the pictures and numbered boxes. Glue them to a piece of construction paper in order from
1 to 6. Glue the captions from the Steps in Martin Luther's Protests activity sheet to the pictures they
match. Add pictures to illustrate the captions with no pictures. Color the other pictures. Use your
finished work to tell Martin Luther's story to someone else.

Illustrating Martin Luther's Protests

Cut out the pictures and numbered boxes. Glue them in the right order on another piece of construction paper. Glue the captions from the box below to Martin Luther's Protests activity sheet in the proper order. Add pictures to illustrate "together with a partner. One of the other pictures of your finished work to tell Martin Luther's story to someone else.

Name   Date

The Steps in Martin Luther's Protests

Glue these captions to the construction paper under the pictures or boxes they match. Add pictures to illustrate the captions with no pictures. Color the other pictures. Use your finished work to tell Martin Luther's story to someone else.

1. Martin Luther writes his 95 theses.	4. Martin Luther won't take back what he said.
2. The pope throws Martin Luther out of the Catholic Church.	5. Martin Luther flees to a prince's castle.
3. Emperor Charles V calls Martin Luther to Worms.	6. The Christian Church splits in two.

Lesson Assessment

A Diet of Worms? The Reformation Splits Christianity

1. What did the Reformation do to the Christian Church?_____

2. What were the two branches of the church called?_____

3. Why were the followers of Martin Luther called Protestants?_____

4. What did Martin Luther's protests do?_____

5. Who protected and supported Luther?_____

Student Guide
Lesson 9: Europe Fractured

What began as an attempt at church reform ended in a series of wars. By 1550 the countries of Europe had divided along religious as well as political lines, some adhering to the new Protestant creeds, others recommitting themselves to the Roman Catholic Church, increasingly referred to simply as "Catholic."

Lesson Objectives

- Recognize that many people (princes, reformers, and ordinary folk) found Luther's ideas appealing.
- State that in Europe, wars over religion followed Luther's break with the church.
- State that after the Reformation and wars over religion, Europe was divided into Catholic and Protestant countries.

PREPARE

Approximate lesson time is 60 minutes.

Materials

> For the Student
>> 🖳 Map of Europe, 1500
>> crayons 8 - red and blue
>> History Record Book

LEARN
Activity 1: Catholic and Protestant Europe *(Online)*

Activity 2: History Record Book *(Online)*

Activity 3: Luther's Great Hymn *(Online)*
Prepare to introduce Martin Luther's most famous hymn.

ASSESS

Lesson Assessment: Europe Fractured (*Online*)
You will complete an offline assessment covering the main objectives of this lesson. Your learning coach will score this assessment.

LEARN
Activity 4. Optional: Europe Fractured *(Online)*

The Protestant church, led by Martin Luther, eventually split into many churches. Do some research to learn about some of them.

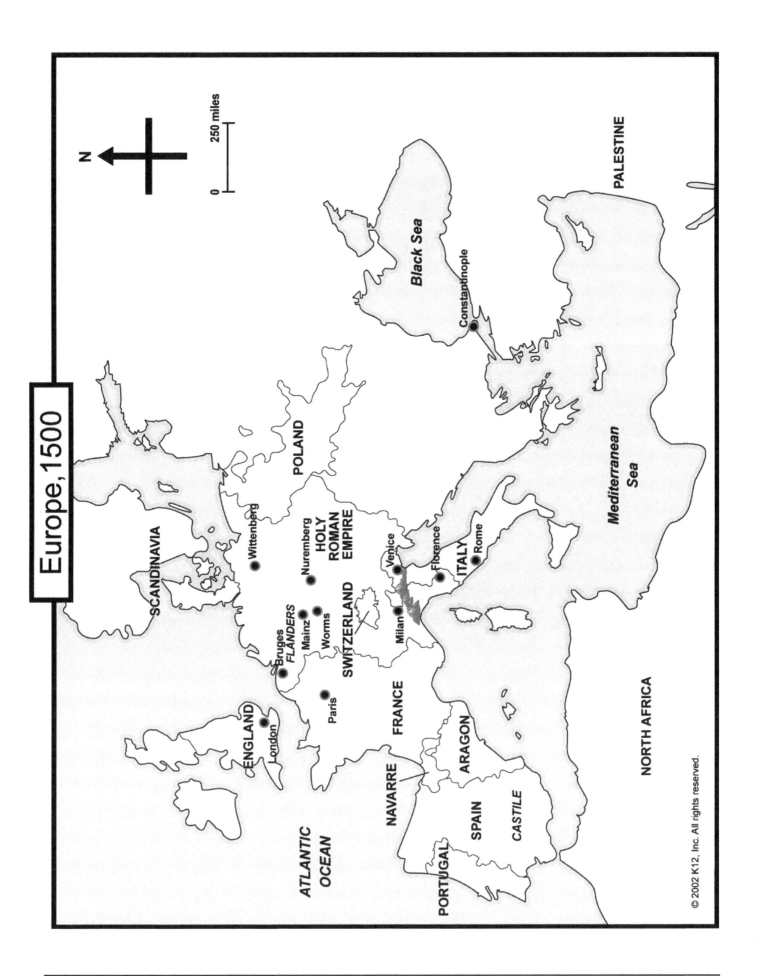

Europe, 1500

250 miles

N

PALESTINE

Black Sea

Constantinople

Mediterranean Sea

POLAND

SCANDINAVIA

Wittenberg

Nuremberg

HOLY ROMAN EMPIRE

Venice

Florence

ITALY

Rome

Bruges
FLANDERS
Mainz
Worms

SWITZERLAND

Milan

Paris

ENGLAND
London

FRANCE

NAVARRE

ARAGON

SPAIN

CASTILE

PORTUGAL

ATLANTIC OCEAN

NORTH AFRICA

Lesson Assessment

Europe Fractured

1. Did many people around Europe support Martin Luther, or just a few?_____

2. What sort of people supported Martin Luther?_____

3. What happened in Europe after Martin Luther broke with the Catholic Church?_____

4. After the Reformation and wars over religion, Europe was divided into two types of countries. What were they?_____

Student Guide
Lesson 10: Henry VIII and England for Protestantism

Henry VIII's desire for a male heir led to one of the most important ruptures in Christianity. He broke with the Roman Catholic Church and formed the Church of England. England would eventually become the standard-bearer for Protestantism.

Lesson Objectives
- Name Henry VIII as the English king who broke with the Catholic Church.
- Explain that Henry VIII's divorce was the reason for England's break with the Catholic Church.
- Identify the Church of England as the new church Henry VIII founded.

PREPARE

Approximate lesson time is 60 minutes.

Materials
For the Student

History Record Book
- 📖 Europe Divided activity sheet
- 📖 Map of Europe, A.D. 1450

Keywords and Pronunciation
heir (air) : One who inherits.
Tudor (TOO-dur)

LEARN
Activity 1: Henry VIII Starts a New Church *(Online)*

Activity 2: History Record Book *(Offline)*
Instructions
Choose either A or B.

A. Written Narration
Write two to four sentences explaining what the lesson was about. If necessary, use the Show You Know questions to help get started. Only include the most important parts of the lesson. Write your name, the date, and the lesson title on your written narration, and put it in your History Record Book.
Sample written narration: "Henry VIII was the king of England. He wanted to divorce his wife. The pope would not let him. So Henry started the Church of England."

B. Picture Narration
Draw a picture of the part of the lesson that interested you most. When you have finished drawing, describe the picture. Below your picture, write a description of what you have drawn. Write your name, the date, and the lesson title on your picture narration, and put it in your History Record Book.

Activity 3: Europe Divided *(Offline)*

Instructions

Martin Luther's attempt to reform the Catholic Church resulted in a series of wars. By 1550 Europe had begun to divide, partly based on religion. Some countries began to practice the Protestant faith, while others remained with the Catholic Church.

Complete the Europe Divided activity sheet to see how Europe divided.

ASSESS

Lesson Assessment: Henry VIII and England for Protestantism (*Online*)

You will complete an offline assessment covering the main objectives of this lesson. Your learning coach will score this assessment.

LEARN

Activity 4. Optional: Henry VIII and England for Protestantism *(Online)*

Learn more about the famous cathedral at Canterbury and the history of its archbishop.

Name

Date

Europe Divided

Use color to show which parts of Europe were Catholic and which parts were Protestant. Fill in the squares on the map legend and use those colors on the map. Then answer the questions using complete sentences.

1. Why did Henry VIII break from the Catholic Church?

2. What is the name of the church Henry VIII founded?

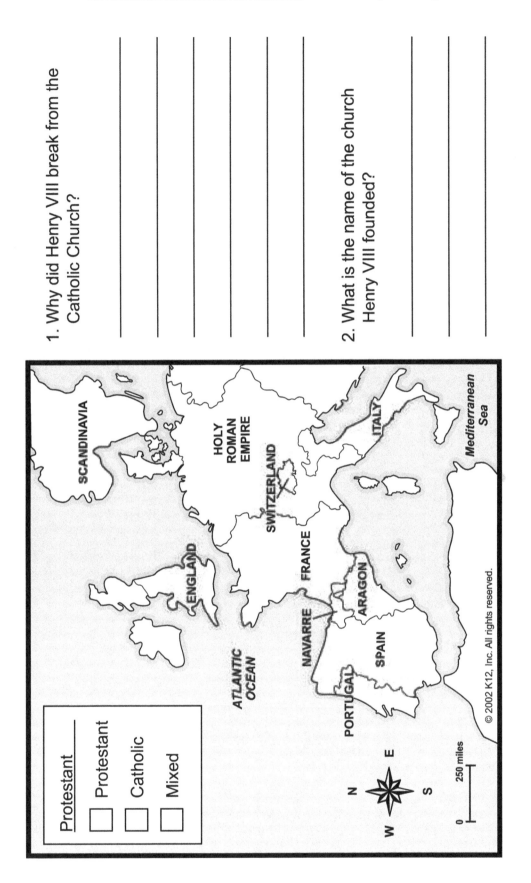

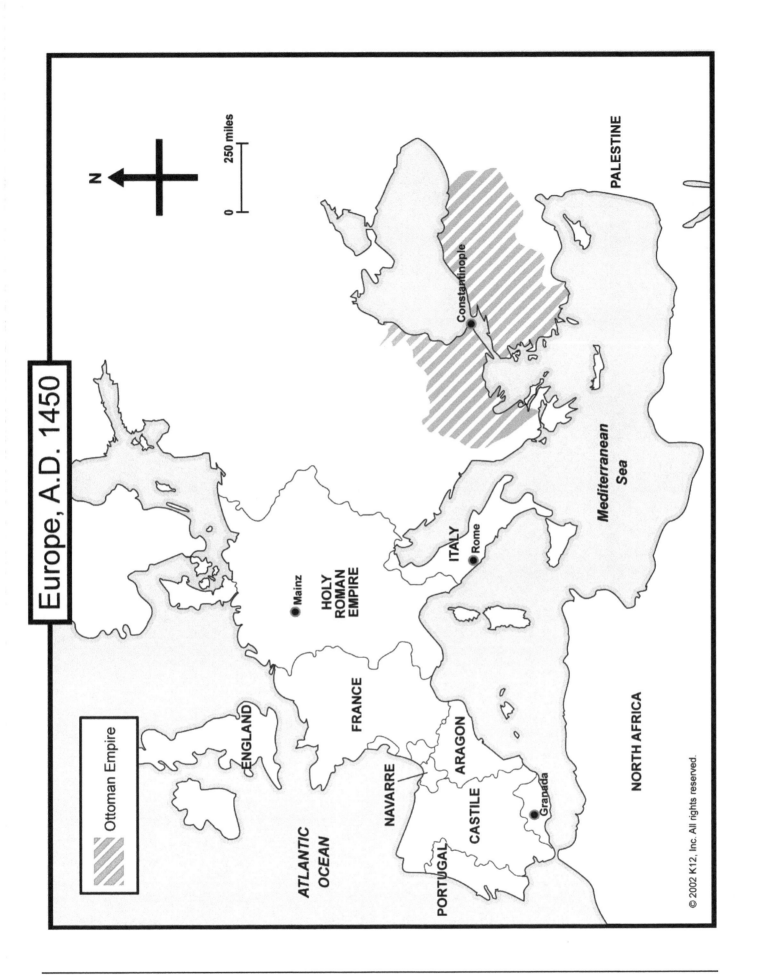

Europe, A.D. 1450

N

250 miles

0

Ottoman Empire

PALESTINE

Constantinople

ITALY
Rome

Mainz

HOLY
ROMAN
EMPIRE

Mediterranean
Sea

FRANCE

ENGLAND

ATLANTIC
OCEAN

NAVARRE

ARAGON

PORTUGAL

CASTILE

Granada

NORTH AFRICA

© 2002 K12, Inc. All rights reserved.

Lesson Assessment

Henry VIII and England for Protestantism

1. Who was the English king who broke with the Catholic Church?_____

2. Why did Henry VIII break with the Catholic Church and start his own church?_____

3. What was the new church founded by Henry VIII called?_____

Student Guide
Lesson 11: The Counter-Reformation

The Reformation led to reform within the Catholic Church itself. A new council and an energetic order of priests helped reinvigorate the beleagured church.

Lesson Objectives
- Identify the Counter-Reformation as a reform within the Catholic Church in response to the Reformation.
- Name Ignatius of Loyola as the founder of the Society of Jesus, which defended the pope and spread Catholicism.

PREPARE

Approximate lesson time is 60 minutes.

Materials
> For the Student
>> History Record Book
>>
>> pencils, colored 12

Keywords and Pronunciation
Ignatius of Loyola (ig-NAY-shuhs of loy-OH-luh)
Jesuits (JEH-zou-uhts)

LEARN
Activity 1: Ignatius of Loyola and the Counter-Reformation *(Online)*

Activity 2: History Record Book *(Offline)*
Instructions
Choose either A or B.
A. Written Narration
Write two to four sentences explaining what the lesson was about. If necessary, use the Show You Know questions to help get started. Only include the most important parts of the lesson. Write your name, the date, and the lesson title on your written narration, and put it in your History Record Book.
Sample written narration: "Ignatius of Loyola was a soldier for the king of Spain. He decided to go to Jerusalem. He started schools for priests called Jesuits. Ignatius of Loyola was part of the Counter-Reformation."

B. Picture Narration
Draw a picture of the part of the lesson that interested you most. When you have finished drawing, describe the picture. Below your picture, write a description of what you have drawn. Write your name, the date, and the lesson title on your picture narration, and put it in your History Record Book.

Activity 3: The Moving Life of Ignatius of Loyola (Offline)

ASSESS
Lesson Assessment: The Counter-Reformation (Online)
You will complete an offline assessment covering the main objectives of this lesson. Your learning coach will score this assessment.

LEARN
Activity 4. Optional: Reformation (Online)
Do some research to find out if Ignatius is a popular name for schools.

Lesson Assessment

The Counter-Reformation

1. What is the name of the Catholic Church's effort to reform itself?_____

2. What is the name of the man who set up the Society of Jesus?_____

Student Guide
Lesson 12: Galileo Faces the Inquisition

Italian astronomer Galileo Galilei (1564-1642) used a telescope to study the heavens and confirmed the Copernican theory that the earth and other planets revolve around the sun. Galileo ran afoul of the Catholic Church, which tried him for heresy.

Lesson Objectives

- Identify Galileo as an astronomer who studied the skies with a telescope.
- State that Galileo's work confirmed Copernicus's theory.
- Explain that Galileo's work conflicted with the church's position and that he was tried for heresy.

PREPARE

Approximate lesson time is 60 minutes.

Materials

> For the Student
>> History Record Book
> Optional
>> Starry Messenger by Peter Sis

Keywords and Pronunciation

Galileo Galilei (gal-uh-LEE-oh gal-uh-LAY-ee)

heresy (HAIR-uh-see) : A religious belief that goes against the teachings of a church.

Inquisition : a special court set up by the Roman Catholic Church to combat heresy

LEARN
Activity 1: Galileo Turns His Eyes to the Stars *(Online)*

Activity 2: History Record Book *(Online)*

It's time to add another chapter to the story of our past. Create a new entry in your History Record Book by completing a written or picture narration.

Activity 3: Galileo's Room *(Online)*

See artifacts from Galileo's life, including his famous telescope.

ASSESS
Lesson Assessment: Galileo Faces the Inquisition (*Online*)

You will complete an offline assessment covering the main objectives of this lesson. Your learning coach will score this assessment.

LEARN
Activity 4. Optional: Galileo Faces the Inquisition *(Offline)*

To read more about Galileo, check your library or bookstore for the beautifully illustrated *Starry Messenger* by Peter Sis (New York: Farrar Straus & Giroux, 1996).

The author tells the famous scientist's story in a simple fashion, but also includes excerpts of Galileo's own writing. This work explains more about both Galileo and the time in which he lived.

Lesson Assessment

Galileo Faces the Inquisition

1. What kind of scientist was Galileo?_____

2. What instrument did Galileo use to study the stars?_____

3. Galileo's work supported the work of another astronomer who lived before him. What was that other astronomer's name?_____

4. What did Galileo say that made the church put him on trial?_____

5. What was the name of a belief that went against the Roman Catholic Church's teachings?_____

Student Guide
Lesson 13: Unit Review and Assessment

You've completed this unit, and now it's time to review what you've learned and take the unit assessment.

Lesson Objectives

- Demonstrate mastery of important knowledge and skills in this unit.
- Name Johannes Gutenberg as the inventor of the printing press.
- Name the Bible as the first important book Gutenberg printed.
- State that wars between Christians and Muslims lasted into the Renaissance.
- Name Ferdinand and Isabella as the king and queen who ousted the Moors from Spain.
- Define a monarch as a single ruler, such as a king or queen.
- Name Francis I as a powerful Renaissance monarch of France who imported Italian artists and ideas.
- Name van Eyck and Dürer as major Renaissance artists from northern Europe.
- Name Martin Luther as a monk who wished to reform the Christian Church.
- Identify the 95 Theses as a document that criticized church practices.
- Define the Reformation as a religious movement that divided the Christian Church into Catholic and Protestant branches.
- Explain the origin of the word *Protestant*.
- State that after the Reformation and wars over religion, Europe was divided into Catholic and Protestant countries.
- Explain that Henry VIII's divorce was the reason for England's break with the Catholic Church.
- Name Ignatius of Loyola as the founder of the Society of Jesus, which defended the pope and spread Catholicism.
- Identify Galileo as an astronomer who studied the skies with a telescope.
- State that Galileo's work confirmed Copernicus's theory.
- Tell that Copernicus believed the Earth moved around the sun.
- Identify the development of the printing press as key to the spread of Renaissance ideas and ideals.
- Recognize the role of Italy in the spread of Renaisssance ideas to northern Europe.

PREPARE

Approximate lesson time is 60 minutes.

Materials

> For the Student
>
> > History Record Book

Keywords and Pronunciation

Albrecht Durer (AHL-brekht DUR-er)

Galileo Galilei (gal-uh-LEE-oh gal-uh-LAY-ee)

Jan van Eyck (yahn van IYK)

Johannes Gutenberg (yoh-HAHN-uhs GOOT-n-burg)

Nicolaus Copernicus (NIK-uh-luhs kuh-PUR-nih-kuhs)

Ottoman (AH-tuh-muhn)

Renaissance (REH-nuh-sahns) : Literally, rebirth; the time in Europe, beginning in the 1300s, when there was a new interest in the civilizations of ancient Greece and Rome.

Tudor (TOO-dur)

LEARN
Activity 1: A Look Back (Offline)
Instructions

We've learned that the Renaissance began in Italy and spread north to the rest of Europe. One inventive German did more to spread the Renaissance than anyone else. His printing press made it possible to print books by the thousands and spread ideas quickly. Do you remember that German's name? [1]

Other energetic rulers, artists, and thinkers helped spread the Renaissance beyond Italy. Let's think about Francis I. How did he bring the Renaissance to France? [2]

And remember Albrecht Dürer? Dürer studied in Venice. Then he went back to Germany and painted with amazing realism and detail. Artists such as Dürer and van Eyck painted the life of their lands in new ways and made the Renaissance their own.

Artists weren't the only ones to try new things. Musicians did the same. They invented new instruments. They wrote new kinds of songs.

Scientists in northern Europe were often inspired by Italy, too. Our friend Copernicus studied in Italy, then went back to his native Poland to continue studying the stars. He had a new theory. What was it? [3]

Years later, a feisty Italian named Galileo built the first telescope to study the stars. He said Copernicus was right.

If you're getting the impression that the Renaissance beyond Italy, like the Renaissance in Italy, was a time of invention and ingenuity, you're correct.

While Italy remained a collection of many city-states, Renaissance France, England, and Spain all became countries united under strong kings and queens. What's another name for a strong single ruler? [4]

What was the name of the strong French monarch who brought the Renaissance to France? [5]

Can you recall the names of the two Spanish monarchs who united Spain? [6]

And does the name of one strong English king stay with you? If you said "Henry VIII," that's a good answer. His family, the Tudors, made England a strong nation.

Those new monarchs built palaces, filled them with Renaissance art, and encouraged study of Latin and Greek, just as the Italian leaders did. And sometimes they fought wars with each other. After all, Francis I brought the Renaissance to France after he marched his army into Italy.

Christian and Muslim empires were often at war, too. Ferdinand and Isabella ousted the Moors from Spain, but the Ottoman Turks triumphed in Constantinople. Even though the medieval Crusades were over, the rivalry between Christian and Muslim powers was not.

Europeans were divided by many things, but they were united in their Christian faith. They even referred to the place they lived as "Christendom." The sense that Europe was united by Christianity lasted a long time--all through the Middle Ages. But the Renaissance had an effect on that, too. We've learned that in 1517 a German monk wrote 95 theses, or reasons, that challenged the practices of the Christian church. He thought the church was becoming too worldly--too concerned with money and power. What was that monk's name? [7]
Do you remember why he was so upset? [8]
Martin Luther worried not just about indulgences, but also about whether there should even be a pope. He decided to break with the church. His worries about the church and the pope were the beginning of a split in Christianity. What do we call that split? [9]
Can you remember why we call it the Reformation? [10]
The printing presses spread Luther's ideas quickly, and some princes sided with Luther. Wars followed. By the end of the Reformation, "Christendom" was divided into two groups: Catholics (those who still followed the pope and the Roman church) and Protestants (those who followed Luther and other reformers).
Look at the word *Protestant.* Can you see the smaller word, *protest,* in it?
Kings and rulers, like our old friend Henry VIII, decided what their country's religion would be. In Europe, there were Catholic countries and Protestant countries. In the Catholic countries, the church took some of Luther's criticisms very seriously. The Catholic Church had its own reformation. What was it called? [11]
Priests and nuns reformed the Catholic Church and worked hard to spread their faith. Can you remember what we call the priests who helped the pope by starting schools and teaching people about Catholicism? [12]
Whew! A lot happened during the 300 years we call the Renaissance. *Renaissance* means "rebirth," but the people of the Renaissance did not just think about the past. The Renaissance was an age of invention and change. In the next unit, we'll see that it was also an age of exploration.

Activity 2: History Record Book Review *(Offline)*

Activity 3: Online Interactive Review *(Online)*

ASSESS
Unit Assessment: The Renaissance Elsewhere and the Reformation *(Offline)*
Complete an offline Unit Assessment. Your learning coach will score this part of the Assessment.

Name   Date

The Renaissance Elsewhere and the Reformation

Read each question and its answer choices. For questions 1 through 20, fill in the bubble in front of the word or words that best answer the question.

1. Who invented the printing press?
   - ⓐ Jan van Eyck
   - ⓑ Johannes Gutenberg
   - ⓒ Martin Luther
   - ⓓ Nicolaus Copernicus

2. Which Spanish monarchs pushed the Moors out of Spain?
   - ⓐ Henry VIII and Elizabeth I
   - ⓑ Francis I and Eleanor
   - ⓒ Ferdinand and Isabella
   - ⓓ Richard and Catherine

3. What is another word for a king or queen?
   - ⓐ monarch
   - ⓑ duke
   - ⓒ pope
   - ⓓ bishop

4. What did Copernicus believe about the Earth and the sun?
   - ⓐ The Earth moved around the sun.
   - ⓑ The sun moved around the Earth.
   - ⓒ The Earth and the sun moved around the moon.
   - ⓓ The sun and the Earth stood still.

5. Wars between what two groups started with the Crusades and lasted into the Renaissance?
   ⓐ Romans and barbarians
   ⓑ Christians and Jews
   ⓒ Europeans and Asians
   ⓓ Christians and Muslims

6. What was the first book printed by Johannes Gutenberg?
   ⓐ *The Book of the Courtier*
   ⓑ the 95 Theses
   ⓒ *English Madrigals*
   ⓓ the Bible

7. What religious movement, sparked by Martin Luther, divided the Christian Church into two branches?
   ⓐ the Renaissance
   ⓑ the Reformation
   ⓒ the Counter-Reformation
   ⓓ the Society of Jesus

8. What happened in Europe after Martin Luther's break with the church?
   ⓐ Wars were fought over religion.
   ⓑ Monarchs became less powerful.
   ⓒ The church supported Galileo's work.
   ⓓ Protestants and Catholics lived peacefully together.

9. In order to get a divorce, King Henry VIII broke with the Catholic Church and founded the _____.
   - ⓐ Counter-Reformation
   - ⓑ Diet of Worms
   - ⓒ Church of England
   - ⓓ Society of Jesus

10. What invention made it possible for large numbers of books and copies of Italian art to spread to northern Europe?
   - ⓐ oil paints
   - ⓑ the telescope
   - ⓒ newspapers
   - ⓓ the printing press

11. What did the Jesuits, or the Society of Jesus, do?
   - ⓐ acted as missionaries for the Catholic Church
   - ⓑ painted detailed oil portraits of Jesus
   - ⓒ printed German Bibles for Martin Luther
   - ⓓ started new forms of music in the church

12. Who was Galileo?
   - ⓐ an artist who painted very realistic and detailed works
   - ⓑ an astronomer who studied the skies with a telescope
   - ⓒ a monk who created illuminated manuscripts by hand
   - ⓓ a monarch in France who built many magnificent palaces

13. Which powerful Renaissance monarch brought Italian artists and ideas to his country?
   ⓐ Francis I
   ⓑ Charles V
   ⓒ Ferdinand
   ⓓ Charlemagne

14. Jan van Eyck and Albrecht Dürer were _____.
   ⓐ French reformers
   ⓑ Renaissance artists
   ⓒ Renaissance scientists
   ⓓ Italian monarchs

15. What document, written by Martin Luther, criticized church practices?
   ⓐ the Diet of Worms
   ⓑ the Inquisition
   ⓒ *The Divine Comedy*
   ⓓ the 95 Theses

16. After the Reformation and wars over religion, European countries were divided into _____ countries.
   ⓐ Catholic and Protestant
   ⓑ Reformation and Jesuit
   ⓒ Anglican and Roman
   ⓓ Muslim and Protestant

17. Who later confirmed Copernicus's ideas about the Earth moving around the sun?
  ⓐ Loyola
  ⓑ Galileo
  ⓒ Luther
  ⓓ van Eyck

18. Which German monk started the Reformation?
  ⓐ Johannes Gutenberg
  ⓑ Albrecht Dürer
  ⓒ Nicolaus Copernicus
  ⓓ Martin Luther

19. Martin Luther's followers protested some of the church's practices. What did those who followed Luther come to be called?
  ⓐ Counter-Reformists
  ⓑ Catholics
  ⓒ Protestants
  ⓓ monarchs

20. Renaissance ideas spread to northern Europe from _____.
  ⓐ Italy
  ⓑ Spain
  ⓒ Constantinople
  ⓓ Arabia

Student Guide
Lesson 1: How Far Away Is It?

- National Geography Standard 1: How to use maps and other geographic representations, tools, and technologies to acquire, process, and report information.
- National Geography Standard 11: The patterns and networks of economic interdependence on Earth's surface.
- National Geography Standard 15: How physical systems affect human systems.

The scale on a map is a useful tool to figure out the distance between places.

Lesson Objectives

- National Geography Standard 1: How to use maps and other geographic representations, tools, and technologies to acquire, process, and report information.
- National Geography Standard 11: The patterns and networks of economic interdependence on Earth's surface.
- National Geography Standard 15: How physical systems affect human systems.
- Explain the purpose of a scale on a map.
- Use the scale on a map to calculate the distance between places.

PREPARE

Approximate lesson time is 60 minutes.

Materials

>   For the Student
>> History Record Book
>> Understanding Geography: Map Skills and Our World (Level 3)

Keywords and Pronunciation

map scale : A measurement guide on a map that helps you figure out the real distance between places.

LEARN
Activity 1: Scales Aren't Just for Weight *(Online)*

ASSESS

Lesson Assessment: How Far Away Is It? (*Online*)

You will complete an online assessment covering the main objectives of this lesson. Your assessment will be scored by the computer.

LEARN
Activity 2. Optional: Beyond the Lesson *(Online)*

Student Guide
Lesson 2: Landforms and Adapting to Where We Live

Explore mountains, hills, valleys, and other landforms and learn how people adapt to where they live.

Lesson Objectives

- Identify and compare major landforms including mountains, hills, plains, and plateaus.
- Locate landforms on a map.
- Identify ways in which people adapt to living in different environments.

PREPARE

Approximate lesson time is 60 minutes.

Materials

For the Student

History Record Book

Understanding Geography: Map Skills and Our World (Level 3)

Keywords and Pronunciation

adapt : To change or adjust your life to fit the world around you.

civilization : A highly developed and organized group of people, often living in cities, marked by achievements in writing, art, and technology.

coast : The land next to the ocean or sea; the seashore.

environment (in-VIY-ruhn-muhnt) : Everything in a certain place: the land, the water, the air, the plants, and animals; the environment affects the way people live, the houses they build, and the clothes they wear.

eucalyp : A dry, often sandy area that gets very little rain.

hill : A raised area on Earth, not as high as a mountain.

island : Land that is completely surrounded by water.

landforms : Physical features on the Earth such as mountains, hills, or islands.

mountain : The tallest type of landform, higher than a hill.

oasis (oh-AY-sis) : A place in the desert where there is water for plants to grow.

plain : An area of mostly flat land.

plateau (pla-TOH) : An area of high, flat land.

valley : A low area between mountain and hills.

LEARN
Activity 1: The Shape of the Land *(Online)*

Activity 2: Adapting to Different Environments *(Online)*

ASSESS

Lesson Assessment: Landforms and Adapting to Where We Live *(Online)*

You will complete an online assessment covering the main objectives of this lesson. Your assessment will be scored by the computer.

LEARN
Activity 3: Landforms and Adapting to Where We Live *(Online)*

Student Guide
Lesson 3: Natural Resources

We use many materials from nature such as plants, animals, minerals, and fossil fuels.

Lesson Objectives

- Use resource maps to get information.
- Identify natural resources as animal, plant, mineral, or fossil fuel.
- Distinguish renewable from nonrenewable resources.

PREPARE

Approximate lesson time is 60 minutes.

Materials

> For the Student
>> History Record Book
>> Understanding Geography: Map Skills and Our World (Level 3)

Keywords and Pronunciation

agriculture : The science of growing plants or raising animals to be sold.

forestry : Growing and taking care of trees, some of which will be cut down for lumber.

mining : Digging into the Earth to remove mineral resources such as coal.

natural resources : Materials we use that come from nature, such as wood from forests, water from rivers, or coal from the ground.

LEARN
Activity 1: Natural Resources (Online)

ASSESS

Lesson Assessment: Natural Resources (Online)

You will complete an online assessment covering the main objectives of this lesson. Your assessment will be scored by the computer.

LEARN
Activity 2. Optional: Natural Resources (Online)

Student Guide
Lesson 1: Prince Henry the Navigator

- Describe the Renaissance as an age of exploration and discovery.
- List key advances in navigation that made voyages of exploration possible (caravel, compass, astrolabe).
- Identify European motivations for voyages.
- Recognize Portugal and Spain as the leading powers at this time.
- Identify key individuals with their important voyages.

The Renaissance was an age of geographic exploration as well as cultural growth. Portugal's Prince Henry the Navigator paved the way: his interest in exploration led to important studies, inventions, and journeys of discovery.

Lesson Objectives

- Describe the Renaissance as an age of exploration and discovery.
- List key advances in navigation that made voyages of exploration possible (caravel, compass, astrolabe).
- Identify European motivations for voyages.
- Recognize Portugal and Spain as the leading powers at this time.
- Identify key individuals with their important voyages.
- Describe the Renaissance as an Age of Exploration.
- Identify Henry the Navigator as a prince of Portugal interested in navigation and exploration.
- Tell how Henry improved navigation.

PREPARE

Approximate lesson time is 60 minutes.

Materials

For the Student

map, world

History Record Book

🖥 Prince Henry Challenges the Unknown activity sheet

glue, children's white

pencils, colored 12

scissors

Keywords and Pronunciation

astrolabe (AS-truh-layb) : an instrument used to observe the positions of stars and other objects in the sky
caravel (KAIR-uh-vel) : A small ship sailed by the Portuguese and others during the Renaissance.
navigation : The science of getting ships from place to place.

LEARN
Activity 1: Henry and His School of Navigation *(Online)*

Activity 2: History Record Book *(Offline)*
Instructions
Choose either A or B.
A. Written Narration
Write two to four sentences explaining what the lesson was about. If necessary, use the Show You Know questions to help get started. Only include the most important parts of the lesson. Write your name, the date, and the lesson title on your written narration, and put it in your History Record Book.
Sample written narration: "Prince Henry wanted Portugal to be able to trade with Africa. He turned his palace into a school of navigation. His sailors used tools like the compass and astrolabe to explore. Prince Henry helped start the Age of Discovery."

B. Picture Narration
Draw a picture of the part of the lesson that interested you most. When you have finished drawing, describe the picture. Below your picture, write a description of what you have drawn. Write your name, the date, and the lesson title on your picture narration, and put it in your History Record Book.

Activity 3: Prince Henry Challenges the Unknown *(Offline)*

ASSESS
Lesson Assessment: Prince Henry the Navigator (*Online*)
You will complete an offline assessment covering the main objectives of this lesson. Your learning coach will score this assessment.

LEARN
Activity 4. Optional: Prince Henry the Navigator *(Offline)*

Name _____   Date _____

Prince Henry Challenges the Unknown

Write a sentence next to each picture to tell how the caravel, the compass, and the astrolabe helped Prince Henry's sailors challenge the unknown.

caravel

_____

_____

_____

compass

_____

_____

_____

astrolabe

_____

_____

_____

Lesson Assessment

Prince Henry the Navigator

1. Because many Europeans set out to explore faraway lands, what do we also call the time of the Renaissance? _____

2. What were Prince Henry's interests? _____

3. What nickname is Prince Henry remembered by today? _____

4. How did Henry improve navigation? _____

Student Guide
Lesson 2: Bartolomeu Dias and the Cape of Good Hope

Generations of sailors trained by Henry the Navigator explored the coast of Africa and pressed south, hoping to find its southernmost end as well as a sea route to India. In 1488, Portuguese explorer Bartolomeu Dias continued the search and rounded the tip of Africa, which the Portuguese named the Cape of Good Hope.

Lesson Objectives

- Identify Bartolomeu Dias as the Portuguese explorer who located the southern tip of Africa.
- Identify the southern tip of Africa as the Cape of Good Hope.
- Explain that Bartolomeu Dias hoped to find a sea route to India.

PREPARE

Approximate lesson time is 60 minutes.

Materials

> For the Student
>> 🖥 Map of the Journey of Dias, 1487
>> globe, inflatable
>> History Record Book
>> pencils, colored 12

Keywords and Pronunciation

Bartolomeu Dias (bahr-tou-lou-MAY-ou DEE-ahsh)

cape : A part of the land that sticks into the sea.

LEARN
Activity 1: Dias Looks South for a Sea Route to India *(Online)*

Activity 2: History Record Book *(Offline)*

Instructions

Choose either A or B.

A. Written Narration

Write two to four sentences explaining what the lesson was about. If necessary, use the Show You Know questions to help get started. Only include the most important parts of the lesson. Write your name, the date, and the lesson title on your written narration, and put it in your History Record Book.

Sample written narration: "The king of Portugal wanted to find a way to trade with Asia. He sent Bartolomeu Dias to sail around Africa. The ships sailed and sailed until they sailed around the southern tip of Africa. The king named it the Cape of Good Hope."

B. Picture Narration

Draw a picture of the part of the lesson that interested you most. When you have finished drawing, describe the picture. Below your picture, write a description of what you have drawn. Write your name, the date, and the lesson title on your picture narration, and put it in your History Record Book.

Activity 3: Traveling with Bartolomeu Dias (Offline)
Instructions

Bartolomeu Dias undertook a bold adventure! He accepted King John's challenge to sail around Africa and find the sea route to India. So he set sail where no one had gone before.

On the map, follow these directions to review Dias's daring journey.

- Color the country of Portugal, and write the words, "Dias's Home Country" underneath its name.
- Draw three ships sailing on the seas between Portugal and the Cape of Good Hope.
- Circle the names of the Atlantic Ocean and the Indian Ocean.
- On the continent of Africa, trace the course of the two rivers shown in blue. Say their names aloud.
- Put a red star on the Cape of Good Hope. Draw dark blue waves nearby to show that it is a very stormy place. Circle its name in red as a sign of the danger in the waters there.
- Write the words "To India" on the east side of the Cape of Good Hope to show where Bartolomeu Dias was headed.

ASSESS
Lesson Assessment: Bartolomeu Dias and the Cape of Good Hope (Online)

You will complete an offline assessment covering the main objectives of this lesson. Your learning coach will score this assessment.

LEARN
Activity 4. Optional: Bartolomeu Dias and the Cape of Good Hope (Online)

Tour the Cape of Good Hope online.

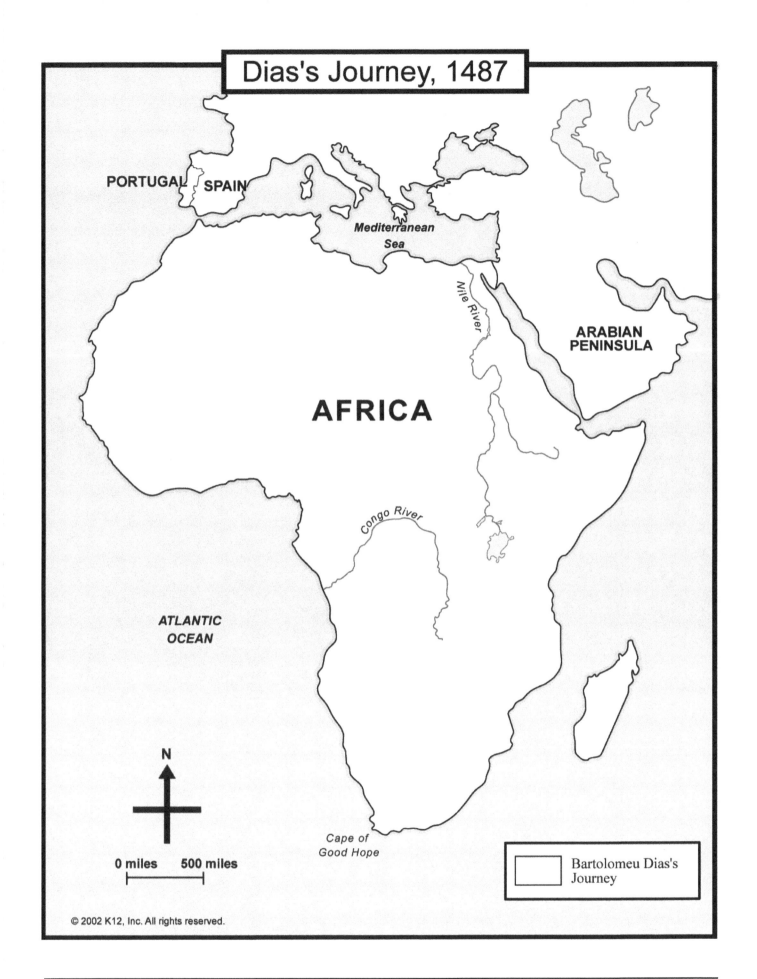

Dias's Journey, 1487

PORTUGAL SPAIN

Mediterranean Sea

Nile River

ARABIAN PENINSULA

AFRICA

Congo River

ATLANTIC OCEAN

N

Cape of Good Hope

0 miles   500 miles

Bartolomeu Dias's Journey

Lesson Assessment

Bartolomeu Dias and the Cape of Good Hope

1. What was the name of the Portuguese explorer who found the southern tip of

    Africa?_____

2. What is the name that the king gave to the southern tip of Africa?_____

3. Why did Dias want to find the tip of Africa?_____

Student Guide
Lesson 3: What Did Columbus Find?

Eager to reach the Indies, Christopher Columbus (1451-1506) had a maverick idea. Knowing the earth was round, he calculated that by sailing west across the Atlantic he would arrive in Asia. His landing in the Americas opened a New World to Europeans.

Lesson Objectives

- Define the *Indies* as the lands of India, China, and Japan.
- Identify Christopher Columbus as an explorer who sought a route to the Indies by sailing west.
- Explain that Columbus discovered the Americas, two continents previously unknown to Europeans, and claimed the lands for Spain.

PREPARE

Approximate lesson time is 60 minutes.

Materials

> For the Student
> > History Record Book

Keywords and Pronunciation

Genoa (JEH-noh-uh)
Niña (NEEN-yah)
Pinta (PEEN-tah)

LEARN
Activity 1: Christopher Columbus: Determined Explorer *(Online)*

Activity 2: History Record Book *(Offline)*
Instructions
Choose either A or B.

A. Written Narration
Write two to four sentences explaining what the lesson was about. If necessary, use the Show You Know questions to help get started. Only include the most important parts of the lesson. Write your name, the date, and the lesson title on your written narration, and put it in your History Record Book.

Sample written narration: "Christopher Columbus wanted to sail west to the Indies. Everyone else thought the Atlantic Ocean was too wide. But Queen Isabella gave him ships. He sailed across the ocean and discovered America."

B. Picture Narration
Draw a picture of the part of the lesson that interested you most. When you have finished drawing, describe the picture. Below your picture, write a description of what you have drawn. Write your name, the date, and the lesson title on your picture narration, and put it in your History Record Book.

Activity 3: Columbus Keeps Trying (Offline)
Instructions

Christopher Columbus didn't give up! That was one of the reasons he eventually made his famous voyages. Think about how Columbus kept trying to reach his goals. Then write a short play about his life to show how he kept trying.

Review the key ideas and events from the lesson first. Then write and perform your play. Here are a few events to help you begin:

- Columbus reads about Marco Polo and dreams of reaching the Indies.
- He tries to persuade rulers in Portugal and Spain to give him money for ships and men.
- Columbus sails west across the Atlantic with three ships and finally reaches land.
- He returns three more times, but never knows quite what he has discovered.

ASSESS
Lesson Assessment: What Did Columbus Find? (*Online*)

You will complete an offline assessment covering the main objectives of this lesson. Your learning coach will score this assessment.

LEARN
Activity 4. Optional: What Did Columbus Find? (Offline)
Instructions

Here's a challenge. Visit your local library or bookstore to find more information about Christopher Columbus and his voyages. Use at least two books to learn more about this famous explorer.

Now make your own list of the top 10 things you think people should know about this man and his work.

Read your list to someone else, starting with number 10 and continuing to the number 1 thing you think everyone should know about Christopher Columbus.

Name_____   Date_____

Lesson Assessment

What Did Columbus Find?

1. Why did Christopher Columbus want to sail west across the Atlantic

    Ocean?_____

2. What were the Indies?_____

3. During his famous voyage, what did Columbus discover?_____

4. Which nation did Christopher Columbus claim the discovered land for?_____

Student Guide
Lesson 4: Da Gama and Cabral Claim More for Portugal

Widely regarded as Portugal's greatest explorer, Vasco da Gama made a voyage around Africa and into the Indian Ocean that showed the way to the Indies. It also gave Portugal a monopoly on trade with the Indies. Pedro Álvares Cabral discovered Brazil by accident and gave Portugal a toehold in the New World.

Lesson Objectives

- Explain that the pope divided the New World between Portugal and Spain.
- Identify Vasco da Gama as a Portuguese explorer whose trip around Africa to the Indies made Portugal a major trading power.
- Identify Pedro Cabral as the Portuguese explorer who claimed Brazil for Portugal.

PREPARE

Approximate lesson time is 60 minutes.

Materials

For the Student

📖 Map of Journeys of Da Gama and Cabral

crayons 8

History Record Book

📖 Mystery Spices activity sheet

Keywords and Pronunciation

Calicut (KA-lih-kuht)

demarcation (dee-mahr-KAY-shuhn)

line of demarcation : A dividing line.

Pedro Cabral (PAY-throo kuh-BRAHL)

scurvy : A disease caused by lack of vitamin C in the diet.

Vasco da Gama (VAHS-koo dah GAH-muh)

LEARN
Activity 1: Da Gama and Cabral *(Online)*

Activity 2: History Record Book *(Offline)*

Instructions

Choose either A or B.

A. Written Narration

Write two to four sentences explaining what the lesson was about. If necessary, use the Show You Know questions to help get started. Only include the most important parts of the lesson. Write your name, the date, and the lesson title on your written narration, and put it in your History Record Book.

Sample written narration: "The Portuguese wanted to trade spices with the Indies. Vasco da Gama led the first trip. Then Pedro Cabral sailed, too. He accidentally discovered South America."

B. Picture Narration

Draw a picture of the part of the lesson that interested you most. When you have finished drawing, describe the picture. Below your picture, write a description of what you have drawn. Write your name, the date, and the lesson title on your picture narration, and put it in your History Record Book.

Activity 3: Spices of Life (Offline)

Add spices to your life--or at least more information about them--by completing the Mystery Spices activity sheet.

ASSESS

Lesson Assessment: Da Gama and Cabral Claim More for Portugal (Online)

You will complete an offline assessment covering the main objectives of this lesson. Your learning coach will score this assessment.

LEARN

Activity 4. Optional: Da Gama and Cabral Claim More for Portugal (Offline)

Instructions

Some people thought the sailors in the Age of Exploration led very exciting lives. Others thought they led very dangerous lives. Maybe there is truth to both ideas.

Think about the people who would want to join a voyage of discovery. What would a good sailor be like? What would a sailor need to know? Who would want to become an explorer?

Try your hand at hiring someone for this job. Review the logs in the lesson. Then use the information in them to write a help-wanted ad for sailors to join one of the voyages of da Gama or Cabral. Hire some sailors for the next exciting voyage of discovery.

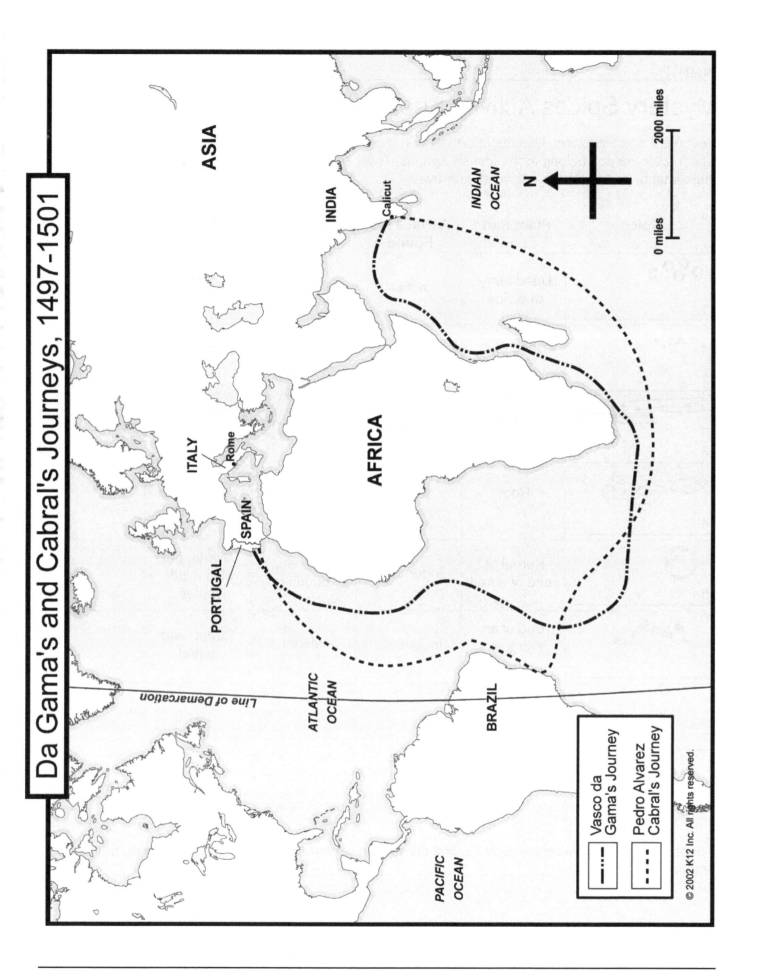

Da Gama's and Cabral's Journeys, 1497–1501

ASIA

INDIA

Calicut

INDIAN
OCEAN

N

2000 miles

0 miles

AFRICA

ITALY
Rome

SPAIN

PORTUGAL

Line of Demarcation

ATLANTIC
OCEAN

BRAZIL

PACIFIC
OCEAN

Vasco da
Gama's Journey

Pedro Alvarez
Cabral's Journey

Name _____   Date _____

Mystery Spices Activity Sheet

Become a spice explorer. Use the information in the table and the words below to help you figure out which spice names belong in the first six spaces. Then add something more about each spice. If there's time, add two more spices of your own.

Spice	Plant Part	A Place It's Found	Use(s) Today	Taste	More
1.	Dried berry of a vine	India	Table seasoning	Hot and sharp	
2.	Seed of a shrub	India	Sauce for hot dogs	Spicy and hot	
3.	Dried bark of a tree	Sri Lanka	Toast, applesauce	Sweet	
4.	Root	China	Cake, soda	Spicy with a strong smell	
5.	Kernel or seed of a fruit	Indonesia	Eggnog, pudding	Sweet, but also a little bitter	
6.	Bud of an evergreen tree	Indonesia	Meats	Strong and sweet	
7.					
8.					

Choose from the following to name the first six spices: cinnamon, cloves, ginger, mustard, nutmeg, and pepper.

Lesson Assessment

Da Gama and Cabral Claim More for Portugal

1. Who drew the line of demarcation?_____

2. What did this line do?_____

3. What Portuguese explorer led this first trip east to the Indies?_____

4. Did this explorer's trip to the Indies make Portugal a major trading power, or did it cause Portugal to become a poorer country?_____

5. What Portuguese explorer followed Vasco da Gama?_____

6. What place, now a country, did he accidentally find and claim for Portugal?_____

Student Guide
Lesson 5: Balboa Sights the Pacific

Spanish explorer Vasco Núñez de Balboa (1475-1519) was the first European to sight the eastern shore of the Pacific. His expedition helped prove that the New World was a large landmass between Europe and Asia.

Lesson Objectives

- Identify Balboa as a Spanish explorer.
- Describe Balboa as the first European to sight the Pacific Ocean from its eastern shore.
- Explain that Balboa's sighting established that there were two oceans and that the New World was a landmass between Europe and Asia.

PREPARE

Approximate lesson time is 60 minutes.

Materials

For the Student

📖 Map of the Journeys of Balboa, 1513

History Record Book

📖 Mapping Balboa's Adventures activity sheet

pencils, colored 12

Keywords and Pronunciation

Hispaniola (his-puh-NYOH-luh)

isthmus (IS-muhs) : A narrow stretch of land that connects larger areas of land.

Pedro Cabral (PAY-throo kuh-BRAHL)

Vasco da Gama (VAHS-koo dah GAH-muh)

Vasco Núñez de Balboa (VAHS-koh NOON-yays day bal-BOH-uh)

LEARN
Activity 1: Balboa Discovers an Ocean *(Online)*

Activity 2: History Record Book *(Offline)*
Instructions
Choose either A or B.

A. Written Narration
Write two to four sentences explaining what the lesson was about. If necessary, use the Show You Know questions to help get started. Only include the most important parts of the lesson. Write your name, the date, and the lesson title on your written narration, and put it in your History Record Book.

Sample written narration: "Balboa wanted to have some adventures. He sailed to the New World. He crossed a narrow stretch of land and saw the Pacific Ocean."

B. Picture Narration

Draw a picture of the part of the lesson that interested you most. When you have finished drawing, describe the picture. Below your picture, write a description of what you have drawn. Write your name, the date, and the lesson title on your picture narration, and put it in your History Record Book.

Activity 3: Where's Balboa Now? *(Offline)*
Instructions

The king of Spain is trying to find Balboa. But where is he? Follow these directions to see if you can report back to His Majesty. Then see what he says about your work.

You've discovered that Balboa stopped somewhere to raise pigs. Put a yellow X on the map to mark this spot. Where are you? [1] Write the name of this place in Clue A.

You've heard that Balboa stowed away on a ship and headed for the mainland. You know he traveled south and landed on a continent. Put a blue X on Santa Maria de la Antigua del Darien, where he stayed for a while. What was special about this place? [2] What is the name of this continent? [3] Write the name in Clue B.

Soon you receive a report that Balboa has left. Next, you learn that he crossed a narrow strip of land where he spied what he thought was a new ocean. Put a red X here. What is the name of this narrow strip of land? [4] Write the name in Clue C.

Balboa called the new ocean the South Sea, but what is it called today? [5] Write that name in Clue D.

Now that you've marked all these important places, you must tell the king what Balboa has been trying to find. Besides the new sea, what was Balboa looking for? [6] Write it in Clue E.

Finally, the king sends you a message to tell you what he thinks of your work. However, you must decode it first. Do this by unscrambling the letters in the boxes. [7]

ASSESS
Lesson Assessment: Balboa Sights the Pacific (*Online*)

You will complete an offline assessment covering the main objectives of this lesson. Your learning coach will score this assessment.

LEARN
Activity 4. Optional: Balboa Sights the Pacific *(Offline)*
Instructions

You learned about some of Balboa's adventures in your History Reader. You found out that Balboa took charge of a settlement in South America. In fact, it was the first permanent European settlement there. But Balboa didn't stay long. Soon he was off to find gold. He crossed the Isthmus of Panama and found the eastern shore of the Pacific Ocean instead.

How do you think Balboa would have described his adventures to the king of Spain? What would he have said about his travels and discoveries? Would he have mentioned the pigs?

Imagine a meeting between Balboa and the king. Use the information you learned in the lesson to write a play about it. Then find some costumes and act out your play for others.

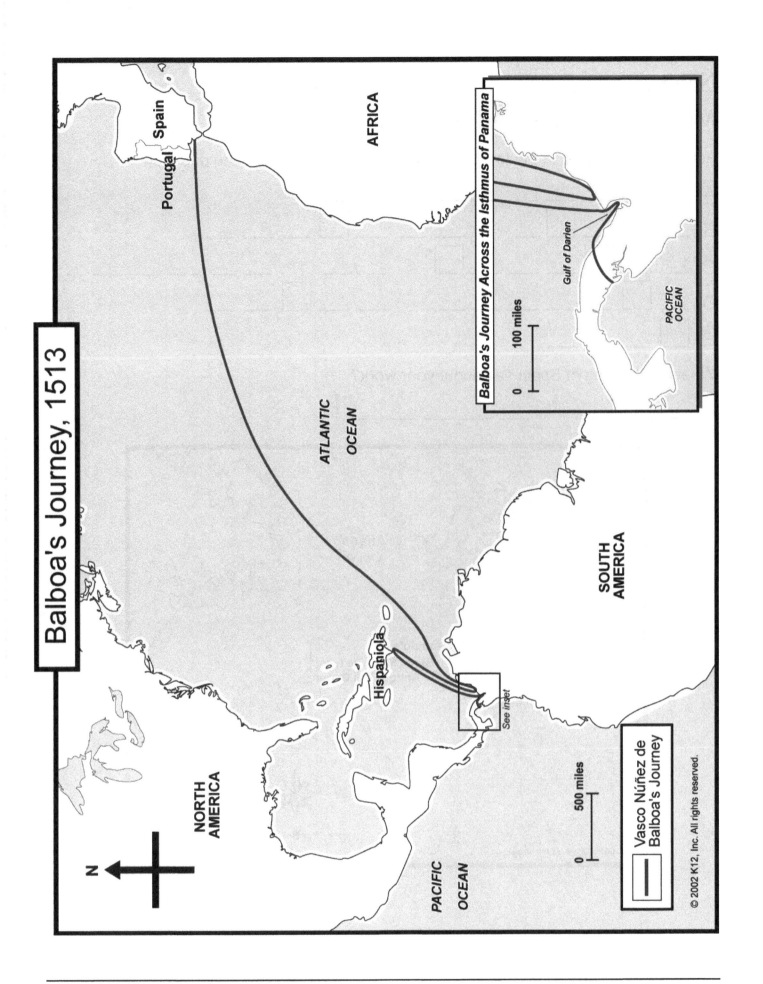

Balboa's Journey, 1513

N

NORTH AMERICA

PACIFIC OCEAN

ATLANTIC OCEAN

Hispaniola

SOUTH AMERICA

Spain

Portugal

AFRICA

See inset

Balboa's Journey Across the Isthmus of Panama

Gulf of Darien

PACIFIC OCEAN

0   100 miles

Vasco Núñez de Balboa's Journey

0   500 miles

© 2002 K12, Inc. All rights reserved.

Name _____   Date _____

Mapping Balboa's Adventures

Follow the directions in the lesson to find the clues and answer the question.

A. ___ ☐ ___ ___ ___ ___ ___ ___ ___ ___ ___

B. ___ ___ ☐ ___ ___   ___ ___ ☐ ___ ___ ___

C. ___ ___ ☐ ___ ___ ☐ ___   ___ ___ ___ ___ ___ ___ ___ ___

D. ___ ☐ ___ ___ ___ ___   ___ ___ ☐ ___ ___ ___

E. ☐ ___ ___ ___

What did the king of Spain say about your work?

___ ___ ' ___   ___ ___ ___ ___ ___ !

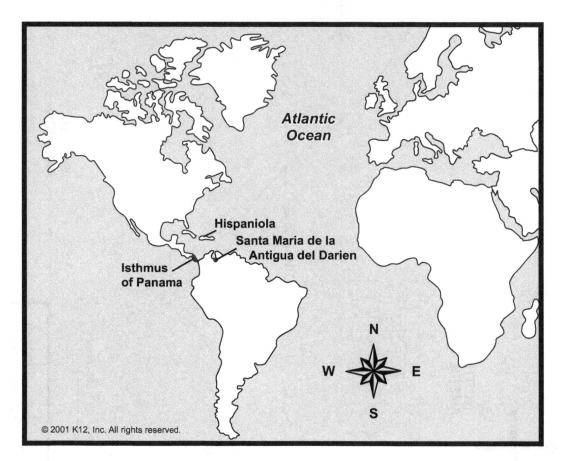

Lesson Assessment

Balboa Sights the Pacific

1. Who was Vasco Núñez de Balboa?_____

2. What did he see that no European in the New World had seen before?_____

3. Why was it important to know there was an ocean on the other side of the

   land?_____

Student Guide
Lesson 6: Circling the Globe: Magellan's Voyage of Discovery

Ferdinand Magellan conceived a daring plan to reach the Indies by sailing west from Spain around the tip of South America, circling the globe. Setting off with five ships and returning with one, the expedition achieved its goals, but at a very high price.

Lesson Objectives

- Name Ferdinand Magellan as the captain of the first expedition to circle the globe.
- Label the Strait of Magellan and explain why it has that name.
- Explain that the Pacific Ocean got its name because Magellan and his sailors thought it was peaceful.

PREPARE

Approximate lesson time is 60 minutes.

Materials

For the Student

    🖥 Map of Journey of Magellan , 1519-1522

    History Record Book

    🖥 Sailing with Magellan activity sheet

    paper, notebook

    pencils, colored 12

Keywords and Pronunciation

Ferdinand Magellan (FUR-dn-and muh-JEHL-uhn)

strait (strayt) : A waterway connecting two large bodies of water.

LEARN
Activity 1: The First Voyage Around the World *(Online)*

Activity 2: History Record Book *(Offline)*

Instructions

Choose either A or B.

A. Written Narration

Write two to four sentences explaining what the lesson was about. If necessary, use the Show You Know questions to help get started. Only include the most important parts of the lesson. Write your name, the date, and the lesson title on your written narration, and put it in your History Record Book.

Sample written narration: "Magellan wanted to sail west to the Spice Islands. He wanted to be the first person to sail around the world. Magellan got killed in the Spice Islands. One of his ships sailed around the world to Spain."

B. Picture Narration

Draw a picture of the part of the lesson that interested you most. When you have finished drawing, describe the picture. Below your picture, write a description of what you have drawn. Write your name, the date, and the lesson title on your picture narration, and put it in your History Record Book.

Activity 3: Sailing with Magellan *(Offline)*
Instructions

Let's remember Magellan's voyage and think about what happened to him, his men, and their ships. Use the Sailing with Magellan activity sheet to follow the voyage and trace the route. Write the numbers 1 to 10 on a separate sheet of paper and fill in the blanks as you go.

Begin by gathering 5 elbow macaroni or other small items to use as ships. If you like, you can use markers to make each piece a different color. Now place all of your ships near Spain on the Sailing with Magellan activity sheet. Begin your voyage by reading "Magellan by the Numbers." As you read the story, figure out your answers and write them on your paper.

Magellan by the Numbers

One morning in 1519 Magellan set sail from Spain with 5 ships and 265 men. It would be 3 years before any would return in the year _____. [1]

Only 1 ship would make the complete trip around the world. _____ [2] ships would not.

First use a colored pencil and trace Magellan's route along the dotted line on the Sailing with Magellan activity sheet. Then have your 5 ships set sail.

Remove 1 ship shortly after setting sail. Unfortunately, this ship disappeared in the Atlantic Ocean, but _____ [3] ships kept going.

The sailors thought they had plenty of food for their trip. They had loaded 3 tons of pickled pork, or _____ [4] pounds. They had packed 5,000 pounds of honey, or _____ [5] tons. It seemed as if they had a lot.

The ships bobbed across the ocean for 10 weeks, or _____ [6] days. Then they sailed south for 2,000 miles, where they hugged the shore of South America and searched for a passage through to the Pacific Ocean. On your map, write the name of the passage they finally found.

Now turn 1 ship around and sail it back to Spain. You have _____ [7] ships left. Sail them on to the Indies. In 3 months and 20 days, or at most _____ [8] days, you will reach the Spice Islands.

You sail on, although Magellan does not. However, danger awaits you, and 2 more ships sink. Remove them from the map. Now you have only _____ [9] ship on its way back to Spain.

When you finally arrive, there are only 18 men left alive. Since you began with 265, this means that _____ [10] have died or left. But despite all this, your expedition has done a remarkable thing. You have become the first human beings to sail around the world.

ASSESS

Lesson Assessment: Circling the Globe: Magellan's Voyage of Discovery
(Online)

You will complete an offline assessment covering the main objectives of this lesson. Your learning coach will score this assessment.

LEARN
Activity 4. Optional: Circling the Globe: Magellan's Voyage of Discovery *(Offline)*

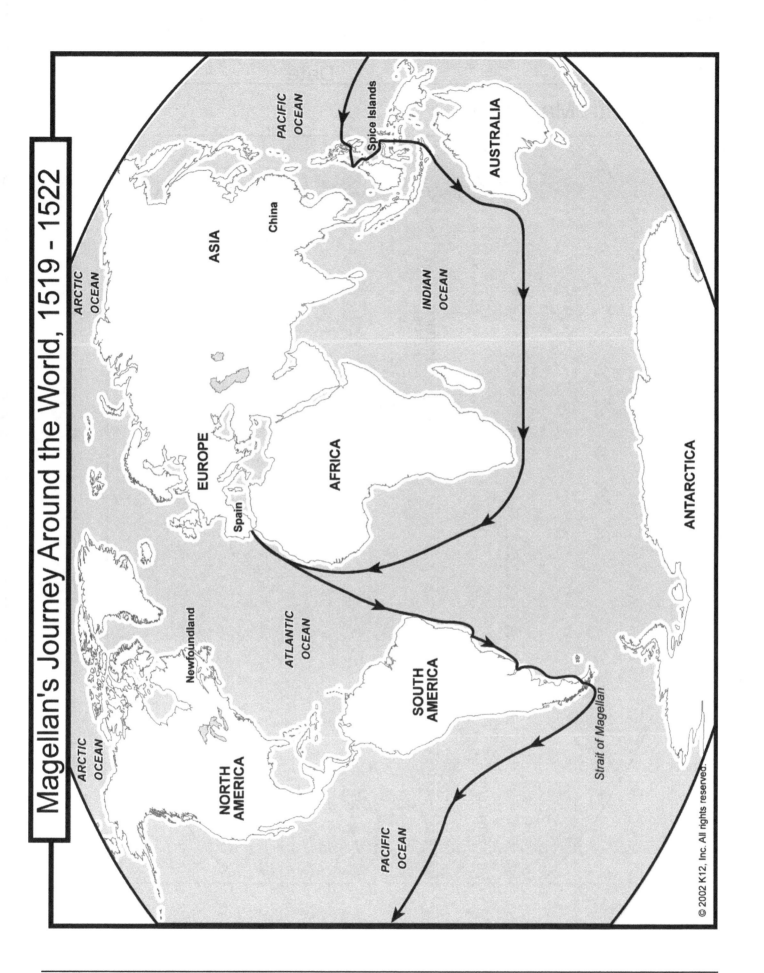

Magellan's Journey Around the World, 1519 – 1522

ARCTIC OCEAN

PACIFIC OCEAN

Spice Islands

AUSTRALIA

China

ASIA

INDIAN OCEAN

EUROPE

AFRICA

Spain

ANTARCTICA

ARCTIC OCEAN

Newfoundland

ATLANTIC OCEAN

NORTH AMERICA

SOUTH AMERICA

Strait of Magellan

PACIFIC OCEAN

Name _____   Date _____

Sailing with Magellan

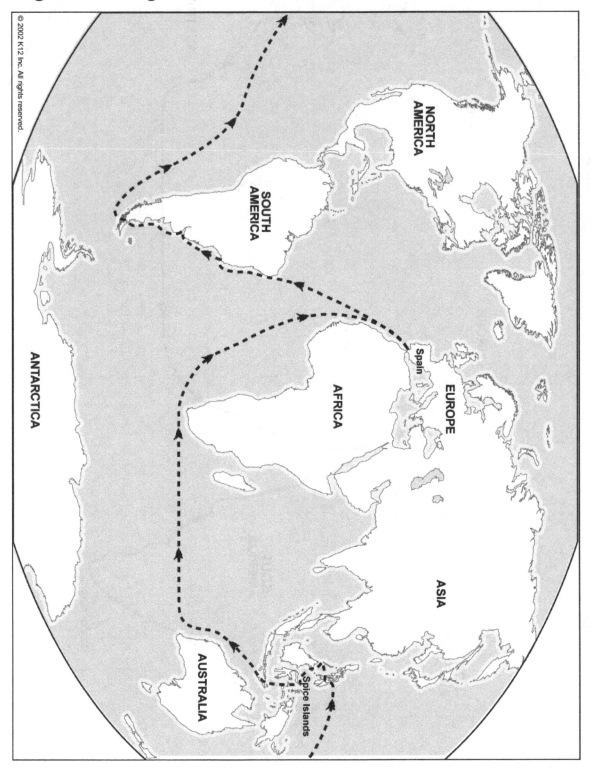

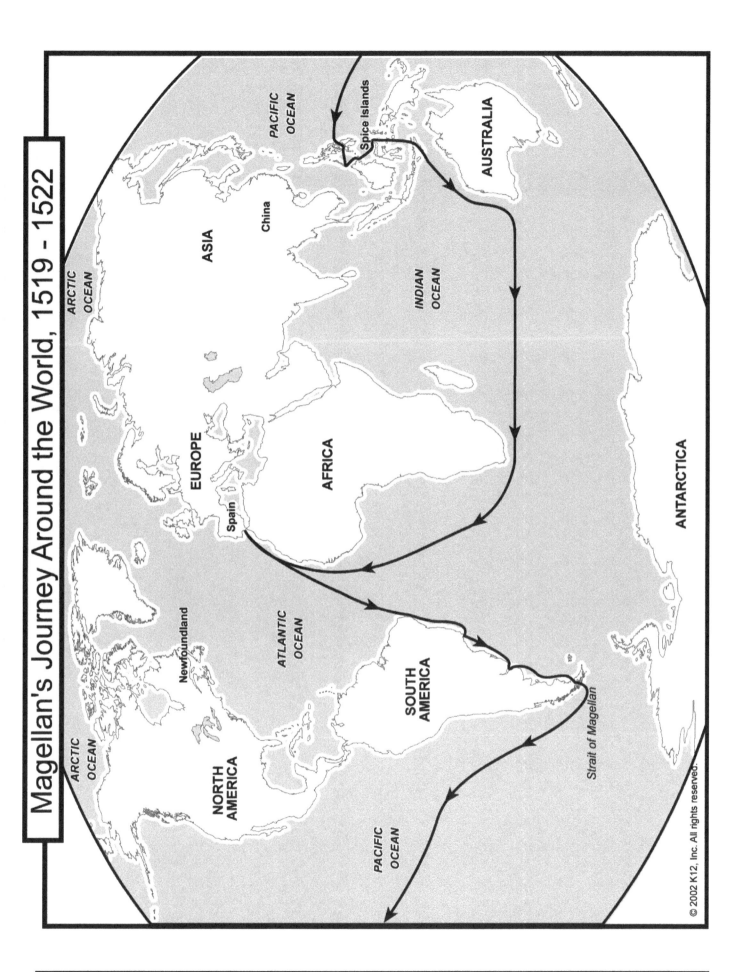

Magellan's Journey Around the World, 1519 - 1522

Spice Islands

PACIFIC OCEAN

AUSTRALIA

ARCTIC OCEAN

ASIA

China

INDIAN OCEAN

EUROPE

AFRICA

Spain

ANTARCTICA

ARCTIC OCEAN

Newfoundland

ATLANTIC OCEAN

NORTH AMERICA

SOUTH AMERICA

Strait of Magellan

PACIFIC OCEAN

Lesson Assessment

Circling the Globe: Magellan's Voyage of Discovery

1. Who was the captain of the first expedition to sail around the world?_____

2. Why did they call this ocean the Pacific?_____

3. **You will need the map of Magellan's Journey Around the World to answer this question.**

   Name and point to the strait that connects the Atlantic Ocean to the Pacific

   Ocean._____

4. Why do we call the Strait of Magellan by that name?_____

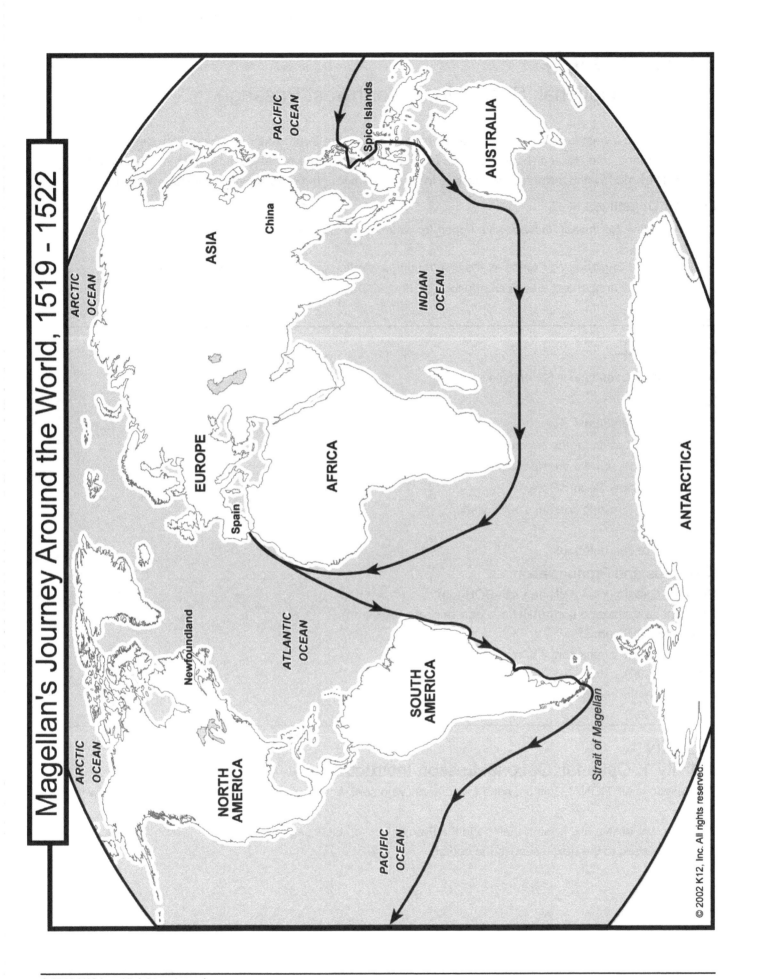

Magellan's Journey Around the World, 1519 - 1522

PACIFIC OCEAN

Spice Islands

AUSTRALIA

China

ASIA

ARCTIC OCEAN

INDIAN OCEAN

EUROPE

AFRICA

Spain

ANTARCTICA

Newfoundland

ATLANTIC OCEAN

SOUTH AMERICA

Strait of Magellan

ARCTIC OCEAN

NORTH AMERICA

PACIFIC OCEAN

Student Guide
Lesson 7. Optional: Search for a Northwest Passage

Magellan found a western route to the Indies by rounding the tip of South America. Spains competitors--England, France, and Holland--hoped to find a faster route through areas free from Spanish or Portuguese control. They tried to find a Northwest Passage to the Indies through the Arctic waters of North America.

Lesson Objectives

- Define *Northwest Passage* as a hoped-for waterway to the Pacific Ocean through North America.
- Name England and France as the first countries wanting a route to the Indies through the north.
- Identify an explorer who searched for a Northwest Passage to the Indies.

PREPARE

Approximate lesson time is 60 minutes.

Materials
For the Student
- Search for the Northwest Passage-1
- Search for the Northwest Passage-2
- History Record Book
- Amazing Journeys activity sheet

Optional
- paper, notebook

Keywords and Pronunciation
Giovanni Caboto (joh-VAHN-nee kah-BOH-toh)
Giovanni da Verrazano (joh-VAHN-nee dah vair-raht-SAHN-oh)
Hurons (HYOUR-uhns)
Jacques Cartier (zhahk kahr-TYAY)
John Cabot (KA-buht)
Montreal (mahn-tree-AWL)

LEARN
Activity 1. Optional: Optional Lesson Instructions *(Online)*

This lesson is OPTIONAL. It is provided for students who seek enrichment or extra practice. You may skip this lesson.

If you choose to skip this lesson, then go to the Plan or Lesson Lists page and mark this lesson "Skipped" in order to proceed to the next lesson in the course.

Activity 2. Optional: Search for a Northwest Passage *(Offline)*

Get Ready

Which two countries led Europe in voyages of discovery during the Age of Exploration? [1]

What did Magellan do? [2]

Why did Magellan sail west around South America? [3]

Magellan wanted to reach the Indies by sailing south and west. Today we're going to learn about some explorers who tried to reach the Indies by sailing north and west.

You remember that Columbus discovered the Americas in 1492, while he was looking for the Indies. Columbus never did figure out that he had found two new continents. Instead, when he returned to Europe, he told everyone that he had reached Asia by sailing across the Atlantic.

Columbus's great adventure made him famous and wealthy. But a sailor from Venice named Giovanni Caboto (joh-VAHN-nee kah-BOH-toh) dreamed of being even more successful than Columbus. He knew that Columbus had sailed west and south across the Atlantic. By sailing north rather than south, Caboto thought he might find a quicker, shorter route to the riches of Asia.

This Italian dreamer asked both the king of Portugal and the king of Spain for help. Both turned him down. So he traveled to England. The English king agreed to help him, which is why he sailed in the service of England. It's also why we know this fellow today as John Cabot (KA-buht) and not Giovanni Caboto. The English couldn't pronounce his name, so they changed it to a name they could pronounce!

In 1497, Cabot sailed across the northern Atlantic in a small ship with only 18 sailors. After a month-long voyage, they sighted land--a rocky coast where huge waves exploded against tall cliffs.

Cabot explored the coast, but he didn't see any people. He was disappointed not to find the cities of Asia, rich with spices and jewels. But he found that the place was rich in something else--fish!

The sea was so crowded with them that all Cabot's sailors had to do was hang a bucket over the side of the ship. When they pulled it up, the pail was full of flapping, squirming fish.

Later, Europeans would settle in this land just because it was so easy to make a living from the sea. Cabot planted the English flag and claimed the land for England.

When Cabot returned to England, he called the place he discovered--a huge island--the "newfound land." Today Newfoundland is part of the nation of Canada.

In the years after Cabot's voyage, Europeans figured out that neither Columbus nor Cabot had really made it to Asia. Instead, the lands they discovered were the continents of North and South America.

But Europeans kept trying to get to the Indies by sailing west. In the early 1520s, Ferdinand Magellan did just that--he reached Asia by sailing around South America and then across the Pacific.

The king of France was especially interested in what Magellan had done. This king's name was Francis I, and you read about him in the lessons on the Renaissance. Francis I tried to bring glory to France by building palaces and supporting great artists like Leonardo da Vinci. Now he decided that he would also bring glory to France another way--by supporting exploration.

Francis hired another Italian sea captain named Giovanni da Verrazano (joh-VAHN-nee dah vehr-uh-ZAH-noh). He told Verrazano, "I want you to find a new route to the Indies through the Americas. You can't go to the south, because Spain and Portugal have already claimed those lands. Find me a water route through North America. I'm looking for a northwest passage." That hunt for the Northwest Passage would go on for many, many years.

Verrazano sailed across the Atlantic until he reached the area that would later be the east coast of the United States. He started in North Carolina and sailed north past Virginia, New York, Massachusetts, and Maine. Along the way he traded with the natives, who were usually very friendly. Once, though, a native who was smoking tobacco in a pipe approached Verrazano's men. The Frenchmen, who had never seen anyone smoking tobacco, were afraid that the pipe was a weapon and fired a shot to scare the smoker away!

Verrazano never found a Northwest Passage through the American continent. By the time he reached the rocky shores of Newfoundland, his ships were running out of food and water. He decided to head back to France.

King Francis was disappointed by Verrazano's failure. But he never lost faith that the Northwest Passage could be found. A few years later he backed another captain, Jacques Cartier (zhahk kahr-TYAY). He sent Cartier on three different voyages to find the passage. On his first voyage, Cartier went to Newfoundland and then explored an area farther south, which was later named Nova Scotia.

Cartier claimed the land he found for France and named the town on the hill *Mont Real*--French for "Mount Royal." Today Montreal (mahn-tree-AWL) is one of the biggest cities in the modern nation of Canada.

Try tracing Cartier's route on the map. First find the big island of Newfoundland off the northeastern coast. Then look south and you'll see Nova Scotia.

Between Nova Scotia and Newfoundland is the Gulf of St. Lawrence, which leads into the St. Lawrence River. Put your finger on the river and trace it down to Montreal, and you'll see how far Cartier went.

Even though he tried three times, Cartier never did find the Northwest Passage. There was no river that cut through North America, making it easy to get to the Indies.

But the search for the Northwest Passage changed history. Cabot, Verrazano, and Cartier brought exciting stories of unknown lands back to England and France. They told of friendly natives, forests full of game, and seas teeming with fish.

The stories made people want to settle in these new, northern lands. The Spanish and Portuguese would settle the new world first, but settlers from France and England would not be far behind.

Show You Know

What was the Northwest Passage that explorers hoped to find? [4]

Which were the first two countries to seek the Northwest Passage? [5]

Name one of the explorers who went searching for the Northwest Passage. [6]

Activity 3. Optional: History Record Book (Offline)

Instructions

Choose either A or B.

A. Written Narration

Write two to four sentences explaining what the lesson was about. If necessary, use the Show You Know questions to help get started. Only include the most important parts of the lesson. Write your name, the date, and the lesson title on your written narration, and put it in your History Record Book.

Sample written narration: "England and France both wanted to find a way to the Indies. They sent explorers to sail north and west. John Cabot, Giovanni Verrazano, and Jacques Cartier all looked for a route called the Northwest Passage."

B. Picture Narration

Draw a picture of the part of the lesson that interested you most. When you have finished drawing, describe the picture. Below your picture, write a description of what you have drawn. Write your name, the date, and the lesson title on your picture narration, and put it in your History Record Book.

Activity 4. Optional: Amazing Journeys *(Offline)*

Instructions

Your journey to learn about the Northwest Passage took you to many places along the east coast of North America and into Canada. You learned about captains and countries, flags and fish. You met many explorers and even a king.

To sort out these amazing journeys, complete the crossword puzzle on the activity sheet. When you finish, see if you can think of two other words and clues you would add if you were making this puzzle.

Activity 5. Optional: Search for a Northwest Passage *(Online)*

Make your own map showing the search for the Northwest Passage.

The Search for the Northwest Passage

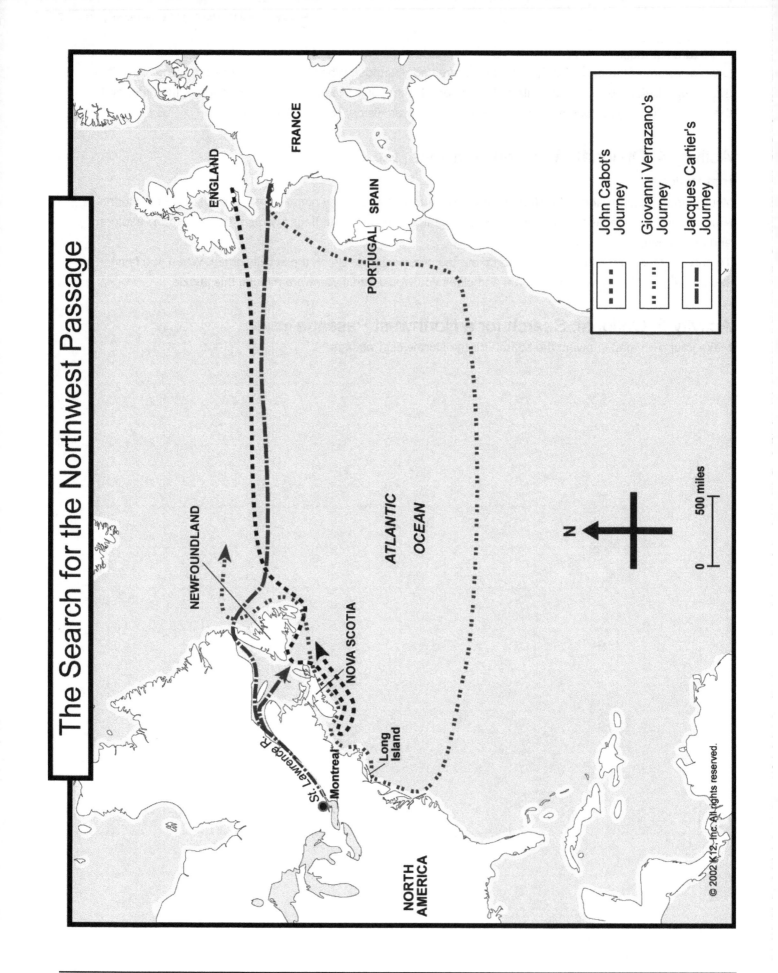

John Cabot's Journey

Giovanni Verrazano's Journey

Jacques Cartier's Journey

ENGLAND

FRANCE

PORTUGAL

SPAIN

NEWFOUNDLAND

NOVA SCOTIA

Long Island

St. Lawrence R.

Montreal

NORTH AMERICA

ATLANTIC OCEAN

N

500 miles

0

© 2002 K12 Inc. All rights reserved.

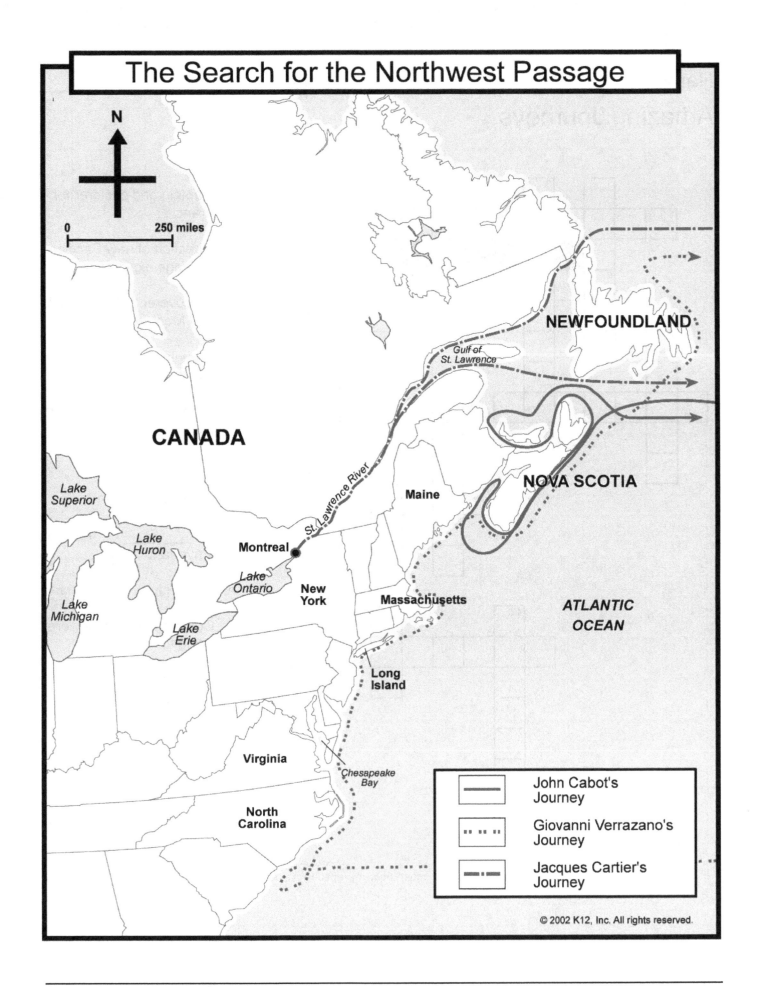

The Search for the Northwest Passage

N

0 ———— 250 miles

NEWFOUNDLAND

Gulf of St. Lawrence

CANADA

Lake Superior

Lake Huron

St. Lawrence River

Montreal

Lake Ontario

Lake Michigan

Lake Erie

New York

Maine

NOVA SCOTIA

Massachusetts

ATLANTIC OCEAN

Long Island

Virginia

Chesapeake Bay

North Carolina

	John Cabot's Journey
	Giovanni Verrazano's Journey
	Jacques Cartier's Journey

© 2002 K12, Inc. All rights reserved.

Name _____   Date _____

Amazing Journeys

Across

3. Captain and explorer for Francis I

6. Direction of new Pacific passage exploration

9. Discoverer of Nova Scotia and Montreal

11. Country once explored by Jacques Cartier

13. English name for Giovanni Caboto

Down

1. Nation ruled by Francis I

2. St. _____, name of a river and a gulf

4. Name given to new island

5. Continent explorers were trying to reach

7. A leading country of exploration

8. A leading country of exploration

10. Round the world explorer

12. 1492 Americas discoverer

Across: 3. Verrazano 6. Northwest 9. Cartier 11. Canada 13. John Cabot **Down:** 1. France 2. Lawrence 4. Newfoundland 5. Asia 7. Portugal 8. Spain 10. Magellan 12. Columbus

Student Guide
Lesson 8: Unit Review and Assessment

You've completed this unit, and now it's time to review what you've learned and take the unit assessment.

Lesson Objectives

- Demonstrate mastery of important knowledge and skills in this unit.
- Describe the Renaissance as an Age of Exploration.
- Identify Henry the Navigator as a prince of Portugal interested in navigation and exploration.
- Tell how Henry improved navigation.
- Identify Bartolomeu Dias as the Portuguese explorer who located the southern tip of Africa.
- Identify the southern tip of Africa as the Cape of Good Hope.
- Define the *Indies* as the lands of India, China, and Japan.
- Identify Christopher Columbus as an explorer who sought a route to the Indies by sailing west.
- Explain that the pope divided the New World between Portugal and Spain.
- Identify Vasco da Gama as a Portuguese explorer whose trip around Africa to the Indies made Portugal a major trading power.
- Identify Pedro Cabral as the Portuguese explorer who claimed Brazil for Portugal.
- Describe Balboa as the first European to sight the Pacific Ocean from its eastern shore.
- Name Ferdinand Magellan as the captain of the first expedition to circle the globe.

PREPARE

Approximate lesson time is 60 minutes.

Materials

> For the Student
>> History Record Book

Keywords and Pronunciation

astrolabe (AS-truh-layb) : an instrument used to observe the positions of stars and other objects in the sky

Bartolomeu Dias (bahr-tou-lou-MAY-ou DEE-ahsh)

caravel (KAIR-uh-vel) : A small ship sailed by the Portuguese and others during the Renaissance.

Ferdinand Magellan (FUR-dn-and muh-JEHL-uhn)

Galileo Galilei (gal-uh-LEE-oh gal-uh-LAY-ee)

Jan van Eyck (yahn van IYK)

Nicolaus Copernicus (NIK-uh-luhs kuh-PUR-nih-kuhs)

Pedro Cabral (PAY-throo kuh-BRAHL)

Vasco da Gama (VAHS-koo dah GAH-muh)

Vasco Núñez de Balboa (VAHS-koh NOON-yays day bal-BOH-uh)

LEARN
Activity 1: A Look Back (Offline)
Instructions

"How wide are the Earth's oceans? How far does the continent of Africa stretch? What's the quickest way to reach the Indies, with all their gold, spices, and silks? How can Europeans spread Christianity? Can human beings sail around the globe?" At the time of the Renaissance, Europe's powerful princes and eager explorers were asking these questions.

You've learned that the Renaissance was a time of new questions and new answers in art, music, and science. Painters such as van Eyck and Dürer wanted to paint the details of the world they saw. Astronomers such as Copernicus and Galileo wanted to know exactly what the universe looked like. Did the sun revolve around the Earth or did the Earth revolve around the sun? It's not surprising that great curiosity about the world spilled over into navigation and exploration. The Renaissance would also be called the Age of Exploration.

You've learned that Portugal and Spain led the way in this great age of exploration. Do you remember the name of the Portuguese prince who was so eager to learn more about sailing? He was called Henry the Navigator, and when he brought sailors, thinkers, and mapmakers to his palace, big things started to happen. The Portuguese designed small, fast ships called caravels. They also designed new versions of instruments such as the compass and astrolabe. Henry sent brave Portuguese sailors south to explore the coast of Africa. He hoped to find the source of the Muslim traders' gold and pepper. He hoped to spread his Christian faith. And he hoped to learn more about an unknown world.

But wait a minute. Why go to all this trouble? Why didn't the Portuguese just send merchants by land to the east? Muslim powers ruled over most of the eastern land routes to India, China, and Japan. The Spanish and Portuguese had thrown the Moors out of their peninsula, but Muslims ruled in North Africa, eastern Europe, and central Asia. Even if Muslim leaders let the European merchants travel in peace, they still made them pay money to travel through their lands.

"How much easier it would be," thought the Europeans, "to find a sea route to the Indies. We need those spices that make our food taste so much better. We need that silk that makes dresses swish and rustle. We need that gold to make us rich."

Within 50 years, the Portuguese and their neighbors, the Spanish, were sailing unknown waters and figuring out the shapes of the continents. The Portuguese explorer Bartolomeu Dias weathered a storm and found Africa's southernmost tip. The Portuguese king named it the Cape of Good Hope, because now he had hope of finding the Indies by sailing around Africa.

Another of the king's explorers, Vasco da Gama, did just that. Da Gama reached India by sailing around Africa, then past Arabia and northeast to India. A third Portuguese explorer, Pedro Cabral, got there that way, too, but he accidentally bumped into the coast of South America along the way. Cabral claimed the land he found for Portugal. Nowadays we call it Brazil.

You know, of course, that Christopher Columbus reached the Americas before Cabral. He found the Americas by accident! Columbus convinced King Ferdinand and Queen Isabella of Spain that they could beat the Portuguese to the Indies. He'd get there faster by sailing west. He said, "The world is round, so if I sail west across the Atlantic, I'm sure to get there."

Columbus sailed off into a vast ocean, but instead of reaching the Indies, he landed in the Americas in 1492. Here were two continents unknown to Europeans. Sadly, they were unknown to Columbus, too. He died convinced he had reached the Indies. Instead, he had found what Europeans would call the New World.

Before long, other adventurers came and helped explore this New World. Vasco Núñez de Balboa, a Spanish explorer, sighted the Pacific Ocean. The explorer Ferdinand Magellan also sailed for the Spanish king. He wanted to be the first to circumnavigate the globe. (That means sail around it.) Magellan didn't make it, but some of his crew did. In the process, they claimed the Spice Islands for Spain.

By and by, other European countries grew interested in exploration and jealous of Spain and Portugal. England and France knew their rivals were claiming all of South America. But what about North America? Could England and France find a way to the Indies by cutting through North America? Could they claim North America for their own? The French and English search for a Northwest Passage was about to begin. They were unsuccessful, but the French and English learned a great deal about North America. And they both claimed parts of the New World for themselves.

What would happen next in this story of ambitious kings, daring adventurers, and unknown continents? Columbus, Balboa, and Cabral did not come to an uninhabited land. In our next unit we'll learn about the world they encountered and the people they met there.

Activity 2: History Record Book Review (Offline)

Activity 3: Online Interactive Review (Online)

ASSESS

Unit Assessment: The Age of Exploration (Offline)

Complete an offline Unit Assessment. Your learning coach will score this part of the Assessment.

Name _____   Date _____

The Age of Exploration

Read each question and its answer choices. Fill in the bubble in front of the word or words that best answer the question.

Questions marked with an asterisk (*) will have more than one correct answer. For these questions, fill in the bubble next to ALL correct answers.

1. Which name best describes the period from 1450 to 1600?
   - ⓐ Age of Exploration
   - ⓑ Age of Faith
   - ⓒ Age of Science
   - ⓓ Age of Democracy

2. What is the Portuguese explorer Bartolomeu Dias known for?
   - ⓐ reaching the Americas by sailing west
   - ⓑ designing a new kind of sailing ship
   - ⓒ reaching the southern tip of Africa
   - ⓓ circumnavigating the globe

3. Why were Europeans looking for a sea route to the Indies?
   - ⓐ Muslim powers controlled most of the land routes.
   - ⓑ Mountains blocked the way from Europe to Asia.
   - ⓒ Camels and donkeys were becoming scarce.
   - ⓓ Merchants liked to travel by sea.

4. Which explorer was the first to sail west across the Atlantic in hopes of reaching the Indies?
   - ⓐ Ferdinand Magellan
   - ⓑ Vasco Núñez de Balboa
   - ⓒ Christopher Columbus
   - ⓓ Vasco da Gama

* 5. Who were the leading powers during the first part of the Age of Exploration? (Select ALL that are correct.)

(a) Spain

(b) France

(c) Portugal

(d) England

(e) Germany

6. Who was the first European to see the Pacific Ocean from its eastern shore?

(a) Vasco Núñez de Balboa

(b) Ferdinand Magellan

(c) Christopher Columbus

(d) Pedro Cabral

7. What is Ferdinand Magellan known for?

(a) He was the first European to land in the New World.

(b) He discovered the Northwest Passage.

(c) He found a sea route to India by sailing around Africa.

(d) He led the first expedition to circle the globe.

8. When Pedro Cabral accidentally landed in South America, what part did he claim for Portugal?

(a) Brazil

(b) Peru

(c) Mexico

(d) Cape Horn

9. Who brought shipbuilders, mapmakers, and sailors to his palace in Portugal to encourage exploration?

    ⓐ Prince Henry the Navigator

    ⓑ Christopher Columbus

    ⓒ King Ferdinand of Spain

    ⓓ Sir Francis Drake

*10. Select the items that Europeans were interested in obtaining in the Indies. (Select ALL that are correct.)

    ⓐ corn

    ⓑ spices

    ⓒ tobacco

    ⓓ gold

    ⓔ lumber

    ⓕ paper

    ⓖ silk

11. If you were standing on the southernmost tip of Africa, where would you be?

    ⓐ at Cape Horn

    ⓑ at the Cape of Good Hope

    ⓒ on Mount Everest

    ⓓ on Mount Kilimanjaro

12. Why did Europeans set off on voyages of discovery and exploration?

    ⓐ to prove the world was round and find new peoples and cultures

    ⓑ to spread Christianity and get spices, gold, and silk

    ⓒ to find new places to build farms

    ⓓ to create jobs for shipbuilders and mapmakers

13. Europeans were interested in spices because they could use them to make _____.
   ⓐ green vegetables last longer
   ⓑ gunpowder for new muskets
   ⓒ oil paints dry faster
   ⓓ bad food taste better

14. Whose trip around Africa to India made Portugal a major European power?
   ⓐ Christopher Columbus
   ⓑ Vasco da Gama
   ⓒ Prince Henry the Navigator
   ⓓ Ferdinand Magellan

* 15. Which of the following helped make voyages of exploration possible? (Select ALL that are correct.)
   ⓐ large, slow ships called galleons
   ⓑ the compass and astrolabe
   ⓒ accurate seagoing clocks
   ⓓ small, fast ships called caravels
   ⓔ new ways to keep food from going bad

Student Guide
Lesson 1: Travel Back in Time: The Mysterious Maya

- Recognize that different civilizations and cultures inhabited the Americas before the arrival of Europeans.
- List the Maya, Aztecs, and Incas as three major pre-Columbian civilizations and describe some of their skills and abilities.
- Describe the motivations of the Spanish in the New World.
- Characterize the conflict of Spanish and Native American civilizations as a clash of civilizations in which the Spanish conquered the Aztec and Inca Empires.
- Identify key figures in the conflict: Moctezuma, Cortés, Atahualpa, Pizarro, and Las Casas.

Explore the amazing civilization of the Maya--one of many groups of people who lived in the Americas before Europeans began to settle there--and learn about their remarkable skill in architecture, writing, and astronomy.

Lesson Objectives

- Recognize that different civilizations and cultures inhabitied the Americas before the arrival of Europeans.
- List the Maya, Aztecs, and Incas as three major pre-Columbian civilizations and describe some of their skills and abilities.
- Describe the motivations of the Spanish in the New World.
- Characterize the conflict of Spanish and Native American civilizations as a clash of civilizations in which the Spanish conquered the Aztec and Inca Empires.
- Identify key figures in the conflict: Moctezuma, Cortés. Atahualpa, Pizarro, and Las Casas.
- Locate the Yucatán peninsula on a map.
- Describe the Maya as an ancient Native American civilization on the Yucatán peninsula.
- Name two achievements of the Maya or aspects of Maya life (such as an accurate calendar, pyramid temples, and writing).

PREPARE

Approximate lesson time is 60 minutes.

Materials

For the Student

    🖳 Map of Maya and Aztecs

    map, world

    History Record Book

    🖳 The Maya Calendar

Optional

    clay

Keywords and Pronunciation
Hunahpu (hoo-NAH-poo)
Maya (MIY-uh)
stelae (STEE-lee)
Yucatán (yoo-kah-TAHN)

LEARN
Activity 1: Discovering the Maya *(Online)*

Activity 2: History Record Book *(Offline)*
Instructions
Choose either A or B.
A. Written Narration
Write two to four sentences explaining what the lesson was about. If necessary, use the Show You Know questions to help get started. Only include the most important parts of the lesson. Write your name, the date, and the lesson title on your written narration, and put it in your History Record Book.

Sample written narration: "The Maya had a great civilization on the Yucatán Peninsula while people in Europe were in the Dark Ages. They knew how to read and write. They built huge temples shaped like pyramids. They wrote about what they did on stone slabs called stelae. No one knows why their civilization ended."

B. Picture Narration
Draw a picture of the part of the lesson that interested you most. When you have finished drawing, describe the picture. Below your picture, write a description of what you have drawn. Write your name, the date, and the lesson title on your picture narration, and put it in your History Record Book.

Activity 3: The Maya Calendar *(Offline)*
Instructions
The Maya achieved many things during their civilization. Do you remember that this was during the time from around 250 to 900?
During this time, the Maya built temples. They carved stone slabs called stelae. They could write, and they were very good at math. They used mathematics to help them keep track of time during the year. In fact, they even created their own calendar.
What did their calendar look like? Not like the 12-month one that you use. Instead, the Maya calendar had 19 months. Each of the first 18 months had 20 days, for a total of 360 days. Can you figure out how many days there were in the last month? (Hint: Start by thinking about how many days there are in one year.) [1]
The Maya also had a symbol, or glyph, for the name of each month. To see both the glyphs and the names of the Maya months, print out the Maya Calendar activity sheet. Then follow the directions to figure out many more things about the Maya calendar.
[1] 5 days (365 days - 360 days = 5 days)
The Maya Calendar Activity Sheet Answers
[1] 80 days
[2] Kankin, Kayab, Kumku; 60 days

304

[3] 65 days

[4] 165 days (Remember that you did not color the last month, Uayeb.)

ASSESS

Lesson Assessment: Travel Back in Time: The Mysterious Maya (*Online*)

You will complete an offline assessment covering the main objectives of this lesson. Your learning coach will score this assessment.

LEARN

Activity 4. Optional: Travel Back in Time: The Mysterious Maya (*Offline*)

Instructions

The Maya carved scenes and people on large stone slabs called stelae. Try making a smaller stela of your own using clay and the picture you see here. You may use a pencil to help you make designs in the clay. When you have finished, show and explain your work to someone else. Be sure to share as much as you can about the Maya civilization. You may want enjoy some favorite Maya foods, such as hot chocolate and cornbread, while you are doing this.

Name _____   Date _____

The Maya Calendar

This is the calendar the Maya used. It had 19 months, each with its own name and symbol, or glyph, to stand for it. Each month had 20 days except for the last month, Uayeb, which had 5 days. Can you find the months called Pop and Pax? See what else you can find out about the Maya calendar by following the directions and answering the questions below.

1. Color all the months beginning with Z the same color. Each of these months has 20 days in it. How many days are there altogether in the months beginning with Z? Show your work.

2. K is another letter that begins the names of several months. Color the months beginning with K a second color. Write their names in alphabetical order. Then figure out how many days there are in all the "K" months added together. Each month has 20 days.

3. Color the months beginning with M another color. Add the days in all the "M" months together with the days in the month of Uayeb. Remember that Uayeb has only 5 days, but the other months each have 20. Show your work.

4. Challenge: How many days are there in the months that you have NOT colored?

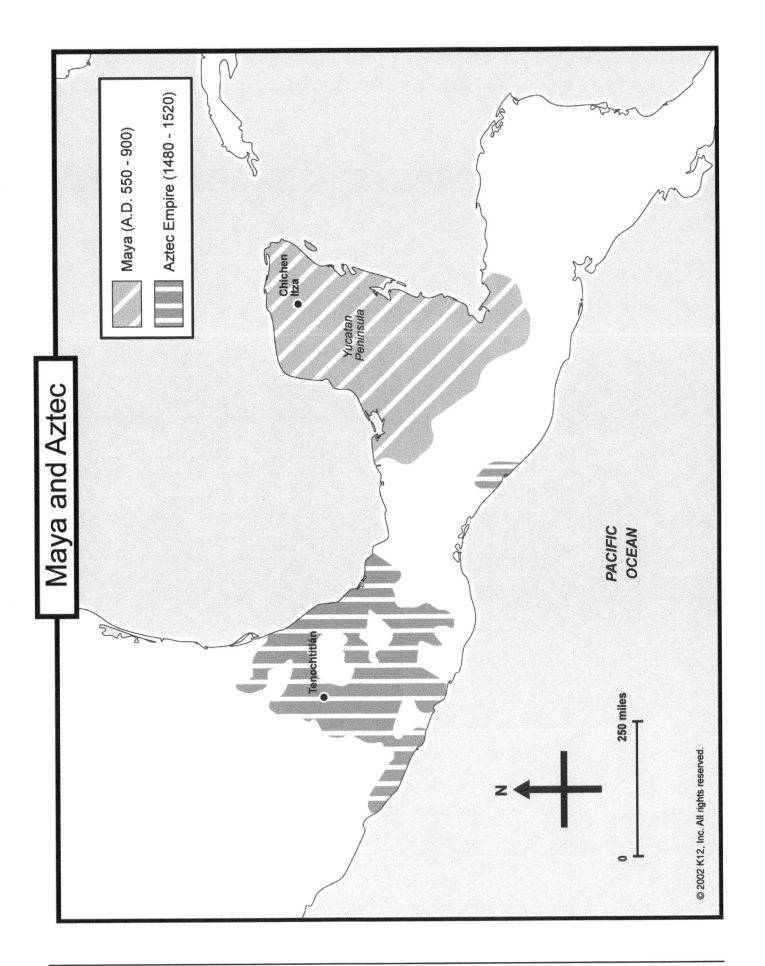

Maya and Aztec

Maya (A.D. 550 - 900)

Aztec Empire (1480 - 1520)

Chichen Itza

Yucatan Peninsula

Tenochtitlán

PACIFIC OCEAN

N

250 miles

0

© 2002 K12, Inc. All rights reserved.

Lesson Assessment

Travel Back in Time: The Mysterious Maya

1. **In order to answer this question you will need to use the map of the Maya and Aztecs.**

    Where is the Yucatán Peninsula?

2. What great ancient Native American civilization existed on the Yucatán peninsula during the Dark

    Ages in Europe?_____

3. Name two things about how the Maya lived and what they achieved?_____

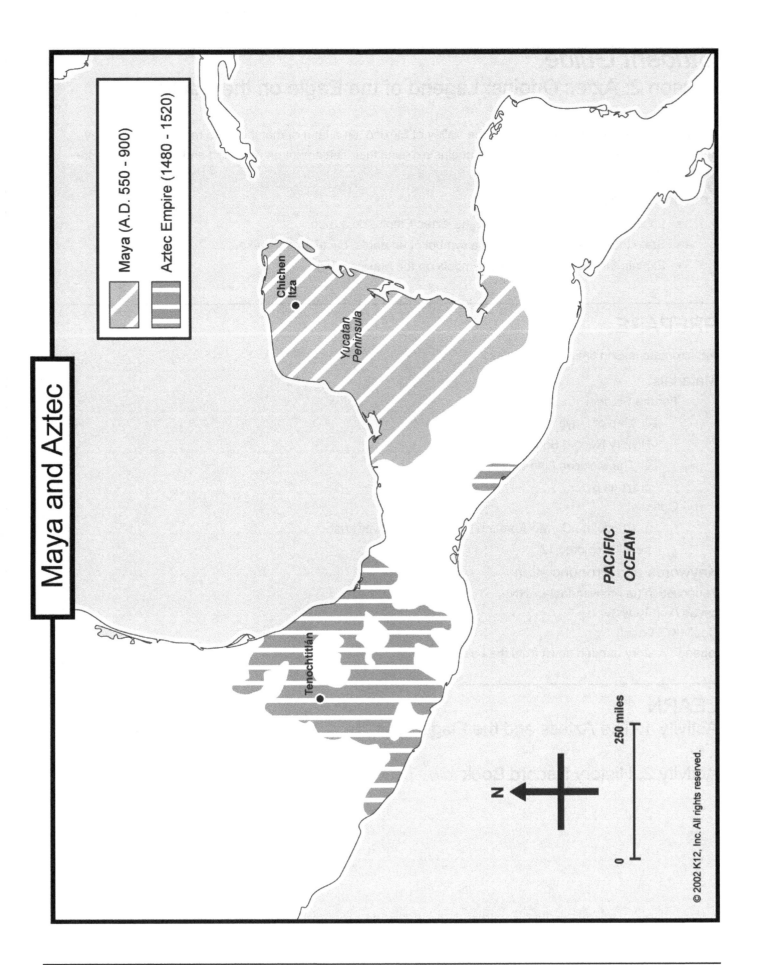

Maya and Aztec

Maya (A.D. 550 - 900)

Aztec Empire (1480 - 1520)

Chichen Itza

Yucatan Peninsula

Tenochtitlán

PACIFIC OCEAN

N

0   250 miles

Student Guide
Lesson 2: Aztec Origins: Legend of the Eagle on the Cactus

The Aztecs built a mighty civilization in the Valley of Mexico, on a land of marshes and reeds. How did they know where to settle? The myth of Aztec origins explains their settlement on an island and the symbol on the Mexican flag.

Lesson Objectives

- Locate the Valley of Mexico and the Aztec Empire on a map.
- State that the Mexican flag has a symbol of an eagle, cactus, and snake.
- Explain the legend behind the symbols on the Mexican flag.

PREPARE

Approximate lesson time is 60 minutes.

Materials

For the Student

- Map of Maya and Aztecs
   History Record Book
- The Mexican Flag activity sheet
   crayons 8

Optional

- Chocolate Comes from the Cacao Tree activity sheet
   pencils, colored 12

Keywords and Pronunciation

Tenochtitlan (tay-nawch-teet-LAHN)

cacao (kuh-KOW)

Copil (KOH-peel)

legend : A story handed down from the past.

LEARN
Activity 1: The Aztecs and the Flag *(Online)*

Activity 2: History Record Book *(Offline)*

Instructions

A. Written Narration

Write two to four sentences explaining what the lesson was about. If necessary, use the Show You Know questions to help get started. Only include the most important parts of the lesson. Write your name, the date, and the lesson title on your written narration, and put it in your History Record Book.

Sample written narration: "The Hummingbird Wizard told the Aztecs to go to a new land. They traveled for a long time and fought a battle. Then they saw a eagle sitting on a cactus holding a snake. The Hummingbird Wizard had told them this was the place to build their city."

B. Picture Narration

Draw a picture of the part of the lesson that interested you most. When you have finished drawing, describe the picture. Below your picture, write a description of what you have drawn. Write your name, the date, and the lesson title on your picture narration, and put it in your History Record Book.

Activity 3: The Story Behind the Flag (Offline)
Instructions

You learned that there's an interesting story behind the symbol on the Mexican flag. This story dates back to the Aztecs and their capital city of Tenochtitlán. Look at this picture of the flag and see whether you can remember the Aztec story. Then print out the Mexican Flag activity sheet and write a caption retelling this famous legend.

ASSESS

Lesson Assessment: Aztec Origins: Legend of the Eagle on the Cactus
(*Online*)

You will complete an offline assessment covering the main objectives of this lesson. Your learning coach will score this assessment.

LEARN

Activity 4. Optional: Aztec Origins: Legend of the Eagle on the Cactus *(Offline)*
Instructions

Do you like chocolate drinks? Both the Aztecs and the Maya thought chocolate was wonderful. They believed it would make them wise and powerful. They even called it the drink of the gods. Chocolate was so valuable to them that they used it as money.

Did you know that chocolate comes from the beans of the cacao (kuh-KOW) tree? Originally the Aztecs crushed the beans and mixed them with hot water and spices to make a bitter drink. Bitter? Yes, that's how the Aztecs drank it. Later the Spanish added other things, such as sugar, to take away the bitter taste.

Want to learn more about chocolate? Begin with the Chocolate Comes from the Cacao Tree activity sheet. Read the information inside the pods. Believe it or not, each pod has about 30 to 40 beans inside.

Then do some research and try to write at least four more facts of your own inside the empty pods on the activity sheet. Use the back of the sheet if you find more. When you have finished, share your information and a cup of hot chocolate with a friend.

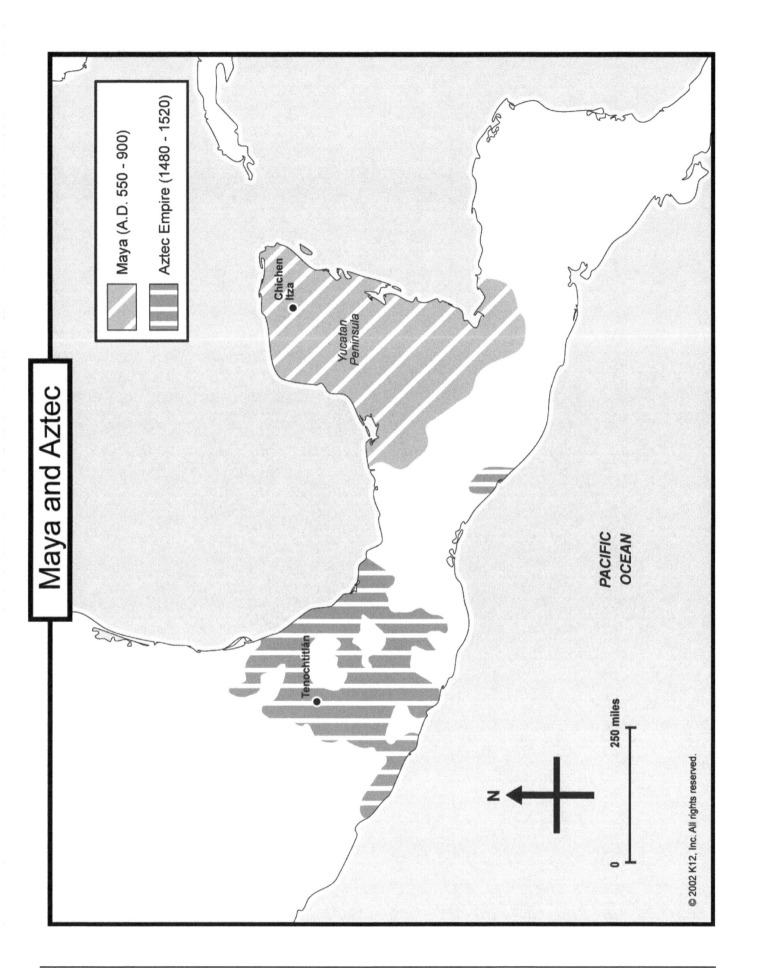

Maya and Aztec

Maya (A.D. 550 – 900)

Aztec Empire (1480 – 1520)

Chichen Itza

Yucatan Peninsula

Tenochtitlán

PACIFIC OCEAN

N

0   250 miles

317

Name _____ Date _____

The Mexican Flag

Here is the flag of Mexico. Use the picture in the lesson to help you color it. Then write a caption below to retell the legend, or story, behind this flag. Remember to mention the cactus, the snake, and the eagle.

_____

_____

_____

_____

_____

_____

_____

Name _____   Date _____

Chocolate Comes from the Cacao Tree

Do some research to learn more about the cacao tree and chocolate. Then fill in the rest of the pods with the facts you find.

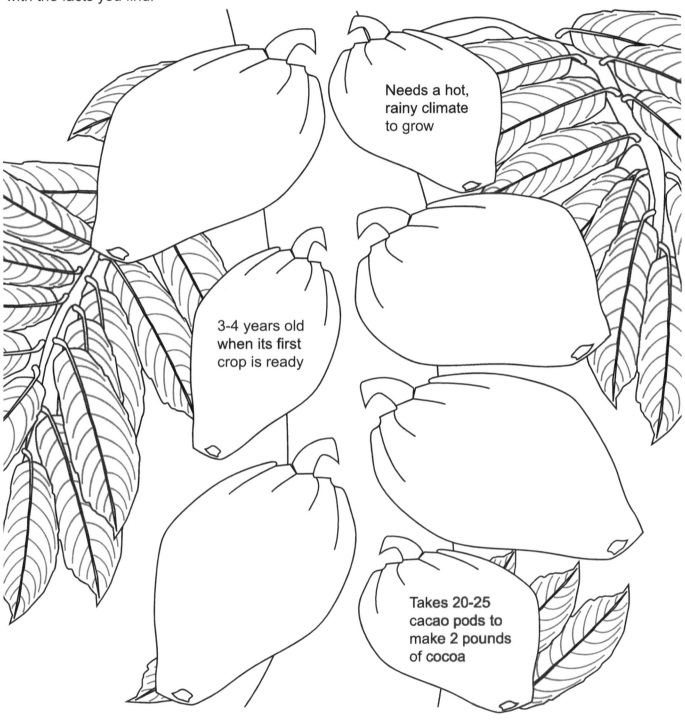

Lesson Assessment

Aztec Origins: Legend of the Eagle on the Cactus

1. **To answer this question, you will need to use the map of the Maya and Aztec Empires.**

   How is the location of the Aztec Empire and the Valley of Mexico indicated on the map?

2. Describe what is on the Mexican flag._____

3. What is the Aztec legend that tells why the cactus, the snake, and the eagle are on the Mexican

   flag?_____

Maya and Aztec

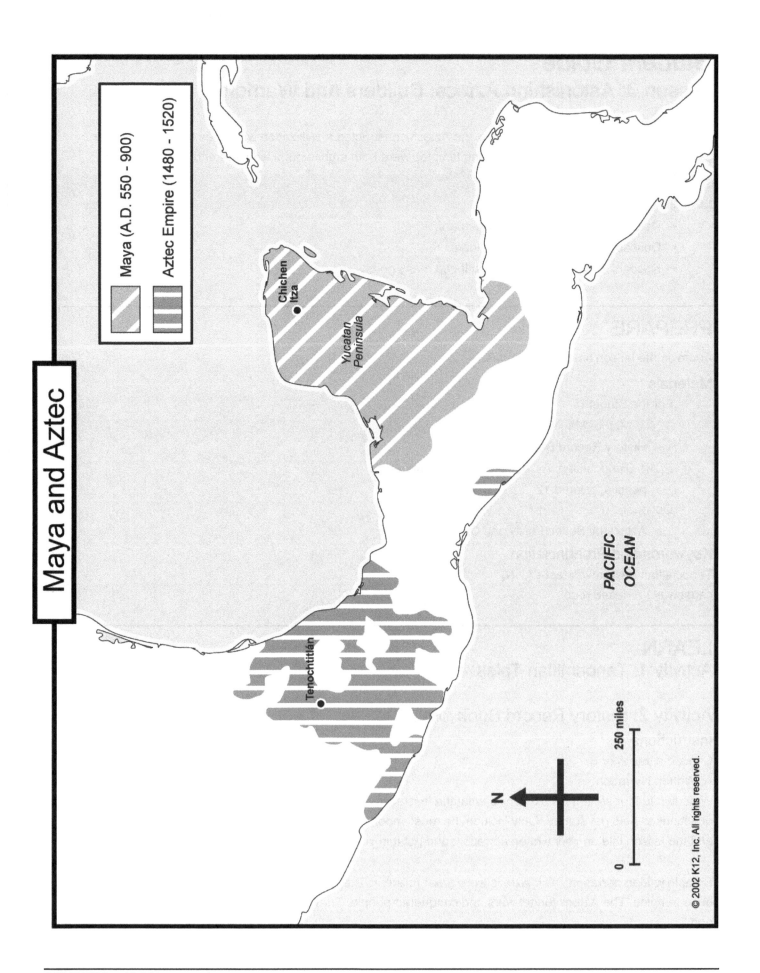

Maya (A.D. 550 - 900)

Aztec Empire (1480 - 1520)

Chichen Itza

Yucatan Peninsula

Tenochtitlán

PACIFIC OCEAN

N

250 miles

0

325

Student Guide
Lesson 3: Astonishing Aztecs: Builders and Warriors

City-builders, warriors, and worshippers, the Aztecs constructed a civilization with cities larger than many European cities of the time. Their towering temples were both architectural wonders and places of great cruelty.

Lesson Objectives

- Describe the Aztecs as fierce warriors.
- Describe the Aztecs as city-builders.
- Recognize that the Aztecs worshipped many gods.

PREPARE

Approximate lesson time is 60 minutes.

Materials

    For the Student
        📖 Map of Maya and Aztecs
        History Record Book
        📖 Tenochtitlán: A Capital City activity sheet
        pencils, colored 12
    Optional
        Aztecs by Susan Purdy and Cass Sandak

Keywords and Pronunciation

Tenochtitlan (tay-nawch-teet-LAHN)

causeway : A raised road.

LEARN
Activity 1: Tenochtitlán Tales *(Online)*

Activity 2: History Record Book *(Offline)*

Instructions

Choose either A or B.

A. Written Narration

Write two to four sentences explaining what the lesson was about. If necessary, use the Show You Know questions to help get started. Only include the most important parts of the lesson. Write your name, the date, and the lesson title on your written narration, and put it in your History Record Book.

Sample written narration: "The Aztecs were great builders. The city of Tenochtitlán had canals, bridges, and huge temples. The Aztecs fought wars and conquered people. They sacrificed prisoners to help their sun god."

B. Picture Narration

Draw a picture of the part of the lesson that interested you most. When you have finished drawing, describe the picture. Below your picture, write a description of what you have drawn. Write your name, the date, and the lesson title on your picture narration, and put it in your History Record Book.

Activity 3: Tenochtitlán - A Capital City (Offline)

Instructions

The Aztecs were great builders, which is easy to see when you look closely at their capital city of Tenochtitlán. Think about all the things you saw and read about in *A Day in Tenochtitlán.*

You might remember that there were canals, bridges, and temples; that people came to trade; that the houses had flower beds; and that craftspeople made baskets, jewelry, and pottery. You might remember much more. After reviewing and thinking about this city, use the Tenochtitlán: A Capital City activity sheet to make a web showing some of the many features of this amazing place.

When you complete your web, use it to write a three- to five-sentence description of the Aztec capital. Share what you learned with someone else.

ASSESS

Lesson Assessment: Astonishing Aztecs: Builders and Warriors (*Online*)

You will complete an offline assessment covering the main objectives of this lesson. Your learning coach will score this assessment.

LEARN

Activity 4. Optional: Astonishing Aztecs: Builders and Warriors (Offline)

Instructions

Visit your library or bookstore for *Aztecs* by Susan Purdy and Cass R. Sandak, illustrated by Pamela Ford Johnson (New York: Franklin Watts, 1982). Then use this book to make some projects that remind you about the Aztecs.

Name _____ Date _____

Tenochtitlán: A Capital City

Think about all the things the Aztecs did to make their capital city great. Then use this web to show what you remember. Next, write three to five sentences about Tenochtitlán, and share what you know with someone else.

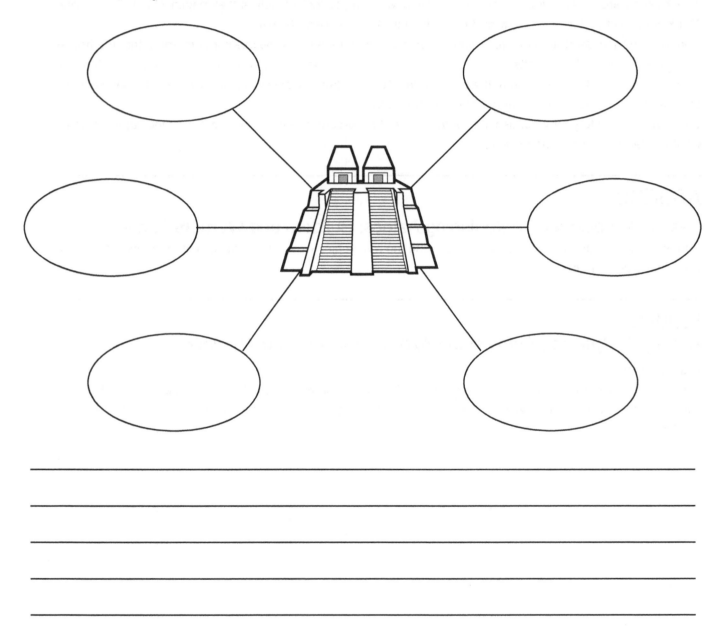

_____

_____

_____

_____

_____

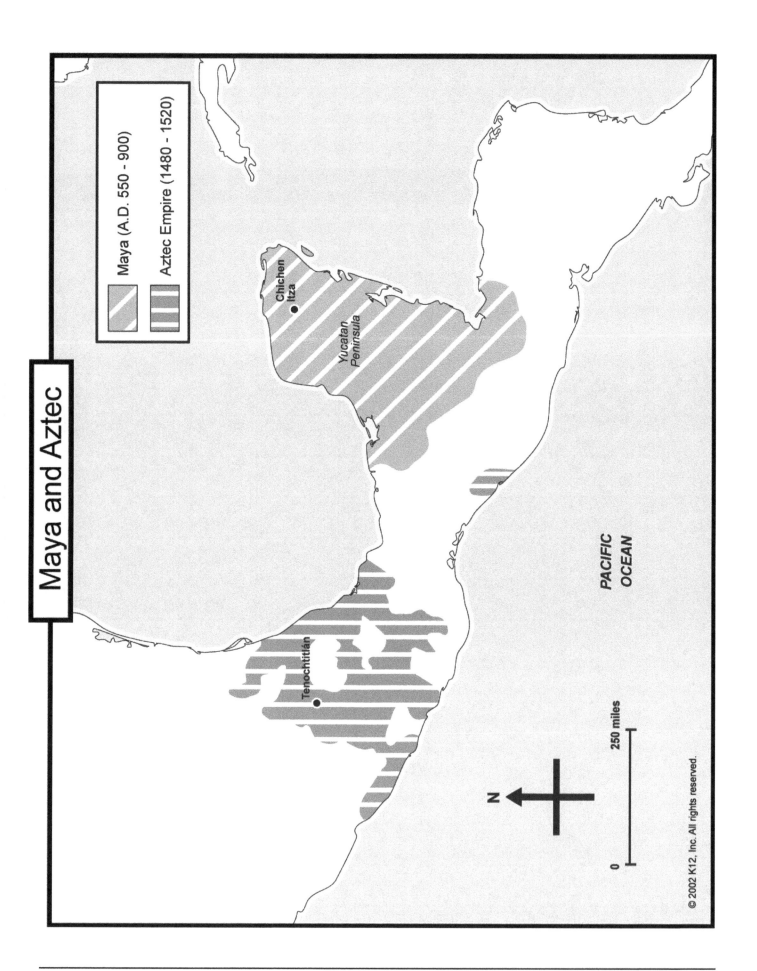

Maya and Aztec

Maya (A.D. 550 - 900)

Aztec Empire (1480 - 1520)

Chichen Itza

Yucatan Peninsula

Tenochtitlán

PACIFIC OCEAN

N

0   250 miles

Lesson Assessment

Astonishing Aztecs: Builders and Warriors

1. Which of these sentences best describes the Aztecs?
    A. The Aztecs were gentle traders.
    B. The Aztecs were fierce warriors.
    C. The Aztecs worshipped one God.

2. What would people learn about the Aztecs by looking at Tenochtitlán and its

    ruins?_____

3. Did the Aztecs worship one God or many gods?_____

Student Guide
Lesson 4: The Inca Empire

While Aztec civilization flourished in Mexico, the Incas prospered in South America. Known for their roads, suspension bridges, couriers, and stonemasonry, the Incas established an empire that began in modern Peru, but eventually stretched from modern Ecuador to southern Chile.

Lesson Objectives

- Locate the Inca Empire on a map.
- Identify the Incas as a civilization located in the Andes mountain range.
- Describe two important characteristics of Inca civilization, such as the use of roads, rope bridges, and couriers.

PREPARE

Approximate lesson time is 60 minutes.

Materials

> For the Student
>> 🖥 Map of the Inca Empire
>>
>> History Record Book
>>
>> 🖥 Inca Message activity sheet
>
> Optional
>> yarn - 5 different colors

Keywords and Pronunciation

Tenochtitlan (tay-nawch-teet-LAHN)

Andes (AN-deez) : A mountain range in South America.

courier : A person who carries messages.

Cuzco (KOOS-koh)

quipu (KEE-poo) : A group of lengths of knotted string that the Incas used to keep records.

quipus (KEE-poos)

Sinchi (SIN-chee)

LEARN
Activity 1: Empire of the Andes *(Online)*

Activity 2: History Record Book (Offline)

Instructions

Choose either A or B.

A. Written Narration

Write two to four sentences explaining what the lesson was about. If necessary, use the Show You Know questions to help get started. Only include the most important parts of the lesson. Write your name, the date, and the lesson title on your written narration, and put it in your History Record Book.

Sample written narration: "The Incas lived high in the Andes Mountains in South America. They had a huge empire. They couldn't write, so couriers remembered messages. Each courier ran very fast and told the message to the next courier. That way the king could know what was going on."

B. Picture Narration

Draw a picture of the part of the lesson that interested you most. When you have finished drawing, describe the picture. Below your picture, write a description of what you have drawn. Write your name, the date, and the lesson title on your picture narration, and put it in your History Record Book.

Activity 3: Remember an Inca Message (Offline)

Instructions

Because the Incas had no written language, Sinchi and the other couriers had to remember all the words in their messages. Do you think this was easy or hard? Try doing it yourself.

Use the Inca Message activity sheet to learn a message about the Inca Empire. Notice that the first letters of the lines in the message spell out the words "Inca Empire." Memorize this message. Then deliver it to someone you know.

If you prefer, write an Inca message of your own and memorize it. Be sure to include as much important information as you can about this early South American civilization.

ASSESS

Lesson Assessment: The Inca Empire (Online)

You will complete an offline assessment covering the main objectives of this lesson. Your learning coach will score this assessment.

LEARN

Activity 4. Optional: The Inca Empire (Offline)

Instructions

The Incas used special knotted strings to keep track of numbers. They tied these strings together into groups called quipus, with different colors to stand for different things. For example, red stood for warriors and yellow stood for gold.

Try making a quipu of your own. Tie four different colors of yarn to a plain-colored string. Although you can use quipus to show any number you want, start by showing the year you were born. Let the first string stand for the thousands place, the second for the hundreds, the third for the tens, and the last for the ones.

Here's an example: If you were born in 1995, you would tie 1 knot in the first string, 9 knots in the second string, 9 knots in the third string, and 5 knots in the last string.

First make a quipu showing the year you were born, and explain it to someone else. Then make another quipu to show the year that person was born.

Name _____   Date _____

Inca Message

Become an Inca messenger. Memorize this message and deliver it to someone you know.

Incas lived in South America long ago,
Near the Pacific coast of the continent.
Couriers carried messages for emperors
Along the steep Andes Mountains,

Even across suspension bridges,
Moving like the wind
Past terraces and up the rocky slopes
Into the emperor's palace and beyond,
Running always as fast as they could,
Even into the capital city of Cuzco.

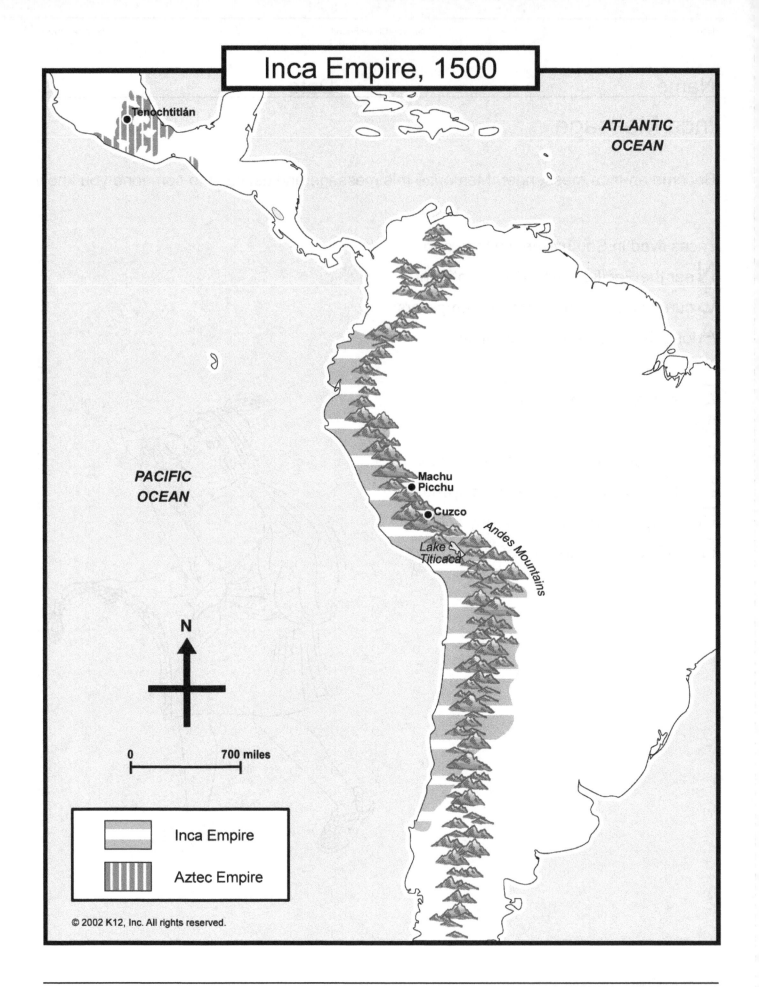

Inca Empire, 1500

ATLANTIC OCEAN

Tenochtitlán

PACIFIC OCEAN

Machu Picchu

Cuzco

Lake Titicaca

Andes Mountains

N

0   700 miles

Inca Empire

Aztec Empire

© 2002 K12, Inc. All rights reserved.

Lesson Assessment

The Inca Empire

1. **In order to answer this question you will need to use the map of the Inca Empire.**
   Where was the Inca Empire?

2. Along what mountain range was the Inca civilization located?_____

3. Name two things you learned about how the Incas lived._____

_____

Inca Empire, 1500

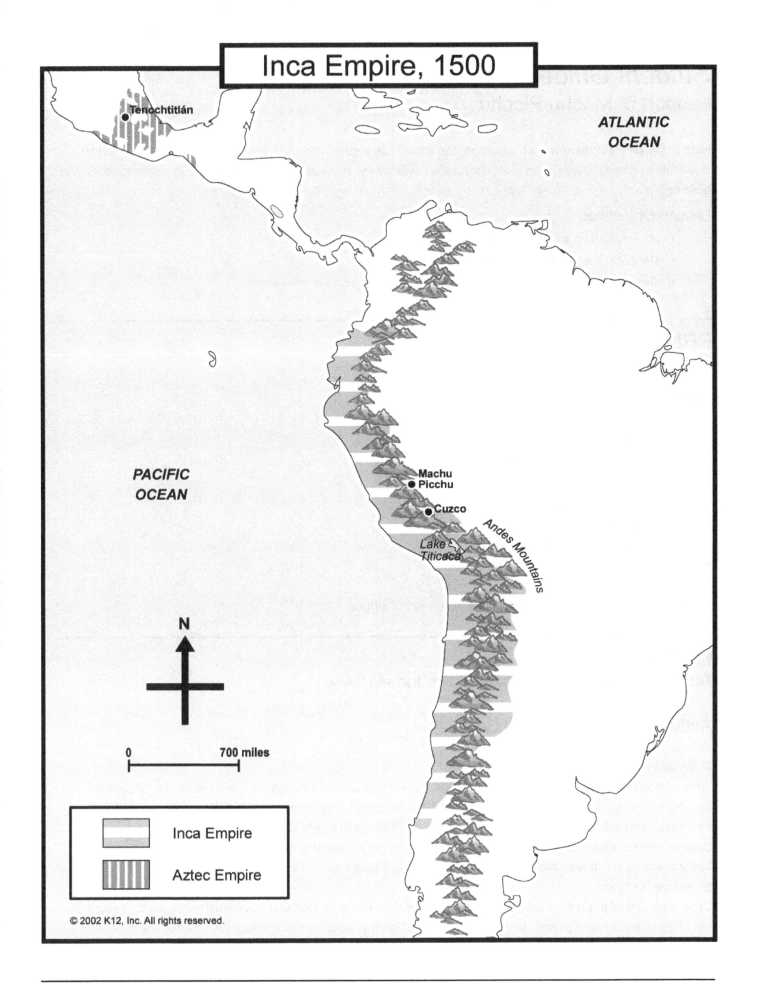

Tenochtitlán

ATLANTIC OCEAN

PACIFIC OCEAN

Machu Picchu

Cuzco

Andes Mountains

Lake Titicaca

N

0   700 miles

Inca Empire

Aztec Empire

Student Guide
Lesson 5: Machu Picchu

High in the peaks of the Andes mountains, the Incas built a stone city. Shrouded in mystery, this city in the clouds is believed to have been a retreat for the royal family. It reveals extraordinary skill in stonemasonry and building.

Lesson Objectives

- Identify Cuzco as the capital of the Inca Empire.
- Describe the Incas as excellent stonemasons.
- Describe Machu Picchu as a stone city built by the Incas in the Andes.

PREPARE

Approximate lesson time is 60 minutes.

Materials

For the Student

📖 Map of the Inca Empire

History Record Book

paper, notebook

Keywords and Pronunciation

Cuzco (KOOS-koh)

Hiram Bingham (HIY-ruhm BING-uhm)

Machu Picchu (mah-choo PEEK-choo)

Sinchi (SIN-chee)

stonemason : A skilled worker who builds things out of stone.

LEARN
Activity 1: The Royal Capital of the Incas (Online)

Activity 2: History Record Book (Offline)

Choose either A or B.

A. Written Narration

Write two to four sentences explaining what the lesson was about. If necessary, use the Show You Know questions to help get started. Only include the most important parts of the lesson. Write your name, the date, and the lesson title on your written narration, and put it in your History Record Book.

Sample written narration: "The Incas built a city high in the Andes Mountains. Then no one could find it for hundreds of years. It was a lost city. An explorer finally found it and called it Machu Picchu."

B. Picture Narration

Draw a picture of the part of the lesson that interested you most. When you have finished drawing, describe the picture. Below your picture, write a description of what you have drawn. Write your name, the date, and the lesson title on your picture narration, and put it in your History Record Book.

Instructions

Choose either A or B.

A. Written Narration

Write two to four sentences explaining what the lesson was about. If necessary, use the Show You Know questions to help get started. Only include the most important parts of the lesson. Write your name, the date, and the lesson title on your written narration, and put it in your History Record Book.

Sample written narration: "The Incas built a city high in the Andes Mountains. Then no one could find it for hundreds of years. It was a lost city. An explorer finally found it and called it Machu Picchu."

B. Picture Narration

Draw a picture of the part of the lesson that interested you most. When you have finished drawing, describe the picture. Below your picture, write a description of what you have drawn. Write your name, the date, and the lesson title on your picture narration, and put it in your History Record Book.

Activity 3: Hiram Bingham's Journal (Offline)

Instructions

Hiram Bingham was an American explorer who discovered the lost city of the Incas. This city, named Machu Picchu, was located high in the Andes mountains northwest of the Inca capital of Cuzco. The Inca emperor is supposed to have spent his summers in Machu Picchu.

While Hiram Bingham was searching for this ancient city, he kept a journal. On July 24, 1911, when he saw Machu Picchu for the first time, he wrote, "Suddenly, I found myself confronted with the walls of ruined houses built of finest Incan stonework."

What else do you think Hiram Bingham wrote about his discovery? Review the lesson. Then complete a journal entry describing Hiram Bingham's exciting find.

ASSESS

Lesson Assessment: Machu Picchu (Online)

You will complete an offline assessment covering the main objectives of this lesson. Your learning coach will score this assessment.

LEARN
Activity 4. Optional: Machu Picchu *(Online)*
Instructions
Visit the ancient Inca city of Machu Picchu.

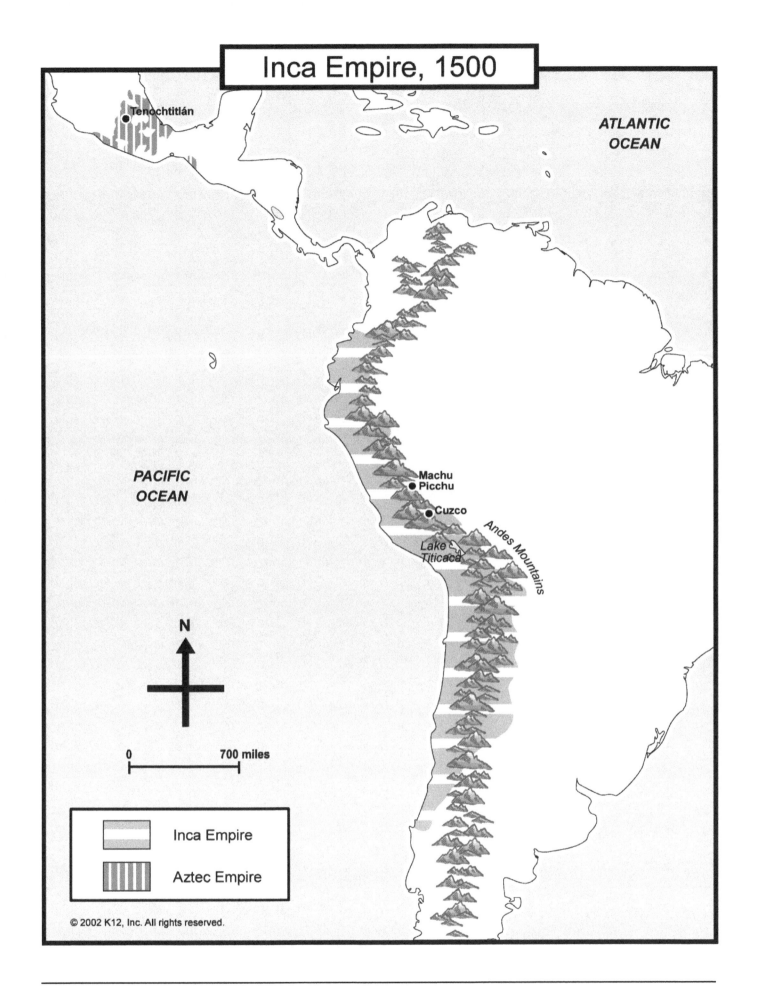

Inca Empire, 1500

Tenochtitlán

ATLANTIC OCEAN

PACIFIC OCEAN

Machu Picchu

Cuzco

Lake Titicaca

Andes Mountains

N

0   700 miles

	Inca Empire
	Aztec Empire

Lesson Assessment

Machu Picchu

1. What city was the capital of the Inca Empire?_____

2. What do their cities, roads, and terraces tell us about the skills of the

    Incas?_____

3. What was Machu Picchu?_____

Student Guide
Lesson 6: Spanish Motivations: Gold, God, and Empire

Gold, faith, and dominion--the same motivations that prompted Spaniards to set off in search of new trade routes--also spurred them to conquer and settle the New World.

Lesson Objectives

- Tell three reasons the Spanish wished to gain control of the Americas (to find gold, build Spain's empire, and spread Christianity).

PREPARE

Approximate lesson time is 60 minutes.

Materials

> For the Student
>> History Record Book
>> 🖥 Drawing on Cortes Experience activity sheet
>> pencils, colored 12

Keywords and Pronunciation
Bernal (behr-NAHL)
Hernán Cortés (ehr-NAHN kor-TAYS)

LEARN
Activity 1: Land of Opportunity *(Online)*

Activity 2: History Record Book *(Offline)*
Instructions
Choose either A or B.
A. Written Narration
Write two to four sentences explaining what the lesson was about. If necessary, use the Show You Know questions to help get started. Only include the most important parts of the lesson. Write your name, the date, and the lesson title on your written narration, and put it in your History Record Book.

Sample written narration: "Cortés wanted to go to Mexico and conquer it. He wanted to make it part of the Spanish empire. He also wanted gold. He wanted to turn the people there into Christians.

B. Picture Narration
Draw a picture of the part of the lesson that interested you most. When you have finished drawing, describe the picture. Below your picture, write a description of what you have drawn. Write your name, the date, and the lesson title on your picture narration, and put it in your History Record Book.

Activity 3: Drawing on Cortés's Experience *(Offline)*
Instructions
There were three main reasons Spain wanted to conquer Mexico. What were they? Show that you know by completing the Drawing on Cortés's Experience activity sheet.

A picture of Cortés is at the bottom, and there is space in three bubbles over his head to write his thoughts. Use the back of the activity sheet to make a drawing illustrating one of Cortés's thoughts.

ASSESS
Lesson Assessment: Spanish Motivations: Gold, God, and Empire *(Online)*
You will complete an offline assessment covering the main objectives of this lesson. Your learning coach will score this assessment.

Name _____   Date _____

Drawing on Cortés's Experience

In the bubbles, write three reasons why Cortés and Spain wanted to conquer Mexico.

Lesson Assessment

Spanish Motivations: Gold, God, and Empire

1. Why did the king of Spain send men and troops to the Americas?_____

2. What did the Spanish church want to do in the Americas?_____

3. What did Cortés and other Spanish adventurers hope to find in the Americas?_____

Student Guide
Lesson 7: Cortés and Moctezuma

Under the Emperor Moctezuma the Aztec empire came to include much of south central Mexico, but the Aztecs were hated by the peoples they conquered. Between 1519 and 1521 Spanish forces led by Hernán Cortés enlisted the aid of neighboring tribes and defeated the Aztecs.

Lesson Objectives

- Define *conquistador* as a Spanish conqueror.
- Identify Hernán Cortés as a Spanish explorer and conqueror of the Aztecs.
- Identify Moctezuma as emperor of the Aztecs.
- Recognize that the Spanish defeated the Aztecs.

PREPARE

Approximate lesson time is 60 minutes.

Materials

For the Student

History Record Book

Optional

The Aztec News by Philip Steele

Keywords and Pronunciation

Tenochtitlan (tay-nawch-teet-LAHN)

conquistador (kahn-KEES-tuh-dor) : The Spanish word for a conqueror.

Hernán Cortés (ehr-NAHN kor-TAYS)

La Villa Rica de la Vera Cruz (lah BEE-yah REE-kah thay lah bay-rah kroos)

Moctezuma (mawk-tay-SOO-mah)

Quetzalcoatl (KET-suhl-koh-AH-tl)

LEARN
Activity 1: Two Worlds Meet *(Online)*

Activity 2: History Record Book *(Offline)*
Instructions
Choose either A or B.
A. Written Narration
Write two to four sentences explaining what the lesson was about. If necessary, use the Show You Know questions to help get started. Only include the most important parts of the lesson. Write your name, the date, and the lesson title on your written narration, and put it in your History Record Book.

Sample written narration: "Cortés wanted gold. He sailed to Mexico and marched toward the Aztec Empire. Moctezuma thought that Cortés might be a god. The Spanish defeated the Aztecs and became the rulers of Mexico."

B. Picture Narration

Draw a picture of the part of the lesson that interested you most. When you have finished drawing, describe the picture. Below your picture, write a description of what you have drawn. Write your name, the date, and the lesson title on your picture narration, and put it in your History Record Book

Activity 3: Retell the Story of Moctezuma's Defeat (Offline)
Instructions

Imagine you're a tourist guide in Mexico City, Mexico. (Remember that Mexico City was built on the ruins of Tenochtitlán.) You come to the ruins of an Aztec temple being excavated by archaeologists. It's time to tell your visitors about the end of the Aztec Empire at the hands of the Spanish conquistador Hernán Cortés. Retell the main events of this story. If you have trouble remembering what happened, reread *The Most Beautiful City in the World*.

ASSESS
Lesson Assessment: Cortés and Moctezuma (*Online*)

You will complete an offline assessment covering the main objectives of this lesson. Your learning coach will score this assessment.

LEARN
Activity 4. Optional: Cortés and Moctezuma (Offline)
Instructions
For a fun and interesting look at the life and times of the Aztec people, check your library or bookstore for *The Aztec News*, by Philip Steele (Cambridge, MA: Candlewick Press, 1997).

Lesson Assessment

Cortés and Moctezuma

1. What is a conquistador?_____

2. Which conquistador defeated the Aztecs?_____

3. Who was the emperor of the Aztecs?_____

4. After Cortés defeated the Aztecs, which nation ruled in Mexico?_____

Student Guide
Lesson 8: Pizarro and Atahualpa

While Cortés triumphed over the Aztecs in Mexico, Francisco Pizarro eyed the Inca Empire in Peru. This ambitious conquistador led 180 men against the wealthy and well-organized Inca Empire and won. Spanish conquest of the Inca empire paved the way for Spanish colonization of South America.

Lesson Objectives

- Describe Atahualpa as the leader of the Incas.
- Describe Francisco Pizarro as the Spanish conquistador who conquered the Incas.
- Explain that the Spanish were able to conquer the Incas with a small force.

PREPARE

Approximate lesson time is 60 minutes.

Materials
> For the Student
>> History Record Book

Keywords and Pronunciation
Atahualpa (ah-tah-WAHL-pah)
Cajamarca (kah-huh-MAHR-kah)
Cuzco (KOOS-koh)
Diego (DYAY-goh)
Francisco Pizarro (fran-SIS-koh puh-ZAHR-oh)
treachery : An abuse of trust; a betrayal of confidence.

LEARN
Activity 1: Spain Conquers the Inca Empire *(Online)*

Activity 2: History Record Book *(Offline)*
Instructions
Choose either A or B.

A. Written Narration
Write two to four sentences explaining what the lesson was about. If necessary, use the Show You Know questions to help get started. Only include the most important parts of the lesson. Write your name, the date, and the lesson title on your written narration, and put it in your History Record Book.

Sample written narration: "Pizarro was a conquistador from Spain. He came to South America to conquer the Incas. Pizarro had a small army, but he used treachery. He killed the emperor and took all the gold from the Incas."

B. Picture Narration

Draw a picture of the part of the lesson that interested you most. When you have finished drawing, describe the picture. Below your picture, write a description of what you have drawn. Write your name, the date, and the lesson title on your picture narration, and put it in your History Record Book.

Activity 3: Retelling the Story of Pizarro's Treachery *(Offline)*

Instructions

It's very likely that after Pizarro overthrew the Inca Empire, surviving Incas told the story of his treachery toward Atahualpa. The story might have been told over and over, passed down from one generation to another.

Imagine you've been told the story and are now ready to practice and tell the story yourself. First, write down the main events from the story, each event on one index card. For example, on the first index card you might write, "Pizarro and his army landed on the coast and marched to Cajamarca."

Now skip a line and write a couple of details about the event. In our example, you might write, "Pizarro wanted to conquer the Inca Empire because of its wealth" and "The king of Spain gave him permission to conquer the Inca Empire."

After you have written down the main events and two details for each event, practice telling a story using the information on your index cards. Imagine people are sitting in front of you, listening. Change your facial expressions and the tone of your voice while speaking. Use hand gestures. Stand up a few times and act out a scene. Make your story come alive!

After you have practiced enough so that you feel comfortable telling the story, invite your family to gather around and listen to your story of Pizarro's treachery.

ASSESS

Lesson Assessment: Pizarro and Atahualpa (*Online*)

You will complete an offline assessment covering the main objectives of this lesson. Your learning coach will score this assessment.

Lesson Assessment

Pizarro and Atahualpa

1. Who was Atahualpa?_____

2. What was the name of the Spanish conquistador who conquered the Incas?_____

3. Did Pizarro have a large army or a small one?_____

Student Guide
Lesson 9: Las Casas Speaks Out Against Indian Enslavement

The Portuguese and Spanish enslaved the native peoples they conquered in Central and South America. The Portuguese also began to import African slaves to Brazil. One priest spoke out against Indian enslavement and worked to improve the native peoples' conditions.

Lesson Objectives

- Locate Brazil on a world map or globe.
- State that Portugal claimed Brazil.
- State that both the Portuguese and the Spanish used slave labor in the Americas.
- Identify Las Casas as a priest who worked to improve the lives of the Indians under Spanish rule.

PREPARE

Approximate lesson time is 60 minutes.

Materials

For the Student

> globe, inflatable
>
> map, world
>
> History Record Book
>
> 🖳 Bartolomé de las Casas Plaque activity sheet

Optional

> clay

Keywords and Pronunciation

Bartolomé de las Casas (bahr-toh-loh-MAY day lahs KAHS-ahs)

brasa (BRAH-zuh)

Pedro Cabral (PAY-throo kuh-BRAHL)

LEARN
Activity 1: Slavery in the Americas *(Online)*

Activity 2: History Record Book *(Offline)*

Instructions

Choose either A or B.

A. Written Narration

Write two to four sentences explaining what the lesson was about. If necessary, use the Show You Know questions to help get started. Only include the most important parts of the lesson. Write your name, the date, and the lesson title on your written narration, and put it in your History Record Book.

Sample written narration: "Portugal and Spain needed people to work in the Americas. They made the Indians slaves. A priest named Bartolomé de las Casas thought it was wrong to make them slaves. He worked to make things better for the Indians."

B. Picture Narration

Draw a picture of the part of the lesson that interested you most. When you have finished drawing, describe the picture. Below your picture, write a description of what you have drawn. Write your name, the date, and the lesson title on your picture narration, and put it in your History Record Book.

Activity 3: In Honor of Bartolomé de las Casas *(Offline)*

Instructions

Imagine someone is creating a statue to honor Bartolomé de las Casas. You've been asked to write the text for a plaque that will be attached to the base of the statue. Write a draft of the text on a sheet of notebook paper and revise it until you're happy with how it sounds. Make sure you've spelled the words correctly and written in complete sentences. When it's finished, copy the text onto the Bartolomé de las Casas Plaque activity sheet.

Reread the story to refresh your memory about the work this Spanish priest did to help improve the lives of the Native Americans living under Spanish rule.

ASSESS

Lesson Assessment: Las Casas Speaks Out Against Indian Enslavement

(Online)

You will complete an offline assessment covering the main objectives of this lesson. Your learning coach will score this assessment.

LEARN

Activity 4. Optional: Las Casas Speaks Out Against Indian Enslavement *(Offline)*

Instructions

Make a statue of Bartolomé de las Casas. Click on the link to to see a picture of him on the web at the Oregon State University website.

362

Name _____   Date _____

In Honor of Bartolomé de las Casas

On a sheet of notebook paper, write a paragraph that honors and commemorates the work of Bartolomé de las Casas. Once you have a final draft of your composition, copy it onto the plaque below.

Bartolomé de las Casas
1474-1566

Lesson Assssment

Las Casas Speaks Out Against Indian Enslavement

1. **In order to answer this question you will need to use the map of the world or the globe.**
   Where is Brazil located?

2. Which European country claimed Brazil?_____

3. How did the Portuguese and Spanish get the workers they needed in the

   Americas?_____

4. Who was Bartolomé de las Casas?_____

Student Guide
Lesson 10: Unit Review and Assessment

You've completed this unit, and now it's time to review what you've learned and take the unit assessment.

Lesson Objectives

- Demonstrate mastery of important knowledge and skills in this unit.
- Demonstrate mastery of important knowledge and skills taught in previous lessons.
- Locate the Yucatán peninsula on a map.
- Describe the Maya as an ancient Native American civilization on the Yucatán peninsula.
- Name two achievements of the Maya or aspects of Maya life (such as an accurate calendar, pyramid temples, and writing).
- Locate the Valley of Mexico and the Aztec Empire on a map.
- Describe the Aztecs as fierce warriors.
- Describe the Aztecs as city-builders.
- Locate the Inca Empire on a map.
- Describe two important characteristics of Inca civilization, such as the use of roads, rope bridges, and couriers.
- Identify Cuzco as the capital of the Inca Empire.
- Describe Machu Picchu as a stone city built by the Incas in the Andes.
- Tell three reasons the Spanish wished to gain control of the Americas (to find gold, build Spain's empire, and spread Christianity).
- Define *conquistador* as a Spanish conqueror.
- Identify Hernán Cortés as a Spanish explorer and conqueror of the Aztecs.
- Identify Moctezuma as emperor of the Aztecs.
- Recognize that the Spanish defeated the Aztecs.
- Describe Francisco Pizarro as the Spanish conquistador who conquered the Incas.
- Explain that the Spanish were able to conquer the Incas with a small force.
- State that Portugal claimed Brazil.
- State that both the Portuguese and the Spanish used slave labor in the Americas.
- Identify Las Casas as a priest who worked to improve the lives of the Indians under Spanish rule.

PREPARE

Approximate lesson time is 60 minutes.

Materials

> For the Student
>> History Record Book

Keywords and Pronunciation

Tenochtitlan (tay-nawch-teet-LAHN)

Andes (AN-deez) : A mountain range in South America.

Bartolomé de las Casas (bahr-toh-loh-MAY day lahs KAHS-ahs)

conquistador (kahn-KEES-tuh-dor) : The Spanish word for a conqueror.

Francisco Pizarro (fran-SIS-koh puh-ZAHR-oh)

Hernán Cortés (ehr-NAHN kor-TAYS)

Machu Picchu (mah-choo PEEK-choo)

Maya (MIY-uh)

Yucatán (yoo-kah-TAHN)

LEARN
Activity 1: A Look Back *(Offline)*

Activity 2: History Record Book Review *(Offline)*

Activity 3: Online Interactive Review *(Online)*

ASSESS
Unit Assessment: The World They Found (*Offline*)

Complete an offline Unit Assessment. Your learning coach will score this part of the Assessment.

Name _____   Date _____

The World They Found

Read each question and its answer choices. Fill in the bubble in front of the word or words that best answer the question. Questions marked with an asterisk (*) will have more than one correct answer. For these questions, fill in the bubble next to ALL correct answers.

* 1. Which of the following describe achievements of the Maya or aspects of Maya life? (Select ALL that are correct.)
  - ⓐ They used an accurate calendar.
  - ⓑ They grew sugar on plantations.
  - ⓒ They traveled on hundreds of miles of paved roads.
  - ⓓ They used a system of writing on stelae.
  - ⓔ They built pyramid temples.

2. Which Native American civilization that built Tenochtitlán was known for its builders and fierce warriors?
  - ⓐ Maya
  - ⓑ Inca
  - ⓒ Aztec
  - ⓓ Brazil

3. True or False: When the Spanish and Portuguese began exploring the New World, they found civilizations and cultures that were exactly the same as their own.
  - ◯ True
  - ◯ False

4. I'm standing high in the Andes Mountains. Llamas carry my supplies. A stone city peeks through the clouds. Where am I?
   - ⓐ Tenochtitlán
   - ⓑ Machu Picchu
   - ⓒ Cuzco
   - ⓓ Yucatán

5. Use the following words to complete the table below. For each row, start on the left and read across to the right. For example, in the row that begins with "Aztec," write the name of the Aztec leader in the second column and the name of the Aztec capital city in the third column.

Francisco Pizarro   Tenochtitlán   Moctezuma   Cuzco

Civilization	Leader	Capital City	Defeated By
Aztec			Hernán Cortés
Inca	Atahualpa		

6. Which country claimed the land that makes up present-day Brazil?
   - ⓐ England
   - ⓑ Spain
   - ⓒ France
   - ⓓ Portugal

7. Which Native American civilization lived in the Andes mountain range and built the stone city of Machu Picchu?
   - ⓐ Maya
   - ⓑ Cuban
   - ⓒ Inca
   - ⓓ Aztec

* 8. Which are characteristics of the Incas? (Select ALL that are correct.)
   ⓐ They built pyramid temples.
   ⓑ They built roads and rope bridges.
   ⓒ They used couriers.
   ⓓ They brought diamonds to the Americas.

* 9. Why was Spain eager to gain control of the Americas? (Select ALL that are correct.)
   ⓐ to learn about the Native American gods
   ⓑ to enlarge the Spanish empire
   ⓒ to convert the Native Americans to Christianity
   ⓓ to grow sugar on large plantations
   ⓔ to find gold, silver, and other riches

10. Write the name of each Native American civilization on the map to show where it was located.

   Maya

   Aztec

   Inca

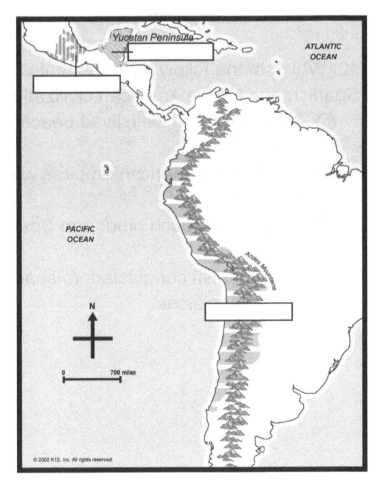

11. Who was a priest who worked hard to improve the lives of the Indians under Spanish rule?
    - ⓐ Hernán Cortés
    - ⓑ Bartolomé de las Casas
    - ⓒ Francisco Pizarro
    - ⓓ Atahualpa

12. As I look around, I see causeways, stair-stepped temples, feathered headdresses, and a busy city. What civilization have I found?
    - ⓐ Inca
    - ⓑ Maya
    - ⓒ Aztec
    - ⓓ Spanish

13. Which of the following statements best describes the meeting of Spanish and Native American civilizations?
    - ⓐ They got along well, lived peacefully together, and learned from each other.
    - ⓑ The Native American empires were allowed to exist but were ruled by Spain.
    - ⓒ They fought each other and Spain conquered the Native American empires.
    - ⓓ The Spanish conquistadors searched for gold but left the Native Americans alone.

14. The Spanish mined gold and silver in the Americas, and the Portuguese grew and harvested sugar on plantations in Brazil. How were they able to get this work done?

ⓐ They hired Portuguese settlers to do the work.

ⓑ They forced Spanish conquistadors to do the work.

ⓒ They invented and built machinery to do the work.

ⓓ They used Native American and African slaves.

* 15. Which of the following helped Cortés defeat the Aztecs? (Select ALL that are correct.)

ⓐ guns

ⓑ bows and arrows

ⓒ spears

ⓓ cannons

ⓔ llamas

ⓕ horses

16. True or False: The continents of North and South America had been home to human beings for a very long time when the Europeans arrived.

○ True

○ False

17. A conquistador is _____.

ⓐ a Spanish conqueror

ⓑ an Inca slave

ⓒ an Aztec warrior

ⓓ a Portuguese priest

Student Guide
Lesson 11: Semester Review and Assessment

You've completed the first semester, and now it's time to review what you've learned and take the semester assessment.

Lesson Objectives

- Demonstrate mastery of important knowledge and skills in this semester.
- Demonstrate mastery of important knowledge and skills taught in previous lessons.
- Explain that *Renaissance* means *rebirth*.
- State that rebirth meant a new interest in the civilizations of ancient Greece and Rome.
- State that Giotto painted realistic figures and showed emotions.
- Give an example of how the Medici family patronized learning and art.
- Name Brunelleschi as the architect of the dome of the cathedral of Florence.
- Define the phrase *Renaissance man* as one who does many things well.
- Name one famous painting by Leonardo da Vinci (*The Mona Lisa* or *The Last Supper*).
- Recognize the Pietà and the David as two of Michelangelo's greatest works.
- Name Johannes Gutenberg as the inventor of the printing press.
- State that wars between Christians and Muslims lasted into the Renaissance.
- Name Martin Luther as a monk who wished to reform the Christian Church.
- Define the Reformation as a religious movement that divided the Christian Church into Catholic and Protestant branches.
- Identify Galileo as an astronomer who studied the skies with a telescope.
- State that Galileo's work confirmed Copernicus's theory.
- Describe the Renaissance as an Age of Exploration.
- Identify Henry the Navigator as a prince of Portugal interested in navigation and exploration.
- Tell how Henry improved navigation.
- Explain that Columbus discovered the Americas, two continents previously unknown to Europeans, and claimed the lands for Spain.
- Identify Vasco da Gama as a Portuguese explorer whose trip around Africa to the Indies made Portugal a major trading power.
- Describe Balboa as the first European to sight the Pacific Ocean from its eastern shore.
- Name Ferdinand Magellan as the captain of the first expedition to circle the globe.
- Tell three reasons the Spanish wished to gain control of the Americas (to find gold, build Spain's empire, and spread Christianity).
- Identify Hernán Cortés as a Spanish explorer and conqueror of the Aztecs.
- Identify Moctezuma as emperor of the Aztecs.
- Describe Atahualpa as the leader of the Incas.
- Describe Francisco Pizarro as the Spanish conquistador who conquered the Incas.
- Identify Las Casas as a priest who worked to improve the lives of the Indians under Spanish rule.

PREPARE

Approximate lesson time is 60 minutes.

Keywords and Pronunciation

Albrecht Dürer (AHL-brekt DYOUR-ur)

Bartolomeu Dias (bahr-tou-lou-MAY-ou DEE-ahsh)

Bartolomé de las Casas (bahr-toh-loh-MAY day lahs KAHS-ahs)

Castiglione (kahs-teel-YOH-nay)

Filippo Brunelleschi (fee-LEEP-poh broo-nehl-ES-kee)

Jan van Eyck (yahn van IYK)

Maya (MIY-uh)

Medici (MED-uh-chee)

Pietà (pee-ay-TAH)

Primavera (pree-muh-VAIR-uh)

LEARN

Activity 1: A Look Back *(Offline)*

Instructions

We're halfway through our course, and we've been halfway around the world. You've been studying the Renaissance, a period from about 1350 to 1600. It was a time when people were asking new questions and making new discoveries. To many who lived during that time, it felt as if spring was in the air.

Remember the painting called *Primavera,* or "spring," that we admired on the very first day? That painting said a lot about the period you've just studied. Can you remember what *Renaissance* means? [1] The Renaissance that started in Italy changed the whole world. It started as a rebirth of interest in two ancient civilizations-- Greece and Rome. People in the civilizations of Greece and Rome thought that if human beings used their heads as well as their hearts, they could do great things. In the Renaissance, people did just that.

By 1600, when our study ends, the Renaissance was not just a rebirth. It was a new growth. Think of all the ways things grew and changed in the Renaissance.

Art

Before the Renaissance, figures in paintings looked flat. Most of the paintings were religious. Most of the people looked weak and fragile. Then came Giotto with his tender expressions and lifelike forms, and art would never be the same.

Soon rich people, called patrons, paid painters and sculptors to create works of art. We met Michelangelo, with his strong and beautiful *Pietà* and *David,* and his frescoes on the Sistine Chapel ceiling. When he painted *The Creation of Adam,* he gave the world something brand-new. We watched Leonardo da Vinci, master of perspective, paint his mysterious *Mona Lisa.* We saw Jan van Eyck and Albrecht Dürer, northern Europeans who painted details so realistic their work seemed to leap off the page.

Who were some of the patrons? Maybe you remember a rich family from Florence, the Medici. Do you remember the name of the temperamental pope in Rome who was Michelangelo's patron? [2] And which patron was a determined king in France? [3]

Architecture

Before the Renaissance, people built stone cathedrals with tall spires and stained glass windows. During the Renaissance, architects remembered the domes of ancient Rome and the way light could pour in through open windows. Domes were popping up everywhere.

- Who designed a famous dome on the cathedral in Florence? [4]
- Who designed the dome for St. Peter's in Rome? [5]
- Who helped design palaces and chateaux for Francis I in France? [6]

Music

Before the Renaissance, music was mostly sacred and sung on a single note. It was called *chant.* During the Renaissance, new instruments were invented, including lutes and recorders. People wrote love songs. *Madrigals* were new songs that had different melodies sung together, making beautiful harmony. Madrigals were sometimes sung at court. Speaking of courts, life changed there, too.

Court Life

In northern Europe, some strong new monarchs emerged. Can you remember some? [7] All the great leaders of the Renaissance, even if they weren't kings, had their own courts. One writer named Castiglione even told courtiers how to behave. He said, "Read Latin and Greek. Write poetry. Play an instrument. Learn to draw. Walk with grace. Fight with skill. Cultivate humor and humility." It sounds as if courtiers needed to be Renaissance men. Do you remember what a Renaissance man is? Someone who can do many things well! How did Castiglione's ideas become so popular? The printing press, of course.

Books

Before the Renaissance, monks copied books by hand. During the Renaissance, an inventive German introduced his printing press, and Europe was never the same again. What was that inventor's name? [8] With Gutenberg's printing press, books, art, and maps were printed by the thousands.

Religion

At the beginning of the Renaissance, most Europeans thought of themselves as Christians. When they worried about another religion, they usually worried about Islam and the Muslims who took over Constantinople. But during the Renaissance, a quarrel began in the Christian Church.

When a German monk named Martin Luther criticized the pope and wrote down his ideas, those thoughts spread like wildfire. The printing press rushed them across Europe. A split began in the Christian Church. What was this split in the Christian Church called? [9] What were the two new branches of Christianity? [10]

Exploration

Before the Renaissance, people were just trying to get by in a dangerous world. They often thought about life after death. But after the Renaissance, people became very curious about this world, the world in which they lived. Who were some of those people?

- **Copernicus and Galileo** studied the stars and showed that the earth revolved around the sun.
- **Prince Henry the Navigator** studied the sea and helped develop ships and instruments that made navigation easier.
- **Explorers and adventurers,** from Bartolomeu Dias to Christopher Columbus, charted the coast of Africa, opened routes to the Indies, found new places where Europeans could trade, and even discovered continents they hadn't known existed.

Clash of Cultures

Before the Renaissance, Europeans knew nothing of the Americas or the people who lived there. Yet great civilizations existed in the Americas. Can you name three? [11]

The Spanish and Portuguese were awed when they came upon these civilizations. What amazing cities the Aztecs had built! What astonishing roads and bridges the Incas made!

But nothing stopped the Spanish and the Portuguese from conquering the Aztecs, Incas, and other native peoples. The conquistadors claimed those areas for their kings, conquered the native peoples, and set up colonies in the New World. It was the beginning of a painful time.

The Spanish and Portuguese enslaved the Indians and took their gold. They set up mines and plantations. When they needed more workers, they enslaved Africans and brought them to the West Indies and Brazil. Some people were already beginning to see that this was wrong. Bartolomé de las Casas spoke out and said, "Christians can't do this!"

The Renaissance, which began in Europe, now reached halfway around the globe. It was a time of new ideas, new discoveries, and new challenges. How could one part of the world rule another? How could different peoples live together? How should they treat each other? Finding the answers to those questions would take a very long time.

Activity 2: End of Semester (Online)

ASSESS

Semester Assessment: History 3, Semester 1 (Offline)

Complete an offline Semester Assessment. Your learning coach will score this part of the assessment.

Name _____   Date _____

Semester Assessment

Read each question and its answer choices. Fill in the bubble in front of the word or words that best answer the question.

Questions marked with an asterisk (*) will have more than one correct answer. For these questions, fill in the bubble next to ALL correct answers.

1. What does the word *Renaissance* mean?
   ⓐ reprint
   ⓑ rename
   ⓒ rebirth
   ⓓ review

2. How did paintings change with Giotto and the beginning of the Renaissance?
   ⓐ People in paintings started to look weak and fragile.
   ⓑ Paintings became flat and unrealistic.
   ⓒ Objects and people in paintings started to look lifelike.
   ⓓ Most paintings became religious in nature.

3. Which two civilizations inspired writers, thinkers, and artists of the Renaissance?
   ⓐ India and China
   ⓑ Mesopotamia and Egypt
   ⓒ Japan and Russia
   ⓓ Greece and Rome

4. Where did the Renaissance begin?
- ⓐ Italy
- ⓑ France
- ⓒ China
- ⓓ Arabia

5. What powerful banking family from Florence supported the arts and learning?
- ⓐ the Tudors
- ⓑ the Medici
- ⓒ the Stuarts
- ⓓ the d'Estes

Match each person on the left with a description of the person on the right.

6. Michelangelo

painted the *Mona Lisa;* helped design palaces for Francis I

7. Leonardo da Vinci

wrote 95 Theses and started the Reformation

designed the dome on the cathedral in Florence

8. Brunelleschi

created the sculpture *David;* painted the Sistine Chapel ceiling

9. Martin Luther

10. A "Renaissance" man is a person who _____.
- ⓐ studies ancient civilizations
- ⓑ does many things well
- ⓒ helps the pope spread Christianity
- ⓓ moves from place to place

* 11. Who were strong monarchs in Europe during the Renaissance? (Select ALL answers that are correct.)

ⓐ Henry VIII

ⓑ Moctezuma

ⓒ Ferdinand and Isabella

ⓓ Julius II

ⓔ da Gama and Cabral

ⓕ Francis I

12. Wars between what two groups started in the Middle Ages with the Crusades and lasted into the Renaissance?

ⓐ Europeans and Native Americans

ⓑ Aztecs and Incas

ⓒ Romans and barbarians

ⓓ Christians and Muslims

13. Which of the following best describes the period from 1350 to 1600?

ⓐ a dark age when few people in Europe could read or write and most lived in castles

ⓑ an age of learning and questioning when Europeans became very curious about the world

ⓒ a time of peace and hope when people from different lands came together

ⓓ a time when the Christian faith was reunited and more people were ruled by the pope

14. What made it possible for Renaissance ideas and art to spread throughout Europe?
- (a) Prince Henry's astrolabe
- (b) Galileo's telescope
- (c) Martin Luther's 95 Theses
- (d) Gutenberg's printing press

15. Which sentence best describes what happened when the European and Native American civilizations met?
- (a) The explorers and conquistadors searched for gold and left the Native Americans alone.
- (b) The two civilizations got along well, lived peacefully together, and learned from each other.
- (c) The Native American empires were left alone but had to pay taxes to Spain and Portugal.
- (d) The two civilizations fought each other and the Native American empires were conquered.

16. What was the Reformation?
- (a) an age of exploration and discovery led by Portugal
- (b) the conquest of the Aztecs and Incas by Spain
- (c) the founding of the Church of England by Henry VIII
- (d) a split in the Christian Church started by Martin Luther

17. What did Copernicus and Galileo do?
- (a) They spread Christianity and showed Native Americans how to read and write.
- (b) They studied the stars and showed that the earth revolved around the sun.
- (c) They printed books and helped spread Renaissance ideas and art.
- (d) They crossed oceans and explored new lands in North and South America.

18. Who helped expand exploration by working with others to design new ships, improve navigation, and chart the African coast?
- ⓐ Prince Henry
- ⓑ Hernán Cortés
- ⓒ Ferdinand Magellan
- ⓓ King Henry VIII

Match each person on the left with a description of the person on the right.

19. Christopher Columbus   first European to see the eastern shore of the Pacific Ocean

20. Vasco da Gama   reached India by sailing south around the tip of southern Africa and then east

21. Ferdinand Magellan   sailed west across the Atlantic to find a shorter route to the Indies

22. Balboa   captain of the first expedition to sail around the world

* 23. At first, why were Spain and Portugal so interested in the Americas? (Select ALL that are correct.)
- ⓐ They wanted to spread Renaissance ideas to the Americas.
- ⓑ They wanted to get rich by finding gold and silver.
- ⓒ They wanted to make their empires larger and more powerful.
- ⓓ They wanted to join forces with the Aztecs and Incas against England.
- ⓔ They wanted to spread Christianity and convert Native Americans.

Match each person on the left with a description of the person on the right.

24. Hernán Cortés   emperor of the Inca Empire

25. Atahualpa   Aztec emperor who ruled from Tenochtitlán

26. Francisco Pizarro   Spanish conquistador who defeated the
                            Aztec Empire

27. Moctezuma   defeated the Inca Empire using treachery

28. What did Bartolomé de las Casas speak out against when Spain and
Portugal started colonies in the New World?
   ⓐ the growing of sugar cane on large plantations
   ⓑ the enslavement of Native Americans
   ⓒ the exploration of Brazil by conquistadors
   ⓓ the attempt by England to settle in South America

Answer Keys

Using Maps and Globes Answer Key

Activity 1: Globes and Maps

1. half of the Earth
2. South America, Africa (You can see Antarctica and Europe on the globe, but they are not labeled.)
3. Atlantic Ocean
4. See the map on page 5.
5. See the map on page 5.
6. You can see the continents North America, South America, Europe, Asia, Australia, Antarctica, and Africa. You can also see the Pacific Ocean, Atlantic Ocean, Arctic Ocean, and Indian Ocean on the map and the globe.
7. Asia = 5
   Africa = 3
   Antarctica = 7
   Australia = 6
   Europe = 4
   North America = 1
   South America = 2
8. Atlantic Ocean = c
   Arctic Ocean = a
   Indian Ocean = d
   Pacific Ocean = b

Optional
9. You can see Africa, Europe, Asia, Australia, and Antarctica.
10. You cannot see North America and South America on the globe and satellite image.
11. Indian Ocean

Optional
Skill Builder
1. A globe is round; a map is flat and can be folded.
2. True
3. False. A *continent* is a large area of land. An *ocean* is a large body of water.

Activity 2: Map Keys

1. See the map on page 8.
2. See the map on page 8.
3. The small dots are cities.
4. The capital of Colorado is Denver.
5. The symbol for a park is a tree.
6. The symbol for a library is a group of books.

7. There are six houses (three on each side of the street) on Main Street.
8. The school is on Peach Street.
9. The police station is on Main Street.
10. The fire station is on Willow Avenue.
11. Rome is the capital of Italy.
12. Venice, Genoa, Rome, Naples, and Palermo are close to major airports. (You only need to name two airports.)
13. Pisa, Florence, Bologna, and Cagliari do not have major airports. (You only need to name two cities that do not have large airports.)
14. Po River, Tiber River
15. France, Switzerland, Austria, and Slovenia are next to Italy. (You only need to name one country.)

Optional

16. Yes, Venice is a tourist attraction. It has a camera symbol near it.
17. See the map on page 10.
18. Answers may vary. Possible answers include the Leaning Tower of Pisa and a gondola.

Optional

Skill Builder

1. True
2. The symbol for a tourist attraction is a camera.
3. A dot represents a city.

Directions and Hemispheres Answer Key

Activity 3: Globes and Maps

1. west
2. south
3. North is at the top.
4. You should go west.
5. Swan Pond is east of the picnic area.
6. You will come to Saddleback Road.
7. The playground is east of the parking lot.
8. There are houses north of Goose Creek.
9. **Optional**: Iowa, Illinois, Wisconsin, Missouri, Michigan, Indiana, Ohio (You only have to name two.)
10. **Optional**: Iowa, Minnesota, Wisconsin, Michigan (You only have to name two.)
11. **Optional**: Illinois, Missouri, Kansas (You only have to name two.)
12. You would travel southwest.
13. You would travel northwest.
14. Chicago
15. Decatur
16. Rock Island, Peoria, Springfield (You only have to name two.)
17. East St. Louis, Quincy, Rock Island, Springfield (You only have to name two.)
18. northeast

Optional

Skill Builder
1. It is important to know your directions so you can understand how to get from one place to another if someone tells you and so you can tell others how to get from one place to another.
2. The cardinal directions are north, south, east, and west.
3. The intermediate directions are northeast, southeast, southwest, and northwest.

Optional

Try It Yourself
Answer may vary—it depends on where you live.

From Washington, D.C. you head southwest to Jackson, Mississippi.
From Jackson, Mississippi, you drive northwest to Portland, Oregon.
From Portland, Oregon, you travel east to Minneapolis, Minnesota.
From Minneapolis, Minnesota, you head southeast to Nashville, Tennessee.
Finally you travel northeast from Nashville, Tennessee, on your way back to Washington, D.C.

Activity 4: The Four Hemispheres
1. Northern Hemisphere
2. Southern Hemisphere
3. both
4. The Arctic Ocean is in the Northern Hemisphere. The Atlantic, Pacific, and Indian Oceans are in both the Northern and Southern Hemispheres.
5. North America and South America are located only in the Western Hemisphere.
6. Eastern Hemisphere
7. The Atlantic and Pacific Oceans are located in the Western Hemisphere. (The Arctic Ocean is also in the Western Hemisphere, but it is not labeled.)
8. The Atlantic, Indian, and Pacific Oceans are in the Eastern Hemisphere. (The Arctic Ocean is also in the Eastern Hemisphere, but it is not labeled.)

Optional
Skill Builder
1. The Equator crosses South America, Africa, and Asia.
2. The prime meridian crosses Europe, Africa, and Antarctica.
3. The Arctic Ocean is in the Northern Hemisphere.
4. Australia is located in the Southern and Eastern Hemispheres.
5. South America is located in the Southern and Western Hemispheres.
6. Europe is closer to the North Pole.
7. South America is closer to the South Pole.

Optional
Try It Yourself
Answer may vary.

The Places We Live Answer Key

Activity 5: The Places We Live

1. The other continent on the globe is South America.
2. You can see the Arctic, Pacific, and Atlantic Oceans.
3. Canada is just to the north of the United States.
4. Answers may vary. Student may mention Mexico, any of the Central American countries, or the Caribbean islands labeled on the map on page 21, except Puerto Rico, which belongs to the United States. (You only need to name two.)
5. See the map on page 22.
6. You would pass through Colorado and Utah.
7. Missouri
8. Florida
9. **Optional:** Idaho, Oregon, and Washington are northwest of Utah.
10. **Optional:** California, Oregon, Washington, Alaska, and Hawaii touch the Pacific Ocean. (You only need to name two.)
11. **Optional:** Louisiana
12. **Optional:** Iowa
13. eastern
14. Schenectady, Albany, Binghamton, Utica, Watertown, Syracuse, Ithaca, Rochester, Niagara Falls, Buffalo, and Jamestown. (You only need to name two.)
15. Lake Erie, Lake Ontario, and Lake Champlain touch New York. (You only need to name one.)
16. Pennsylvania and New Jersey
17. **Optional:** Canada
18. **Optional:** You would drive west to Niagara Falls.
19. **Optional:** Albany is the capital of New York.
20. **Optional:** Vermont, New Hampshire, Massachusetts, and Connecticut are all east of New York.(Rhode Island also appears on the map but it is not labeled.)
21. You could visit the Staten Island Zoo, Statue of Liberty, Bronx Zoo, Brooklyn Children's Museum, Coney Island, or Jamaica Arts Center. (You only need to name two.)
22. La Guardia Airport, John F. Kennedy International Airport
23. Shea Stadium, Yankee Stadium
24. The red lines show highways.
25. Coney Island is in Brooklyn.
26. Harlem includes Lenox Avenue, 125th Street, St. Nicholas Street, Broadway, Henry Hudson Parkway, 145th Street, 155th Street, Harlem River Drive, and Central Park North. (You only need to name two.)
27. Abyssinian Baptist Church, Apollo Theater, Columbia University
28. 125th Street

Skill Builder
1. Answers may vary. North America is the most likely answer.
2. Answers may vary. The United States is the most likely answer.
3. continent
4. Answers may vary. You may mention any three of the countries on the map on page 21. (Remember, Puerto Rico is not a country—it is a commonwealth associated with the United States.)
5. Answers may vary.

Activity 6: Countries , States, and Borders
1. Ottawa, Canada; Mexico City, Mexico; Havana, Cuba
2. Honduras, Costa Rica
3. See the map on page 26.
4. Guatemala, Honduras, Nicaragua, Costa Rica, Panama (You only need to name two.)

5. Canada
6. United States, Mexico
7. Idaho, Nevada, Arizona, New Mexico, Colorado, and Wyoming border Utah. (You only need to name two.) People probably created the borders because they are all straight lines.

Optional
8. Pacific Ocean
9. Missouri River
10. Louisiana, Mississippi, Arkansas, Tennessee, Kentucky, Missouri, Illinois, Iowa, Wisconsin, and Minnesota border the Missouri River. (You only need to name two.)
11. Lakes form the border between Michigan and Canada.
12. The Río Grande passes through Colorado, New Mexico, and Texas.
13. California, Arizona, New Mexico, and Texas are on the Mexican border.

Skill Builder
1. True
2. Political maps show countries, states, cities, borders, and capitals.
3. Mississippi River
4. Myanmar, Bangladesh, Bhutan, China, Nepal, and Pakistan border India. (You only need to name two.)
5. France, Portugal, and Andorra border Spain. (You only need to name two.)
6. Albania, Macedonia, Bulgaria, and Turkey border Greece. (You only need to name two.)
7. Sudan

Name _____   Date _____

Lesson Assessment Answer Key

The Places We Live, Part 2

Answer:

1. Answers will vary, but the student should point to their correct continent, country, city, and state in which they live.

2. Ottawa

3. Santo Domingo

Lesson Assessment Answer Key

Renaissance Means Rebirth

Answers:

1. rebirth
2. Greece and Rome

Lesson Assessment Answer Key

A Dangerous Feudal World

Answers:

1. a dangerous and hard time.
2. feudalism
3. Almost everyone there believed in the Christian religion.
4. castles
5. cathedrals
6. a place where monks lived and worked together

Lesson Assessment Answer Key

Monks, Islam, and the Light of Classical Learning

Answers:

1. monks
2. Islam
3. Aristotle

Lesson Assessment Answer Key

Dante Writes a Book

Answers:

1. Dante
2. life after death
3. their Christian faith

Lesson Assessment Answer Key

Giotto Breaks with the Past

Answers:

1. Giotto

2. The people in his paintings looked more real and lifelike. Their faces showed emotions.

3. Possible answers: Giotto's people looked real, not flat. Giotto's paintings showed how people were feeling.

Name _____   Date _____

Lesson Assessment Answer Key

Petrarch: The Treasure Hunter

Answers:

1. Possible answers: for being a writer, a poet, a scholar, and a person who wrote many letters.

2. Possible answers: Cicero and Virgil, classical writers.

3. humanism

4. Petrarch

Unit Assessment Answer Key

Background to the Renaissance

Answers:

1. rebirth
2. Greece and Rome
3. danger and hardship
4. ancient Greek writers
5. Giotto di Bondone
6. Islam
7. humans can do great things
8. monks
9. the Middle Ages
10. feudalism
11. Dante Aligihieri
12. Christianity

Lesson Assessment Answer Key

The Hub of the Renaissance

Answers:

1. The Italian peninsula is shaped like a boot.
2. city-states
3. Merchants went there to trade.
4. Florence, Venice, Rome, or Milan

Lesson Assessment Answer Key

Florence and the Medici

Answers:

1. Florence is located in northern Italy on the Arno River.

2. the Medici family

3. cloth and banking

4. Accept any of the following: They rebuilt a monastery; gave monks a library; built new buildings; started a school; brought scholars to the city; helped artists.

Lesson Assessment Answer Key

Brunelleschi's Dome

Answers:

1. the great dome
2. Ancient Rome
3. the dome of the cathedral of Florence
4. Brunelleschi

Name _____   Date _____

Lesson Assessment Answer Key

Lorenzo the Magnificent

Answers:

1. Florence
2. the banking business
3. because he loved them and wanted people to read them
4. Possible answers: He wrote songs and poems; he discussed Plato; he had copies made of ancient Greek manuscripts.

Lesson Assessment Answer Key

Venice: Queen of the Adriatic

Answers:

1. Venice is the only city on the map in the Venice Empire.
2. The Adriatic Sea is between Italy and the land to the east.
3. People travel around Venice on canals. They used boats called gondolas.
4. the Doge
5. to trade and make Venice an empire

Lesson Assessment Answer Key

Rome Revived

Answers:

1. that Rome had once been the center of a great civilization

2. It was home to the popes.

3. The popes returned.

4. They tried to improve the city, built libraries, art collections, better roads and monuments.

Lesson Assessment Answer Key

Da Vinci: The Renaissance Man

Answers:

1. art and invention
2. a person who does many things well
3. *The Mona Lisa* or *The Last Supper*

Name _____   Date _____

Michelangelo Discussion Questions: Answers

1. They are closed.

2. They make it seem that the statue has wrinkles or lines on its face.

3. Some possible answers might include the following: Giotto—the way the angel is reaching out to St. John; Masaccio—the way the figures are in color, but the background isn't; Donatello—the way St. Mark's clothing is draped so that it looks as if he's moving; Ghiberti—the way it feels as if the figures are coming out of the art.

4. One possible answer: The baby's hand looks real.

5. Possible answers: The hands and feet look real; the clothing looks wrinkled; it makes you feel as if this just happened.

6. They imagined that this statue of David was a symbol for them—strong, brave, and clever.

7. Possible answers: His eyes seem to be looking at something; his hair seems as if you could touch it; he seems as if he's ready to do something.

8. He thought he was only a sculptor, not a painter.

9. Accept any reasonable answers.

10. His feet make him look ready to go somewhere; his arms have muscles; he has a long beard.

11. Accept any reasonable answers.

Lesson Assessment Answer Key

Meet Michelangelo

Answers:

1. Florence
2. as a great painter and sculptor
3. as lifelike and realistic
4. the *Pietà*
5. the *David*

Lesson Assessment Answer Key

Julius II, Michelangelo, and the Sistine Chapel

Answers:

1. Julius II
2. The pope didn't pay him.
3. Michelangelo painted the ceiling more slowly than the pope thought he should.
4. fresco
5. *The Creation of Adam*

Name _____   Date _____

Lesson Assessment Answer Key

Isabella d'Este: Renaissance Woman

Answers:

1. Isabella d'Este
2. Mantua
3. Possible answers include: she filled the palace with art; she filled the library with books; she invited musicians, artists and writers to visit: she started a school for young women.

Name _____ Date _____

Lesson Assessment Answer Key

Rebuilding St. Peter's

Answers:

1. St. Peter's Basilica
2. Pope Julius II
3. Michelangelo
4. yes

Unit Assessment Answer Key

The Italian Renaissance

Answers:

1. Italy

2. rebirth

3. St. Peter's Basilica

4. Medici

5. Brunelleschi

6. Venice

7. He was a patron of the arts in Florence.

8. *The Creation of Adam*

9. lifelike

10. *The Last Supper*

11. a person who does many things well

12. Michelangelo

13. Pope Julius II

14. an important leader of Mantua who made it a center of art and learning

15. the *David* and the *Pietà*

16. Greece and Rome

17. study of classical writers, ability to paint and draw, humility

18. cloth and banking

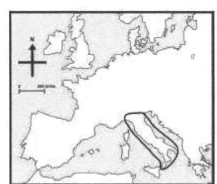

19.

20. the cathedral in Florence

Lesson Assessment Answer Key

Gutenberg Breaks into Print

Answers:

1. Johannes Gutenberg
2. the Bible
3. Large numbers of books could be printed.

Lesson Assessment Answer Key

Crescent Versus Cross

Answers:

1. They lasted into the Renaissance.
2. the Ottoman Turks
3. Ferdinand and Isabella
4. The Christians controlled Europe and the Muslims controlled the land farther East.

Lesson Assessment Answer Key

Renaissance Monarchs and the Changing Face of Europe

Answers:

1. a single person, such as a king or queen, who rules a kingdom

2. Possible answers: They had large armies; they built beautiful palaces.

3. Francis I

Lesson Assessment Answer Key

An Eye for Detail: Van Eyck and Dürer

Answers:

1. from travel or from books made available by the printing press
2. van Eyck and Dürer
3. very realistic and detailed

Lesson Assessment Answer Key

Copernicus Moves the Earth

Answers:

1. They believed the sun moved around the Earth.
2. He believed that the Earth revolves around the sun.
3. No, they wanted to explore and understand more; it was an age of learning.

Name _____   Date _____

Lesson Assessment Answer Key

Martin Luther and the 95 Theses

Answers:

1. Martin Luther.
2. a document in which Martin Luther criticized Church practices
3. the printing press

Name _____ Date _____

Lesson Assessment Answer Key

A Diet of Worms? The Reformation Splits Christianity

Answers:

1. It divided Christianity into two branches.
2. Catholic and Protestant
3. because they protested against the practices of the church
4. They caused a break with the Catholic Church.
5. some German princes

Lesson Assessment Answer Key

Europe Fractured

Answers:

1. many people
2. all sorts of people: princes, priests, peasants
3. There were many wars over religion.
4. Protestant countries and Catholic countries

Lesson Assessment Answer Key

Henry VIII and England for Protestantism

Answers:

1. Henry VIII
2. so that he could get a divorce
3. the Church of England

Lesson Assessment Answer Key

The Counter-Reformation

Answers:

1. the Counter-Reformation
2. Ignatius of Loyola

Lesson Assessment Answer Key

Galileo Faces the Inquisition

Answers:

1. an astronomer
2. the telescope
3. Copernicus
4. He said the Earth moved around the sun, which went against the teachings of the church.
5. a heresy

Unit Assessment Answer Key

The Renaissance Elsewhere and the Reformation

Answers:

1. Johannes Gutenberg
2. Ferdinand and Isabella
3. Monarch
4. The Earth moved around the sun.
5. Christians and Muslims
6. the Bible
7. the Reformation
8. Wars were fought over religion.
9. Church of England
10. the printing press
11. acted as missionaries for the Catholic Church
12. an astronomer who studied the skies with a telescope
13. Francis I
14. Renaissance artists
15. the 95 Theses
16. Catholic and Protestant
17. Galileo
18. Martin Luther
19. Protestants
20. Italy

How Far Away Is It? Answer Key

Activity 7: Scales Aren't Just for Weight
1. 300 miles
2. 180 miles
3. 750 feet
4. **Optional** 400 meters
5. **Optional** 1,200 meters
6. 2,500 feet

<u>Skill Builder</u>
1. A map scale could help you figure out how far you would have to walk, drive, or travel from one place to another.
2. It is probably on the map of a continent. If one inch stands for 500 miles, the map is showing a big area in a small amount of space.
3. It is probably a map of a city. If one inch on the map stands for 100 meters, the map is showing a relatively small area.
4. A mile is longer than a kilometer.
5. A meter is longer than a foot.

Landforms and Adapting to Where We Live Answer Key

Activity 8: The Shape of the Land

1. A hill is lower than a mountain.
2. A plateau is higher than a plain.
3. No, a valley is a low area between hills or mountains.
4. hills
5. plateau
6. plain
7. mountain
8. island
9. valley
10. The mountains are orange.
11. The plains are green.
12. The Deccan Plateau is between the Western Ghats and Eastern Ghats.
13. The islands are east of India.
14. New Delhi is in the plains.
15. **Optional:** Bangalore, Nagpur, and Madurai are on the Deccan Plateau. (You only need to name one.)
16. **Optional:** Pakistan
17. **Optional:** northern
18. India, Bangladesh, and Myanmar border the Bay of Bengal. (You only have to name two.)
19. Ganges River
20. **Optional:** Pakistan and India border the Arabian Sea. (You only need to name one.)
21. **Optional:** The Gulf of Kutch and the Gulf of Khabhat are on India's west coast. (You only need to name one.)
22. **Optional:** Indian Ocean

Optional
Skill Builder
1. plateau
2. valley
3. mountain
4. sea
5. ocean

Activity 9: Adapting to Different Environments

1. The houses were probably made of stone because the land was rocky so it was hard to grow trees and plants.
2. It is hard to grow crops in Greece because the land is rocky and there is little rain.
3. Nile River
4. Mesopotamia was between the Tigris and Euphrates rivers.

5. Yellow River and Yangtze River
6. Indus Valley Civilization
7. The people drank the water, used it to grow plants, and gave it to their animals to drink.

Optional
<u>Skill Builder</u>
1. False
2. They needed water to live. The people drank the water, used it to grow plants, and gave it to their animals to drink.
3. Answers may vary. I would wear warm clothing and raise animals that can live in the cold.
4. Answers may vary. I would dig deep wells for water or find an oasis.

Natural Resources Answer Key

Activity 11: Natural Resources

1. a = plant
   b = plant
   c = animal
   d = mineral
2. Cattle, sheep, and fish are among the animal resources you find in South America. (You only need to name two.)
3. Bananas, cacao, citrus, coffee, corn, cotton, trees (forestry), fruit, rice, sugarcane, and wheat are among the plant resources you find in South America. (You only need to name two.)
4. Argentina
5. Coffee is grown in Peru, Ecuador, Colombia, Venezuela, and Brazil. (You only need to name three.)
6. Peru
7. Brazil
8. In Colombia you can find corn, cattle, oil, trees (forestry), sugarcane, rice, coffee, bananas, cacao, and fish. (You only need to name three.)
9. In Brazil you can find corn, cattle, cotton, minerals (mining), citrus, trees (forestry), oil, sugarcane, rice, coffee, bananas, cacao, and fish. (You only need to name three.)
10. In Chile you can find fruit, fish, minerals (mining), wheat, cattle, sheep, and oil. (You only need to name three.)
11. Canada's animal resources include cattle, hogs, and fish. (You only need to name two.)
12. Canada's plant resources include trees (forestry), fruit, wheat, and other grains. (You only need to name two.)
13. Ontario
14. Alberta
15. Fruit is grown in Nova Scotia and Ontario.
16. Fish are important in New Brunswick, Nova Scotia, Newfoundland, Ontario, and British Columbia. (You only need to name two.)
17. Forestry is important in New Brunswick, Newfoundland, Québec, Ontario, Saskatchewan, Alberta, British Columbia, and Yukon Territory. (You only need to name two.)

Optional
Skill Builder
1. copper
2. raising chickens
3. coffee
4. cacao
5. lumber
6. oil

Lesson Assessment Answer Key

Prince Henry the Navigator

Answers:

1. the Age of Exploration or the Age of Discovery

2. navigation, exploring

3. Prince Henry the Navigator

4. Possible answers: He invited mapmakers, sailors and shipbuilders to his palace; he made his palace like a school of navigation; he had shipbuilders make better ships; he made his men keep careful records of the places they had been.

Lesson Assessment Answer Key

Bartolomeu Dias and the Cape of Good Hope

Answers:

1. Bartolomeu Dias
2. the Cape of Good Hope
3. He wanted to find a sea route east to lands in Asia such as India and China.

Lesson Assessment Answer Key

What Did Columbus Find?

Answers:

1. He was looking for a quicker route to the Indies.

2. the lands of Asia: India, China, Japan

3. the Americas

4. Spain

Name _____ Date _____

Lesson Assessment Answer Key

Da Gama and Cabral Claim More for Portugal

Answers:

1. the pope
2. It divided newly discovered lands between Portugal and Spain.
3. Vasco da Gama
4. a major trading power
5. Pedro Cabral
6. Brazil

Lesson Assessment Answer Key
Balboa Sights the Pacific

Answers:

1. a Spanish explorer
2. the Pacific Ocean
3. It meant that there were two big oceans divided by continents.

Lesson Assessment Answer Key

Circling the Globe: Magellan's Voyage of Discovery

Answers:

1. Ferdinand Magellan
2. This ocean was peaceful when they first saw it, and the word pacific means peaceful.
3. The Strait of Magellan is at the southern tip of South America.
4. Magellan and his ships sailed through it to reach the Pacific Ocean.

Name _____ Date _____

Unit Assessment Answer Key

The Age of Exploration

Answers:

1. Age of Exploration
2. reaching the southern tip of Africa
3. Muslim powers controlled most of the land routes.
4. Christopher Columbus
5. Spain
   Portugal
6. Vasco Núñez de Balboa
7. He led the first expedition to circle the globe.
8. Brazil
9. Prince Henry the Navigator
10. spices
    gold
    silk
11. at the Cape of Good Hope
12. to spread Christianity and get spices, gold, and silk
13. bad food taste better
14. Vasco da Gama
15. the compass and astrolabe
    small, fast ships called caravels

Lesson Assessment Answer Key

Travel Back in Time: The Mysterious Maya

Answers:

1. The Yucatán Peninsula is the only peninsula on the map.

2. the Maya

3. possible answers: temple pyramids; writing; the study of the stars; an accurate calendar; worship of many gods; corn and chocolate as food and drink; carved stelae

Name _____ Date _____

Lesson Assessment Answer Key

Aztec Origins: Legend of the Eagle on the Cactus

Answers:

1. The Aztec Empire and the Valley of Mexico are where the vertical striped area is on the map.

2. The flag has an eagle at its center, sitting on a cactus and eating a snake.

3. The Aztecs believed that they should build their city at a place where they saw an eagle sitting on a cactus eating a snake.

Lesson Assessment Answer Key

Astonishing Aztecs: Builders and Warriors

Answers:

1. The Aztecs were fierce warriors.
2. The Aztecs were city-builders.
3. many gods

Name _____   Date _____

Lesson Assessment Answer Key

The Inca Empire

Answers:

1. The Inca Empire surrounds the Andes Mountains.

2. the Andes Mountains

3. Possible answers: They built roads and robe bridges; they used couriers; they carried quipus; they built terraces on mountainsides; they used llamas as beasts of burden.

Lesson Assessment Answer Key

Machu Picchu

Answers:

1. Cuzco
2. The Incas were excellent builders and stonemasons.
3. a stone city built by the Incas in the Andes mountains

Lesson Assessment Answer Key

Spanish Motivations: Gold, God, and Empire

Answers:

1. to make it part of Spain's empire
2. convert the native people to Christianity
3. gold and glory

Lesson Assessment Answer Key

Cortés and Moctezuma

Answers:

1. a conqueror, or a Spanish conqueror
2. Hernán Cortés
3. Moctezuma
4. Spain

Lesson Assessment Answer Key

Pizarro and Atahualpa

Answers:

1. the emperor of the Incas
2. Francisco Pizarro
3. He had a small army.

Lesson Assessment Answer Key

Las Casas Speaks Out Against Indian Enslavement

Answers:

1. Brazil is on the Northeast side of South America.
2. Portugal
3. They made the Indians slaves.
4. a priest who worked to improve the lives of the Indians

Name _____ Date _____

Unit Assessment Answer Key

The World They Found

Answers:

1. They used an accurate calendar.
    They used a system of writing on stelae.
    They built pyramid temples.

2. Aztec

3. False

4. Machu Picchu

5.

Civilization	Leader	Capital City	Defeated By
Aztec	**Moctezuma**	**Tenochtitlán**	Hernán Cortés
Inca	Atahualpa	**Cuzco**	**Francisco Pizarro**

6. Portugal

7. Inca

8. They built roads and rope bridges.
    They used couriers.

9. to enlarge the Spanish empire
    to convert the Native Americans to Christianity
    to find gold, silver, and other riches

10.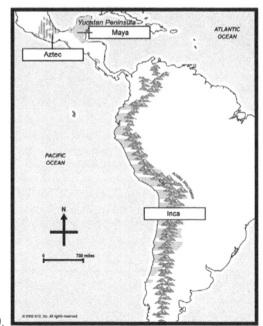

11. Bartolomé de las Casas

12. Aztec

13. They fought each other and Spain conquered the Native American empires.

14. They used Native American and African slaves.

15. guns
    cannons
    horses

16. True

17. a Spanish conqueror

Semester Assessment: Answer Key

1. c

2. c

3. d

4. a

5. b

6. created the sculpture *David;* painted the Sistine Chapel ceiling

7. painted the *Mona Lisa;* helped design palaces for Francis I

8. designed the dome on the cathedral in Florence

9. wrote 95 Theses and started the Reformation

10. b

11. a, c, f

12. d

13. b

14. d

15. d

16. d

17. b

18. a

19. sailed west across the Atlantic to find a shorter route to the Indies

20. reached India by sailing south around the tip of southern Africa and then east

21. captain of the first expedition to sail around the world

22. first European to see the eastern shore of the Pacific Ocean

23. b, c, e

24. Spanish conquistador who defeated the Aztec Empire

25. emperor of the Inca Empire

26. defeated the Inca Empire using treachery

27. Aztec emperor who ruled from Tenochtitlán

28. b